Greek and Roman Mythology

Third Edition

Kirk Summers

University of Alabama

KENDALL/HUNT PUBLISHING COMPANY
4050 Westmark Drive   Dubuque, Iowa 52002

Cover art supplied by author.

Excerpts on pages 14–15 from *Ovid Metamorphoses* translated by Rolfe Humphries, 1955, published by Indiana University Press. Reprinted by permission of the publisher.

Hymn I, pages 24–27, from Lombardo, Stanley and Diane Rayor, eds. and trans. *Callimachus: Hymns, Epigrams, Select Fragments*, pp. 3–6. © 1987 Reprinted by permission of Johns Hopkins University Press.

Photos of coins found throughout book provided by Classical Numismatic Group, Inc. Reprinted by permission.

Pages 65–66 from *The Love Songs of Sappho*, translated by Paul Roche. Copyright 1966, 1991 by Paul Roche. Used by permission of Signet Classic, a division of Penguin Putnam Inc.

Art on chapter openers © paradoks_blizanaca, 2008. Used under license from Shutterstock, Inc.

Contents

Preface

This book, now in its third edition, is intended as a concise introduction to the basic myths of the Greeks and the Romans. It is meant to be tied to specific course lectures where certain interpretations of the myths can be applied, but it also stands alone as a guide to gods and heroes.

The outlines at the end of the book support the lectures of the author's course at the University of Alabama. Students will find ample space there for note-taking. A web site that is open to anybody provides additional support for the course by collecting images from antiquity and linking to additional information on the web:

http://bama.ua.edu/~ksummers/cl222/

One will see that images of ancient coins appear throughout the text to illustrate the various stories. I chose coins specifically because as illustrations in myth books they are notably underused and underrated. But most importantly they are *ancient* images, rather than Renaissance or modern, so they best complement the web images of vases and sculptures for recreating the context in which these myths once thrived.

CHAPTER ONE
Introduction to Myth

"Through the humanities we reflect on the fundamental question: What does it mean to be human? The humanities offer clues but never a complete answer. They reveal how people have tried to make moral, spiritual, and intellectual sense of a world in which irrationality, despair, loneliness, and death are as conspicuous as birth, friendship, hope, and reason."

—from *The Humanities in American Life*, a report of the 1980 United States Rockefeller Commission on the Humanities

Humanities. We hear the term bandied about. At the university we could choose an academic course of study in the Humanities, which would land us in Classics, Philosophy, Religion, History, or English, among other fields. Some universities have a department or college of Humanities, or house Centers for Humanistic Studies, such as The Center for Clinical Ethics and Humanities in Health Care at SUNY-Buffalo or the Harry Ransom Humanities Research Center at the University of Texas. The federal government is involved in the Humanities as well. The National Endowment for the Humanities is a big supporter of National Public Radio. It gives grants to individuals for major research initiatives, funds the development of digital media for the Humanities, and organizes summer seminars for further scholars and teachers to delve deeper into specific humanistic subjects. Every state has an official entity that supports the Humanities in that state, such as the Alabama Humanities Foundation. Many private Humanities institutes exist on many levels. So why all this interest in Humanities? What is Humanities, exactly?

To answer this it will be helpful to look back several centuries to the Renaissance period of our history. The word "Renaissance" means "rebirth," and in this case the rebirth of Classical learning. In other words, during the Renaissance, educated men and women were gaining a greater interest in the intellectual ideas of ancient Greece and Rome than had existed during the previous great period of history, the Middle Ages. During the Middle Ages, the greatest trend among the educated elite was to focus their intellectual energy on discussions about the nature of God and his will for mankind. In the Renaissance, this tendency shifted more towards man himself. With the renewed interest in the Classical past,

A 4th Century Corinthian silver stater depicting Pegasus and Aphrodite, whose cult on the Corinthian citadel was renowned throughout the world.

people began to think more humanistically. Now, the term "humanistic" has taken on negative connotations in recent times, especially in religious circles, but at its most basic sense it need not evoke such ire. It simply means that Renaissance scholars, writers, educators, and elite began to think more about what it means to be a human being. What is the most successful means of achieving a happy life? What are our duties toward other human beings and what is the best form of government? Is love just an emotion that makes us foolish, or is it a noble expression of our soul's desire to unite with another? They found a discussion of these ideas and many more in twelve hundred years of Greco-Roman literature and art. It was a treasure trove of intellectual history, where ideals were proposed, problems debated, and the human experience laid bare in a variety of ways. One of those ways, the one that concerns us in this Humanities textbook, is myth.

Quite simply put, myths are traditional stories. By "traditional" we mean that they are handed down from generation to generation until they become part of the fabric of a society, both influencing and being influenced by the way a certain people think and live. The Greeks had a particularly rich story-telling culture even long before they learned how to record those stories with writing. Preliterate Greeks depended on myths to communicate certain values and social structures among themselves and to pass them along to their descendants. How should we think about marriage? What motives enable us to wage war on another people or defend our cities? With what attitude should we face death? The traditional act of storytelling provides a vehicle for raising and discussing such questions as these. Undoubtedly, mythic communication took place on the personal level, with parents telling the stories to the children, and on the communal level, when traveling bards came to town and sang songs about the adventures of gods and heroes. But wherever or however they were told, we can be sure that both speaker and listener were swapping views about the way the world works.

Why should we study myths today, though? The ancient Greeks' inter-generational exchange of world-views and *mores* surely cannot contribute to our own discussions about life, can they? Obviously, scholars can use myths to reconstruct the way that the ancient Greeks comprehended and ordered their lives, but myths have other layers of meaning that have immediate relevance to us even today. Myths offer observations on the human condition that transcend any one culture or era. In the noise of our modern society, in the mad rush to earn more money and climb the ladder of success, amid the constant demands on our time and attention, sometimes we are not prepared to face the more perennial issues that touch as all as human beings. Myth has the ability to refocus our thoughts on the experience and meaning of our life journey.

Joseph Campbell, the famous mythologist of the previous generation, gives a succinct rationale for studying myth in his book *Power of Myth:*

> "One of our problems today is that we are not well acquainted with the literature of the spirit. We're interested in the news of the day and the problems of the hour. It used to be that the university campus was a kind of hermetically sealed-off area where the news of the day did not impinge upon your attention to the inner life and the magnificent human heritage that we have in our great tradition—Plato, Confucius, the Buddha, Goethe, and others who speak of the eternal values that have to do with the centering of our lives. When you get to be older, and the concerns of the day have all been attended to, and you turn to the inner life—well, if you don't know where it is or what it is, you'll be sorry."

> "Greek and Latin and Biblical literature used to be part of everyone's education. Now, when these were dropped, a whole tradition of Occidental mythological information was lost. It used to be that these stories were in the minds of the people. When the story is in your mind, then you see its relevance to something happening in your own life. It gives you perspective on what's happening to you. With the loss of that, we've really lost something because we don't have a comparable literature to take its place. These bits of information from ancient times, which have to do with the themes that have supported human life, built civilizations, and informed religions over the millennia, have to do with deep inner problems, inner mysteries, inner thresholds of passage, and if you don't know what the guide signs are along the way, you have to work it out for yourself. But once this subject catches you, there is such a feeling, from one or another of these traditions, of information of a deep, rich, life-vivifying sort that you don't want to give it up."

Campbell was moved by mythical stories because he believed strongly that they sprang from the human psyche and therefore reveal something of the universal human experience. No one has to be left to wander through life's puzzle without a map: Myths are the "guide signs" put there by people who have traveled the same road, asked the same questions, and fought the same fights.

The Swiss psychiatrist Carl Jung (d. 1961), in his investigations of anthropology and the occult, came to similar conclusions. Struck by the universality of many themes, images, patterns and stories among varying cultures, he theorized about a collective unconscious that contains universal predispositions that he called archetypes. For Jung, the collective unconscious is the deepest, most inaccessible level of our psyche, a communal memory representing the accumulated experiences of mankind. This communal memory predisposes us to apprehend the world in particular ways because it contains archetypes. A psychological archetype is basically a pattern of thinking, that is, an inherited predisposition to respond to certain aspects of the world. We are all born with blueprints for perceiving and behaving. In essence, this is a microcosm of Plato's theories about the ideal forms. But instead of there being independently existing archetypes that we must contemplate to understand the world around us, Jung believed that these archetypal patterns are imbedded within our psyche from birth. And just as the eye is predisposed to respond to light, our psyche is predisposed to be sensitive to the categories of experience that all human beings have experienced, including birth, death, sun, moon, mothers, fathers, heroes, demons, wise men, and so on. It is in myth and dreams, Jung believed, that we can begin to identify what the patterns are and thus understand why we behave and respond to the world as we do.

Jung himself provided a clear definition of what he meant in a lecture delivered in 1936 entitled "The Archetypes and the Collective Unconscious" and subsequently published in his collected works. He explains his terms as follows:

"The collective unconscious is a part of the psyche which can be negatively distinguished from a personal unconscious by the fact that it does not, like the latter, owe its existence to personal experience and consequently is not a personal acquisition. While the personal unconscious is made up essentially of contents which have at one time been conscious, but which have disappeared from consciousness through having been forgotten or repressed, the contents of the collective unconscious have never been in consciousness, and therefore have never been individually acquired but owe their existence exclusively to heredity. Whereas the personal unconscious consists for the most part of complexes, the content of the collective unconscious is made up essentially of archetypes."

"The concept of the archetype, which is an indispensable correlate to the idea of the collective unconscious, indicates the existence of definite forms in the psyche which seem to be present always and everywhere. Mythological research calls them "motifs"; in the psychology of primitives they correspond to Levy-Bruhl's concept of "representations collectives," and in the field of comparative religion they have been defined by Hubert and Mauss as "categories of the imagination." Adolf Bastian long ago called them "elementary" or "primordial thoughts." From these references, it should be clear enough that my idea of the archetype—literally a pre-existent form—does not stand alone, but is something that is recognized and named in other fields of knowledge."

"My thesis, then, is as follows: In addition to our immediate consciousness, which is of a thoroughly personal nature and which we believe to be the only empirical psyche (even if we tack on the personal unconscious as an appendix), there exists a second psychic system of a collective, universal, and impersonal nature which is identical in all individuals. This collective unconscious does not develop individually, but is inherited. It consists of pre-existent forms, the archetypes, which can only become conscious secondarily and which give definite form to certain psychic contents."

Whether Carl Jung is right or not when he speaks of the universal unconscious, his theories do provide a useful way for reading myths and making them relevant to us today. We could dismiss myths as merely random stories vaguely reflecting an ancient religion that made little sense to the adherents or simply tales told for entertainment around a campfire, but that would be to miss certain insights about human nature and experience gained from their study. The imaginative, fantastic nature of myths has a poetic quality to it: It speaks a language that shakes the mind loose from the confines of a rational existence that threatens to choke it or minimize it and elevates it to an irrational plane where the perspectives are new and possibilities are wider.

✳ THE TIMETABLE OF MYTH ✳

Although myths are not so bound up with history that we can attribute a date to them, it is important to view the time line of ancient Greece and Rome to see loosely how the myths fit in. The following table includes some information about the dates of events taking place in the Bible to provide some recognizable context:

2100–1500 B.C.	The height of the non-Greek Minoan civilization on Crete; their main symbols were the bull and an earth goddess with snakes; the earliest Greeks came into contact with their civilization, and told stories about them, including the stories of King Minos and the minotaur. Daedalus and his son Icarus were Greeks held captive on that island. The Minoans wrote using a script we now call Linear A; it is indecipherable for the most part.
c. 1500 B.C.	The capital city, Knossos, was burned, though the circumstances are unclear. The Mycenean Greeks are beginning to dominate the Aegean, mainland Greece, and Crete. This is the beginning of the period we think of as the "Heroic Age."
2000–1300 B.C.	Most Greek myths are thought to take place during this period.
1300 B.C.	The fall of Troy at the hands of the Greeks. About the same time, Moses leads the Israelites out of Egypt (usually estimated to be 1280 B.C.).
1200–1150 B.C.	The Mycenean civilization fades, perhaps replaced by Dorian Greeks and maybe crushed by other invaders from the north now often called the Sea Peoples who were causing general upheaval through the world.
1150–800 B.C.	Usually called the "Dark Ages" of Greece, mainly because we have so little information from this period due to the lack of writing (lost when the Myceneans disappeared).
800 B.C.	Homer, the oral poet, composes the _Iliad_ and _Odyssey;_ possibly a Phoenician script was introduced during this time and adapted to the Greek language.
753 B.C.	Traditional date for the founding of Rome by Romulus and Remus, descendants of the Trojans.
612 B.C.	The Babylonians (Medes and Chaldeans) defeat the Assyrians at Nineveh; the Lydians (the source of some aspects of the Cybele and Dionysus cults) are becoming the major power in Asia Minor.

586 B.C.	The Babylonian King Nebuchadnezzar destroys Jerusalem; builds the Hanging Gardens (one of the 7 wonders of the world).
547 B.C.	The Persians defeat the Lydians (Cyrus def. Croesus) and comes into contact with the Greeks on the Ionian coast of Asia Minor.
539 B.C.	Cyrus the Persian defeats Babylon and frees the Jews.
500 B.C.	Greeks begin to write tragedies.
323 B.C.	The death of Alexander the Great; the Hellenistic Age begins, during which Greek culture is spread throughout much of the world.
300–100 B.C.	Rome gradually conquers the Mediterranean world.
44 B.C.	Julius Caesar is assassinated; the Republican period of Rome comes to an end. Civil wars in Rome reach their height.
27 B.C.	Augustus Caesar, adopted son of Julius, becomes the first real Emperor of Rome, beginning the Imperial period of Rome.
4 B.C.	Possible if not probable date for the birth of Jesus. "Augustus decreed that all the world should be taxed . . ."
29 A.D.	Probable date of Jesus' crucifixion in Jerusalem. Although Christianity begins slowly to rise from this date on, the belief in the Greco-Roman gods persists for another 450 years or so.
392 A.D.	Edict of Theodosius, prohibiting all forms of pagan worship, even private. Still, it would be another 100 years before paganism was completely eradicated or absorbed.

CHAPTER TWO
Creation According to the Greeks

"From the Heliconian Muses let us begin to sing, who hold the great and holy mount of Helicon, and dance on soft feet about the deep-blue spring and the altar of the almighty son of Cronos, and, when they have washed their tender bodies in Permessus or in the Horse's Spring or Olmeius, make their fair, lovely dances upon highest Helicon and move with vigorous feet."

—Hesiod's *Theogony* 1 ff.

Every race of people have a creation story. The bushmen of the Kalahari Desert in southwest Africa believe that a giant praying mantis called the "kaggen" created everything from nothing. The Huron Indians believed that the world is really just a turtle with dirt on its back, put there by some toad who found it underneath the primeval waters. The Aztecs believed that two snakes ripped apart the primal mother to create Earth and Sky, and that the mother from then on demanded human hearts as repayment. Among the Greek tribes we find many versions of the creation story within a general framework. The most famous and influential version, however, was that of Hesiod, who tells how the world developed from Chaos to an ordered structure controlled by the Olympian gods.

Hesiod appears to have flourished in the 8th century B.C., perhaps shortly after the time of Homer. His brother, Perses, had cheated him out of his inheritance, so he spent most of his life working hard as a farmer and shepherd while composing poetry. He may have lived in Orchomenos near Thebes and tended his sheep on Mt. Helicon, a favorite haunt of the nine Muses. Mt. Helicon lies between Thebes and the Gulf of Corinth and was thought to be inhabited by various gods. There Hesiod says that he received poetic inspiration from the Muses by drinking at the sacred Hippocrene spring.[1] The winged horse Pegasus, offspring of Poseidon and Medusa, had caused this spring to flow by a kick of its hooves (notice the root

---

[1]The Muses, who often form choruses with Apollo and the Graces, tended other springs as well from which they could inspire poetry and prophecy. The Castalian spring on Mt. Parnassus just above Delphi was one of their most famous sanctuaries. The Muses sometimes receive the title "Pierian" from their birthplace Pieria at the foot of Mt. Olympus.

Severus Alexander bronze medallion of Perinthos, Thrace. On the reverse is depicted the wheel of the Zodiac; in center, Zeus enthroned holding patera and scepter, eagle at his feet; to upper left, Helios right in quadriga, with crescent moon above; to upper right, Selene left in biga of bulls, with star above. At Zeus's feet recline Gaia, holding cornucopiae, and Thessala, holding rudder.

"hippo"). Around and around it the Muses move their graceful bodies in dance, exalting the gods of Olympus and telling tales of their exploits, the adventures of heroes, and the creation of the world. No poet can say anything about the gods unless the Muses first fill them with the oracular power. "Tell me, Muse, of the man of many turns," prayed Homer as he began his epic the *Odyssey*. "Help me, O Muse, recall the reasons why," asked Vergil at the beginning of the *Aeneid*. Poets are nothing but a mouthpiece through which the Muses disclose the mysteries of the universe. Here are the words that the nine daughters of Zeus first spoke to Hesiod:

> "Listen, you country bumpkins, you swag-bellied yahoos, we know how to tell many lies
> that pass for truth, and we know, when we wish, to tell the truth itself."

With those words they plucked a branch from a laurel tree in full bloom and gave it to Hesiod for a staff. Then they breathed into him the divine song so that he could spread the fame of the deathless gods, past and future. The songs themselves are said to fill Mt. Olympus with sweet sound and gladden the heart of father Zeus, while the earth resounded with harmonious hymns. All creation and all the conflicts of the gods have led to their father's reign as supreme god.

With the Muses singing through him, Hesiod begins to compose his epic poem. After praising the nine Muses and their sweet songs, the shepherd-poet describes their birth from Mnemosyne and Zeus. If the Muses love a man, he is blessed, because they relieve him of troubles and sorrows through song. Hesiod then asks the Muses to tell him how the earth and the gods came to exist, as well as how the sea, the stars and the universe came to be created. He records in chronological order the births of the gods and the generations that sprang from them:

> "Chaos was born first and after her came Gaia
> the broad-breasted, the firm seat of all

the immortals who hold the peaks of snowy Olympos,
and the misty Tartaros in the depths of broad-pathed earth
and Eros, the fairest of the deathless gods."

He begins with Chaos and Gaia (Earth), who existed first, along with Eros (Love), who conquers the souls of men and gods. Chaos gives birth to Erebus (primeval darkness) and Night, and they in turn bear Aether (the upper air) and Day. Gaia gives birth to Ouranos (Sky), and then the two unite to produce the Titans (including Kronos and Rhea), the Cyclopes and the Hecatoncheires (hundred-handed giants).

Ouranos' children are so powerful that the very sight of them coming down the birth canal frightens him. In his cruelty he refuses to let them be born, shoving them back into the mother's womb. Gaia elicits the help of one of them, the Titan Kronos, to usurp the throne from Ouranos. Kronos lies in wait for his father and at an opportune moment (or inopportune, depending on the perspective) slashes his father in the groin. From the blood and genitals of Ouranos are born the Erinyes (Furies), who spring from the earth as vicious doglike creatures who avenge murders, and Aphrodite, the "goddess of the fluttering eyelids," whose coquettishness the poet seems to linger over:

"As soon as Kronos had lopped off the genitals with the sickle
he tossed them from the land into the stormy sea.
And as they were carried by the sea a long time, all around them
white foam rose from the god's flesh, and in this foam a maiden
was nurtured. First she came close to god-haunted Kythera
and from there she went on to reach sea-girt Cyprus.
There this majestic and fair goddess came out, and soft grass
grew all around her soft feet. Both gods and men
call her Aphrodite, foam-born goddess, and fair-wreathed Kythereia."

Sexual imagery surrounds the goddess. The names attached to Aphrodite indicate that she washed ashore at the island of Kythera (Cytherea) though some say Kypris (Cyprus); on both islands she received special veneration. But particularly noteworthy is the connection between the foam of the genitals and the foam of the sea. Aphrodite derives life and her raison d'etre from the sexual energy inherent in the male sky god and the turbulent sea. Some men apply another name to her, Hesiod continues, Philommedes, which probably means "laughter-loving" but which the poet interprets as meaning, "lover of genitals." "From her come young girls' whispers and smiles and deception and honey-sweet love and its joyful pleasures." Eros and Desire become her companions.

The second generation gods are called Titans. Now Kronos marries his sister Rhea and they become king and queen of the second generation. Together they produce children who are destined to become the third generation (the Olympians). Like his father, though, Kronos feared his own children. Each time Rhea presented him with a new child, he swallowed him or her without hesitation, until finally Rhea grew tired of the situation. When she gave birth to the last child, Zeus, she hid him away on the island of Crete and entrusted his care to a nymph named Amalthea. Meanwhile, she presented Kronos with a stone wrapped in swaddling clothes as a substitute for the real child. The monstrous Kronos had become so accustomed to swallowing his children that he ingested the bundle he was given without even examining it first. This stone would one day become sacred to the Greeks, who believed it ended up at Delphi as the omphalos (navel stone), marking the center of the world.

Eventually, Zeus grew old enough to challenge his father, though he had to proceed with some measure of caution. The first thing he had to do was free his brothers and sisters from the belly of Kronos himself. To achieve this end he solicited the support of Metis, one of the Titanesses who had grown weary of Kronos' brutality. During one of the banquets of the gods she slipped an emetic into the drink of the king. This caused him to vomit up the children he had swallowed as well as the rock with which Rhea had tricked him. From this the Titanomachy ensued, the "clash of the Titans." Some of the Titans and their children sided with Zeus and his siblings in the hope that with victory they would have some position of authority in the new world order. Most notably, Prometheus, son of one of the Titans, helped Zeus by encouraging him to let the Kyklopes (Cyclopes) out of prison so they can forge him his thunderbolts for weapons. The thunderbolts prove to be decisive. Zeus defeats his father and his allies and locks them up in Tartarus, deep in the belly of Mother Earth. He sets the Hecatoncheires over them as guards. But here develops another problem: Gaia was angry that Zeus had deposed her favored son, Kronos, and determined to take revenge. She unleashed several fire-breathing giants against him that she unilaterally generated from her womb. The battle that followed came to be known as the Gigantomachy, or "clash of the giants." With the help of the other Olympians and his thunderbolts, Zeus was able to subdue the giants by heaping mountains upon them. These mountains became the volcanoes that dot the Mediterranean even today.

At this point, it is also useful to know the story of the *Prometheus Bound*, a play usually attributed to the ancient Greek playwright Aeschylus. We must also make a digression on the story of Io. According to the *Prometheus Bound*, Zeus has become angry with Prometheus, his former friend and helper, because Prometheus stubbornly helped humans by giving them fire and teaching them to keep the best part of the sacrifice for themselves. He also strengthened their emotional confidence by taking away their ability to know the future. So Zeus sent his two henchmen, Power and Force, along with Hephaistos, to take Prometheus to Scythia, a barren region on the far reaches of the Black Sea. There they bound Prometheus to a rock with "adamantine" steel so that he can undergo the endless tortures and pain that Zeus has in store for him, all because he loved mankind too much. Zeus sent his vulture by day to gnaw at the liver of Prometheus, but by night the liver would grow back, so that the process would start over again the next day. Prometheus, because he can see into the future, predicted to those standing around him that one day he will be released from his bonds. Even Zeus, he said, must submit to the laws of Fate.

Then the maiden Io, in the form of a heifer and tormented by a gadfly, encountered him on her travels. She had once been a priestess of Hera in Argos near Mycenae whom Zeus had seen and fallen in love with. Zeus began having an affair with the girl, who submitted to him from fear that he would harm her family if she did not. Zeus used to come to her as a dark cloud that both shielded his actions from Hera and symbolized his role as a fertile weather god, bringer of rain. When Hera became suspicious of this strange cloud and decided to investigate, Zeus protected the girl Io by transforming her into an exceptional white heifer. When Hera found Zeus standing suspiciously next to a heifer, she demanded the animal as a pet, and Zeus could do nothing but relent. Hera put the hundred-eyed monster Argus, who never fully sleeps (only fifty eyes close at any given time), in charge of watching the animal.

Zeus felt sorry for the girl, so he sent Hermes to rescue her from this sorry state. Hermes used his gift for gab to put Argus to sleep, all one-hundred eyes at once (some say he used a flash from his magic bracelet), and then struck him over his head with his wand (called a caduceus). Hera had loved Argus; she wept for him and honored him by placing his hundred eyes on the tail of a peacock, which thereafter became the goddess' symbol. Against Io, however, she vented her rage. She sent a gadfly to torment her and drive her all over the earth. After many wanderings, she eventually made it to Egypt, where the gods finally took pity on her and turned her back into a human. She eventually bore a child of Zeus, named Epaphus. It was during her wanderings throughout the world that she met up with Prometheus in Scythia.

When Io came upon Prometheus, she described her sufferings and asked Prometheus if he knows what will happen to her. The story of her future wanderings, however, was almost too much for Io to bear and she cried out in agony. Prometheus pointed out that his own woes are greater because he can never die and can only know freedom if Zeus is overthrown. When Io enquirers whether Zeus will really be overthrown, Prometheus says that he will unless he releases Prometheus, who alone knows how to avert this disaster. The problem is that Zeus will one day have a child that will be greater than his father, but only Prometheus knows what marriage or union it is that will produce the child and how Zeus can avoid the pitfall. Io wants to know who could free Prometheus from his bonds, and, as it turns out, that will be a descendant of Io herself. Prometheus predicts that Herakles, a distant descendant of Io, will one day arrive, slay the eagle, and free him from his bonds.

Once Io has heard the prophecy, her tortures by the gadfly resume and she continues her wanderings. Prometheus speaks to the chorus of bystanders about the marriage that will destroy Zeus if he is not warned and declares that no god but himself can warn him. Only Prometheus possesses the secret knowledge to avert Zeus' downfall. Zeus, overhearing this, sends Hermes to extract the secret from Prometheus, but Prometheus says that he does not fear Zeus or his thunderbolts, even if Zeus should decide to smash him down into hell.

It should be obvious that the story of Prometheus, the great benefactor of mankind, and Zeus, the king of the gods, expresses a rift or a tension between god and the creator of mankind. Someone special must come along who can free Prometheus from his bondage and thereby reconcile gods and men. That unique individual, as it turns out, combines the lineage of Io, as her descendant, and the seed of Zeus, as his child.

TRANSLITERATION

Note that in transliterating mythic names into English there are important spelling differences between the older Greek versions of names and the Latinized ones. This chart may be of some help:

Greek	Latin	Example
I	J	Iason → Jason
K	C	Kalypso → Calypso
AI	AE/E	Gaia → Gea
final E	final A	Athene → Athena
final OS	final US	Kronos → Cronus

Consistency in spelling is difficult to achieve, even in the span of one book, since sometimes one form of a name has gained general acceptance over another for whatever reason. The reader should keep in mind the interchangeability of letters and make the necessary adjustments.

CHAPTER THREE
Ovid's Creation Story

"On earth the brute creation bends its gaze,
but man was given a lofty countenance
and was commanded to behold the skies:
and with an upright face may view the stars:
and so it was that shapeless clay put on
the form of man till then unknown to earth."

—Ovid, *Metamorphoses* 1.114ff.

Like the Greeks, the Romans had no consistent story about the creation and beginnings of the universe. The mythic version that carried the most weight was that penned by Publius Ovidius Naso, better known as Ovid. He was a Roman poet born in 43 B.C., was trained in Rome and Athens, and joined the circle of writers and thinkers that included Vergil, Propertius and Tibullus. He flourished during the reign of Augustus Caesar and overlapped the birth of Jesus in Bethlehem.

Ovid's poem *Metamorphoses* comprises fifteen books (chapters). In it the poet collects and retells hundreds of important Greco-Roman myths, almost all of which involve some sort of physical transformation of a character (e.g., Narcissus transforms into a flower). Ovid begins his lengthy poem with these words: "My intention is to tell of bodies changed to different forms; the gods, who made the changes, will help me—or I hope so—with a poem that runs from the world's beginning to our own days." The first book then starts off with the creation story, followed by fourteen more books of specially selected myths. Each myth is connected to the previous one by Ovid's clever weaving together of chronological and psychological intracacies, and the poet's wit and insight shines through everywhere. The common theme that runs throughout is metamorphosis, change. Everything changes. No shape, no mode of existence, no status or relationship remains constant and predictable. We can never step into the same river twice. We can never expect to be tomorrow what we are today. And most of all, simplistic descriptions and explanations of the world and life forever fail us.

We may wonder if Ovid sees himself as a philosopher or a moralist. Perhaps we are better off seeing Ovid in terms of the Roman "vatic" concept. The Romans of Ovid's day

Q. Pomponius Musa. Silver denarius. 56 B.C. Obverse: Laureate head of Apollo right. Reverse: Terpischore, the Muse of dancing, standing right, holding lyre and plectrum.

viewed poets of Ovid's caliber as playing the part of a *vates*, that is, a poet-priest. In the absence of any kind of church, to use an anachronistic term, where ministers and authoritative scriptures serve as moral guides, people looked to intellectuals in their midst to instruct them about proper *mores* and right ways of thinking. Poets, therefore, fulfilled the role of priest. They used the lofty, almost heavenly language of poetry, with its subtleties, beautiful metaphors, and musical qualities, to speak a language that seemed to come directly from the gods and that had the power to stir the soul and elevate human thinking to a new plane. Thus the ancient poets, Ovid included, often appeal to the gods for inspiration and dwell on the many facets of human behavior in their writings.

What follows here is a summary of the creation story as it appears in the first book. We should note how Ovid's world-view exhibits itself in the very making of the universe and its inhabitants. The pieces of the universal puzzle fall together in such a way that they manifest, or predict, or perhaps cause the constant principle of change.

SUMMARY OF THE CONTENTS OF BOOK ONE

The story begins. Ovid describes the original condition of the universe as chaos, by which he means a discordant confusion of atoms that "war" with one another.

> Before the ocean was, or earth, or heaven,
> Nature was all alike, a shaplessness,
> Chaos, so-called, all rude and lumpy matter,
> Nothing but bulk, inert, in whose confusion
> Discordant atoms warred . . .
> . . . land on which no man could stand, and water
> No man could swim in, air no man could breathe,
> Air without light, substance forever changing,
> Forever at war: within a single body
> Heat fought with cold, wet fought with dry . . .

—trans. by Rolfe Humphries

But then some "god, or kindlier Nature" (Ovid is vague here about the precise identity and nature of this prime mover) imposed order amid the chaos, and began to give shape to the universe as we know it. His *modus operandi* was to create boundaries to separate the different kinds of atoms. But god felt something or someone was needed to maintain the order that he created, so he (or perhaps some other divinity) created man, a *sanctius animal*, or "holier animal," whose godlike mind and capacity for complex reasoning would guarantee that the world would not descend into its original chaotic state. This was the hope, at least, but Ovid could never be satisfied with such a simple, philosophical view of things. The poet seems to envision that the original "god" commissioned the old familiar characters to carry out the act of creation while he himself disappeared from the stage. Ovid describes the events as follows:

> "Still a holier animal was lacking,
> one that was capable of more rational thought,
> and that could rule over the other creatures.
> Humankind was born, perhaps made from divine seed
> by that artisan of the universe, as a source of a better world,
> or from the newly-made earth, which,
> until recently connected to the fiery ether,
> still retained in it the seeds of the kindred heaven.
>
> It was this earth, mixed with water,
> that Prometheus, child of Titan Iapetus,
> fashioned into the image of the gods who control everything.
> Although all other animals look downward at the earth,
> he gave to humans a lofty posture and bid them to look at heaven
> and to raise their countenances upward to the stars.
> In this way, earth, which until now had been simple and without form,
> changed and
> clothed itself with the unknown shape of humankind."

We notice how Prometheus, a divinity from Greek myth, steps in to carry out the actual fashioning of mankind. Now, he proceeds with his task by doing the very thing that the original god had tried to prevent: Prometheus creates mankind by *mixing together* again the elements, a formula for disaster that intimates to the reader that human beings are doomed from the start in their efforts to govern creation in an orderly fashion.

With the creation of human beings finished, Ovid then launches into a description of the four ages of mankind. Hesiod had also spoken of the "ages of man," but he envisioned five, placing after the Bronze Age a Heroic Age, probably to satisfy the Greek fascination with the honor and glory of the warriors who, according to popular myth, fought during the Trojan War. At any rate, it had become traditional to talk about the decline of human morality and conduct with reference to the gradation of metals, gold being the best, iron being the worst. Daniel, in the Bible, added "feet of clay" in his vision, which indicates that we are dealing with the actual progress of man from the stone age to the bronze and iron ages, as you might expect. The remarkable thing is that metalworking itself became widespread as early as 3700 B.C. in the Mesopotamia region, about 3000 years before Hesiod himself wrote of the "ages of man." Somehow, this process of evolution was still ingrained in the human subconscious and is reflected in even so simple a convention as the medals that are awarded at the Olympic games: Gold, Silver, Bronze. Iron is left out as too degenerate.

In Ovid's description of the four ages we can easily see the parallels with the book of Genesis in the Bible. Paradise is lost, humans become increasingly belligerent toward one another, giants are in the land producing children who incite rebellion against the gods, until finally the gods decide to destroy mankind with a flood. First, humans lived in a golden age (gold is found in a natural state and does not oxidize), a kind of Garden of Eden experience:

> . . . a time that cherished
> of its own will, justice and right; no law,
> No punishment, was called for; fearfulness
> Was quite unknown, and the bronze tablets held
> No legal threatening . . .

But when Kronos (Saturn) was overthrown by Zeus (Jupiter), the silver age was ushered in, when humans first began to have to work for their food and livelihood in a world of changing seasons. Men built houses to hold out the winter chill or to protect them from summer's heat. Oxen groaned under the yoke as farmers planted seeds in rows; no longer did food grow abundantly everywhere at all times. A much worse age ensued, called the bronze age, when men were more aggressive and quick to arm, but retained some measure of nobility. All was not evil. Then, the worst of all, the iron age came, when humans gave themselves totally over to debauchery, to the point that the goddesses Piety and Justice abandoned the earth.

It is important to note that throughout his description of the ages, Ovid maintains a negative attitude to certain basic human institutions and activities: war, the cutting of trees from mountains to make boats for sailing, digging natural resources out of the deep dark ground to bring them to the light of day, and all kinds of technological advancements. All of these activities involve some measure of mixing and boundary crossing and thus bring humans closer and closer to the original chaos. Ovid considers sailing the worst example of this: Men cross over natural barriers of ocean to spy the lands and possessions of others and covet them for themselves.

At the peak of this time of moral degeneration, in the iron age, Jupiter called a meeting of the gods in heaven. He thunders and rages about humans, particularly about a certain Lycaon, who had insulted Jupiter himself during a recent visit by the god to earth and whom the king of the gods had changed into a wolf to reflect his true character. Jupiter considers him the epitome of how corrupt humans have become and how much they deserve the ultimate punishment from the gods.

Jupiter explains to the other gods that he is determined to wipe humans off the face of the earth and start over again, and prepares to hurl his thunderbolts against the earth. The gods shriek and plead with him to stop, first, because as usual they are worried about who will worship them if mankind is destroyed, and second, because they are worried that if the world is consumed by fire (a conflagration), Olympus itself might be caught up in the flames. Ironically, the philosophers of Ovid's day almost all taught that the world would end with a general conflagration. But Jupiter has to agree that such a plan of destruction carries with it too many drawbacks, and so he instead decides to send a flood.

With the flood came the destruction of all living creatures except, by chance, two righteous people, husband and wife, named Deucalion and Pyrrha. Jupiter saw them fighting against the flood in a small boat, and decided to save them so that they could repopulate the earth with humans. But when the two of them finally settled on dry land again and the waters receded, they had no confidence that they could repopulate the earth on their own. Consulting an oracle of Themis, goddess of eternal laws, they received the strange command to loosen their belts and throw the bones of their mother behind their back. After some deliberation, they decided that the bones of their mother were the rocks of "mother" earth, and so they threw these behind their back. Sure enough, children grew from the tossed rocks. Thus the first and most radical transformation is complete: Human beings begin to repopulate the earth, but their natures are complex and difficult to reduce to any one summary description. They look back to a complicated, tangled ancestry with its roots in many different ages and many different types of characters, some good, some bad. It is not surprising, then, that the rest of the first chapter and all the remaining chapters of Ovid's work tries to describe the human experience in terms of metamorphosis. Book One ends with the stories of Apollo and Daphne, who turns into a laurel tree, and the story of Jupiter and Io, who turns into a cow.

CREATION AND BELIEF

We may wonder if the Romans actually *believed* such a creation story as described here. While there may have been a stratum of people ready to embrace poetic fancies, Roman religion, and especially Roman myth, rarely required anyone to believe in something in the Judaeo-Christian sense of the word. They were part of the dialogue, a very public and intellectual dialogue, about what it means to be a human being. As stated in the introduction to this book, the ancient Greeks and Romans were less interested in dogmas and more interested in groping their way toward the principles observable in the universe. Metamorphosis was one of those great principles. As such, it is reasonable to expect that somehow, in some way, however the universe came into being, that the principle was at work from the beginning. For human beings trying to find a peaceful, harmonious place in a vast and abstruse cosmos, the comprehension of nature's driving mechanism of change promised an almost spiritual awakening.

CHAPTER FOUR
Zeus and Hera

I will sing of Zeus, the best and greatest of the gods, far-seeing, mighty, fulfiller of designs who confides his tight-knit schemes to Themis as she sits leaning upon him. Have mercy, far-seeing son of Kronos, most glorious and great!

—Homeric Hymn to Zeus

Zeus rose to power after leading his brothers and sisters the Olympians, along with some disaffected Titans, against his father Cronus. This was a battle, not of angry gods against angry gods, but one of ideologies. The Titans had been violent and brutish, representatives of nature in the raw, unsettled and furious. The Olympians, and in particular Zeus, rebelled against this disorder and introduced a natural order that was more predictable and settled. The Olympian generation reined in creation, as best as their personalities would allow, thus providing an environment time more hospitable for the appearance of humankind.

When Zeus and his brothers, Hades and Poseidon, divided up the universe they had won, Zeus received the heavens as his portion. This was fitting for the god who would serve as the king over the Olympian generation and who, in his most elemental nature, was a weather god. He is the sky itself, whence comes the rain and the seasons that effect the productivity of mother earth. The heavenly power of Zeus is needed in all aspects of nature, for water in the streams, acorns on the mighty oaks, the lushness of nature. And because of his involvement with the seasons and weather, and because of his role as guide and director of the universe, he became too the greater defender of rules and norms. The god who brings the regular seasons and predictable patterns of the sky must also, the thinking went, be interested in maintaining an orderliness and justice in every corner of creation. Zeus protects the various organizations of men, whether it be the courts, the governmental bodies, or the family unit. Zeus himself guarantees the structure on which society depends.

Besides the story of Zeus' birth and rise to power, the myths of the king of the gods mostly revolve around his many amorous affairs, both with other divinities (he had no problem

Alexander III, Sicyon mint, Silver tetradrachm, c. 225–215 B.C. Head of Alexander the Great as Heracles wearing lion's skin. On the reverse, Zeus enthroned holding scepter and eagle; dove on right leg of Zeus.

having romantic trysts with aunts, sisters and the like), including the nymphs of the forests and streams, and with human beings of exceptional beauty. It is odd to us that the king of the gods has so many erotic encounters, though we have to remember that, as the sky god who sends the fertilizing rain, Zeus naturally had a strong sexual component. The myths simply reflect the basic nature of the sky itself. But even more than that, the Greeks were interested in expressing something about the relationship between Zeus and his numerous lovers and offspring. Through his relationship with other divinities, for example, Zeus brought a degree of unity to the heavenly family (some of whom were originally minor divinities of small Greek tribes), and assumed many otherwise disparate functions under his umbrella and control. Ultimately, children must obey their parents. Thus, if most of the gods of heaven are the children of Zeus, we can understand that their powers are subservient to his central authority. Furthermore, through his relationship with human parents, Zeus introduced the divine and heroic seed into many families of ancient Greece, or, at least, that is what those families would have their fellow countrymen believe. If they could claim that their ancestors descended from Zeus, they could more easily dispel charges that they have no right to the throne or to some measure of prestige.

Here is a chart showing the relationship of Zeus with numerous females and the offspring produced:

With gods:

ZEUS + Metis → Athena
ZEUS + Themis → Seasons (Horae) and Fates (Moirai)
ZEUS + Eurynome → Three Graces
ZEUS + Demeter → Persephone
ZEUS + Mnemosyne → Nine Muses
ZEUS + Leto → Apollo and Artemis
ZEUS + Hera → Hebe, Ares, and Eilithyia
ZEUS + Maia → Hermes

With mortal women:

ZEUS, as a human male, + Semele → Dionysus
ZEUS, as a bull, + Europa → Minos, Sarpedon, Rhadamanthys
ZEUS, as a dark cloud, + Io → Epaphus
ZEUS, as golden rain, + Danae → Perseus
ZEUS, as a swan, + Leda → Helen, Polydeuces (Pollux)

We will examine Zeus' erotic encounters with mortal women in more detail when we learn about the offspring themselves. In regard to his affairs with other divinities, one overarching principle stands behind them all: To the Greeks, Zeus represents the fulfillment or triumph of order over disorder. His sovereignty over the universe and the way that he exercises his power symbolizes the fact that the universe runs on established principles and on a design. The Greeks recognized that, although the world in which they lived is varied and complex, it is also predictable and works according to certain universal patterns. All the myths of the individual affairs with other divinities shows Zeus coupling with goddesses who preside over these universal patterns and producing children who exhibit further concern for order.

Zeus' earliest encounter with another goddess appears to have been with Metis, a goddess whose name means "intelligence." Before Zeus went to war with Cronus (Kronos), he courted this Titaness and convinced her to put an emetic in his father's drink. By this, Cronus vomited the five children (Poseidon, Hades, Hera, Demeter, Hestia) that he had swallowed upon birth in a brutish show of force. He also vomited the stone which had been wrapped in swaddling clothes and substituted for Zeus. This is the same stone, by the way, that was placed at Delphi to mark the center of the earth. Later, when Zeus received a prophecy saying that Metis was pregnant and that her child would be above him, he swallowed his lover, hoping to thwart the oracle. In essence, you see, by swallowing Metis he is assimilating intelligence itself as his own special quality. Later, Zeus complained of having a terrible headache, to which Hephaestus responded by splitting his head open with an axe. Out sprang Athena, fully armed and shouting the war cry. It is to be noted that Athena herself, the first child of Zeus, is the goddess of wisdom, and she presides over crafts and strategic warfare.

After this initial encounter, Zeus had an affair with Themis, the goddess of eternal law. She gives birth to the Horae, whose name literally means "hours" and in the broad sense stand for the passage of time in cycles and seasons. The names of the Horae are variously given, sometimes Discipline, Justice, Peace, sometimes Budding, Growth, Ripening. They controlled the growth of plants through the seasons and they also maintained the stability of society.

Next, Zeus mated with Eurynome, the daughter of Ocean, and produced the three Graces. The Graces are the symbols of happiness and loveliness, or, more precisely, the feminine qualities that attract male to female. Attraction is the most basic principle in the universe: Men are drawn to women because of their loveliness and thus perpetuate the cycle of life.

Zeus also had a brief affair with Demeter, the "Mother Goddess" who watched over the growth of grains and other crops. She is the power of growth itself in the plants. Together they produce Persephone, and, as we shall see in a later chapter, mother and daughter represent a unique aspect of the cycle of birth, growth, death, and rebirth found in nature.

Mnemosyne, whose name means "memory," was Zeus' next conquest. The Greeks believed that memory is the fundamental requirement for the production of arts. Not surprisingly, the two produced the nine Muses that oversee various kinds of arts, such as music, poetry writing, astronomy, and the like. It is said that once the musical, birdlike Sirens challenged the Muses in the arts, and the Muses, out of annoyance, plucked them of all their feathers. The Sphinx learned her riddle from them.

Zeus was also the father of Apollo and Artemis by Leto. Apollo's functions are manifold, but basically he serves as the chief god of the arts and is known as the "leader of the Muses." He is also responsible for driving the chariot of the sun across the sky in a regular fashion. Artemis, as we shall see, presides over the transitions into and out of childhood.

Up to this point, all of Zeus' sexual relationships have resulted in children who represent some sort of orderly system. It is not clear from the myths whether or not we are to imagine that Zeus actually married these divinities (probably he married Metis and Themis), or just carried on an affair with them. We can say for certain, however, that he was married to Hera, his sister. Their marriage was anything but orderly, though, and the children coming out of it all exhibit some chaotic characteristics or have some disconcerting aspect to them. Ares is a wild and savage god who loves the battlefield, especially when noisy confusion and chaos take hold. Hebe's name means "the bloom of youth." Originally, she served as the cupbearer of the gods, but, alas, just as the bloom of youth always fades, so Hebe is replaced when Zeus begins to favor a young Trojan boy named Ganymede. Eilithyia, the third child, presides over childbirth, which itself is a violent, chaotic time. Plutarch, a late Greek writer, expresses the Greek view of childbirth best when he writes in his *Moralia*, "Nothing is as imperfect, needy, naked, shapeless, and soiled as a human being at the moment of birth . . . all covered with blood, full of filth, he looks more like a slaughtered creature than a newborn child." Childbirth only happens with much pain, screaming, blood, and, of course, the constant threat of death.

The *Iliad* (1.396ff.) records one story about Zeus that catches our attention. According to Homer, Hera, Athena, and Poseidon plotted the overthrow of Zeus and attempted to chain him up, but the sea nymph Thetis appealed to Aegeon, one of the hundred-handed giants, for help. His imposing presence was enough to thwart their plan. Here is the Greek hero Achilles in the *Iliad* addressing his mother Thetis and reminding her of the story:

"Time and again I heard your claims in father's halls, boasting how you and you alone of all the immortals rescued Zeus, the lord of the dark storm cloud, from ignominious, stark defeat. That day that Olympians tried to chain him down, Hera, Poseidon lord of the sea, and Pallas Athena—you rushed to Zeus, dear Goddess, broke those chains, quickly ordered the hundred-hander to steep Olympus, that monster whom the immortals call Briareus but every mortal calls the Sea-god's son, Aegaeon, though he's stronger than his father. Down he sat, flanking Cronus' son, gargantuan in the glory of it all, and the blessed gods were struck with terror then, they stopped shackling Zeus."

—taken from Robert Fagles' translation of the *Iliad*

Although Zeus continued to have many relationships with females, after he formally married Hera, making her the queen of the gods, he never divorced. Their wedding took place in the Garden of the Hesperides at the ends of the earth, a kind of fertile Garden of Eden where all things grow lush and effortlessly. Gaia, Mother Earth, gave to Hera golden apples as a wedding present, which she in turn planted in the Garden of the Hesperides. This resulted in the famous tree of the golden apples where Herakles would one day gather fruit as part of his labors. The tree and the garden symbolize one of Hera's main functions, shared later with her daughter Eileithyia: she oversees childbirth. Most of the myths about Hera stem from her jealousy over Zeus' affairs. These she particularly despises because they threaten the stability of the family that she most wants to protect (as does Zeus, but that does not prevent him from also wanting to spread his seed far and wide). It is to Hera that matrons turn for success in bed, for stature in their home, and for the wisdom to run it well.

Although Hera is angry at Zeus for infidelity, she typically punishes the girl, the easier target. Zeus never wavers in his authority of his wife, no matter how many vows he broke. Hera also became enraged at the Trojans when in a beauty contest Paris, son of the Trojan king Priam, decided to pronounce Aphrodite the most beautiful of the goddesses. For this reason in particular she helped the Greeks in their fight against the Trojans then, and when the Trojan prince Aeneas was trying to escape to Italy, she did everything in her power to sink his ship and disrupt his journey. She complains of her "spurned beauty" during the contest, the responsibilities taken from her daughter Hebe and given over to the Trojan boy Ganymede (he becomes cupbearer in heaven), and the general disrespect that her plans receive from Zeus.

Like the other gods and goddesses, Hera receives her own praise among the *Homeric Hymns*:

> "Of golden-throned Hera I sing, born of Rhea,
> queen of the gods, unexcelled in beauty,
> sister and glorious wife of loud-thundering Zeus.
> All the gods on lofty Olympos reverence her
> and honor her together with Zeus who delights in thunder."

—*Homeric Hymn to Hera*, transl. by A. N. Athanassakis

It is important to note from this passage, as complimentary as it seems at first glance, that Hera derives her status and worthiness from her relationship to a man. The gods honor her *together with Zeus*, who is her brother and her husband. This secondary status never quite sits well with Hera, and much of what drives her activity is her resistance to this subjugated role.

SOME HYMNS TO ZEUS

You have already been exposed to the *Homeric Hymn to Zeus* in the opening quote of this chapter. Despite the name, the *Homeric Hymns* were not written by Homer at all, but in a style reminiscent of him. They appear gradually centuries after Homer composed his works and were eventually brought together into a collection that someone attempted to earn credibility for by attaching the name of Greece's great poet.

Besides the *Homeric Hymn* collection, other poets of Greece in other time periods wrote poems and hymns to the gods, each with their own purpose and take on the subject. Here are two more later hymns of Zeus that reveal a developing concern for more humanistic matters. In other words, these hymns constantly raise the question, "How should we then live?"

1. Callimachus was a talented poet of the court of the Ptolemies during the Hellenistic Age, shortly after the time of Alexander the Great, when the Greeks built the great city of Alexandria in Egypt. His *Hymn to Zeus*, given in full below, may strike us as odd in that it devotes so much space to recounting the story of Zeus' birth, until we remember that much of Christian worship (and the worship of other faiths) hinges on the retelling of stories of the divinity: at Christmas, e.g., we retell the story of Jesus' birth as a way of worshiping him (note the song "Away in a Manger" and other carols of that sort). There are many place names here. This list may help:

Dikte and *Lykaion* are mountains in Crete and *Arkadia* (in the Peloponessus) respectively. *Parrhasia* is a mountainous region in Arkadia.

Ladon, Eurymanthos, Iaon, Melas, Karneion, Krathis, Metope are rivers in Arkadia.

Lepreion is a city in Arkadia where the descendants of Kaukon rule.

Thenai-by-Knossos: there were two Thenai, one in Arkadia, the other a small town near Knossos in Crete.

Kydonia was in northwestern Crete.

Hymn I: To Zeus

"What song but of Zeus for the God's libations?[1]
Eternal Lord, eternally great, mythic scourge
of the Sons of Earth,[2] lawgiver to the Sons of Heaven,
Diktaian, Lykaian—how praise the mountain-born god?
Disputed nativity
divides the mind in doubt.
Cretan hills of Ida, Zeus?
Arkadia?
Of these claimants, which has lied, Father?
Cretans are always liars.
And your Cretan-built tomb, my Lord,
will never hold your immortal essence.

---

[1]Libations are being poured to Zeus at a symposium (drinking party) when Callimachus breaks into song.
[2]The Giants sprung from Mother Earth.

On Parrhasia, Rhea bore you, in Arkadia, where
the mountain is shaded with thickest thornbush.
That is holy ground now. No creeping thing,
no woman in labor seeks Eileithyia[3] in that
immemorial Apidanian birthbed of Rhea.
There mother deposited you from the laps and folds
of her body divine, and sought running water
to cleanse herself after birth's defilement
and to wash your skin Zeus.

But mighty Ladon
was not a flow yet, nor Eurymanthos
whitest of rivers,
and all of Arkadia was a waterless parch
which hereafter was called well-watered and -streamed.
At the moment when Rhea slackened her clothes
old hollow oaks
shaded Iaon's moist surge,
Melas was creaking with traffic of wagons,
and serpents coiled and swarmed in their lairs
above Karneion's wetness,
and a man on foot
might pass above Krathis and pebbled Metope,
thirsty for all of the water beneath him.
And Lady Rhea, in the grip of distress, said:

"Earth, dear, deliver—your birth pains are easy!"

Poised in her speech with great arm held high,
the goddess struck: staff to the mountains and water asunder
poured from the rift. In this, O my Lord,
she brightened your flesh, and swaddled and gave you
to Neda,[4] your escort to Crete and a secret upbringing,
Neda, the eldest of those midwifing nymphs
in that earliest birth after Philyra and Styx.
No idle grace repaid this service:
the goddess named that river Neda.
Full in its course
it passes close
to the Kaukonian city

---

[3]Goddess of childbirth, daughter of Hera.
[4]Neda is the daughter of Ocean, born after Styx and Philyra. She assisted at Zeus' birth.

known as
Lepreion,
then
mingles with Nereus,[5]
river with sea,
its ancient waters
drunk by Arkadians
the Sons of the Bear.[6]

Carrying you to Knossos
the nymph left Thenai,
and at that point, Zeus-Father,
near Thenai-by-Knossos,
your navel, Divine One,
dropped to the ground,
on the Umbilical Plain
as the Kydonians still call it.

But your godself the hetairae[7] of the Korybants cradled,
the ash-nymphs of Dikte, and Adrestaia[8] tucked you
in the golden crib, and you sucked butterfat milk
from the goat Amaltheia, and consumed honeycomb sweets,
spontaneous generation of the Panakrian bee
on those hills of Ida known as Panakra.
And the Kuretes orchestrated an armor dance round you,
beating shields like cymbals so that Kronos would hear
bombilating weaponry, but not you playing baby.

You were a lovely child, Zeus: well fed, you grew tall,
swift adolescence, rapid fuzz to your cheeks.
But your youth was wise: you were a young Perfect Master.
And for this your high kindred, though of the Elder Race,
conceded you the sky as your rightful home.
Old poets lie when they say that the lot
assigned triplicate homes to the sons of Kronos.
Who would play dice for Olympos and Hades

---

[5]Nereus is an old sea god.
[6]Arkadians are called "bear people" because they descend from a relationship between Zeus and Callisto, who was transformed into a bear.
[7]The word, often translated "prostitutes," suggests that they were the consorts of the Korybants.
[8]Adrestaia is a sister of the Kuretes, semidivine beings who attend Rhea along with the Korybants (sometimes they are treated as one).

except a green novice? The stakes should be equal
for a gamble like this. These were whole worlds apart.

A poet's fiction should at least be plausible.

Not the luck of the draw made you shah of the gods
but Strength in your hands;
Force crouched by your throne
and Power beside it.
And as for your portent you drafted the most
magnificent of birds (may he flash on my right)
so also of men you chose the greatest as yours,
not sea captains, not soldiers, no, not even poets—
these you dismissed to lesser divinities,
other wards for other gods—but reserved for yourself
kings, rulers of cities,
under whose hands are
landowners,
oarswingers,
spearmongers,
tradesmen
and whatnot.

So we say: blacksmiths belong to Hephaistos,
mercenaries to Ares,
hunters to Artemis Chiton,[9]
and to Apollo those who strum tunes on a lyre.
But kings are from Zeus, and there is nothing more divine
than God's own lords.
And so you chose them to sponsor,
gave them cities to guard, and took your position
in the high citadels, a monitor of judgments
straight and crooked, to see how they govern.
And you lavished wealth
and prosperity on them, on all, but not equally
if we may judge by our monarch,
for Ptolemy Philadelphos is preeminent by far.
he accomplishes by dusk what he thinks of at dawn—
the monumental by dusk, the minor in a trice—
while the projects of others drag on for years,
their programs curtailed by your executive order.

---

[9]A chiton was a tunic that Artemis wore while hunting.

A Royal Salute to the Son of Kronos most high!
Benefactor and Savior, who could hymn your works?
That poet hasn't been born,
inconceivable poet of the works of Zeus.

A second salute, Father! Dispense goodness and wealth:
Wealth without goodness is a worthless increase,
and goodness needs substance.
Bless us with both, Zeus."

2. The Greek philosophers of the Hellenistic Age (late 4th Century B.C. and on) were not so quick to dismiss Zeus or any of the other mythological gods, so as not to make themselves appear to be atheists or subverters. Instead, they preferred to retain the name of the god while offering some alternative way of interpreting and understanding the activities of the divine nature. The Stoic philosophers followed this trend, even though their ideas about divine beings had little to do with popular mythological gods. One interesting example of this adaptation of mythological names appears in the Stoic Cleanthes' *Hymn to Zeus*. Although his hymn sounds typical and devout, it even seems Christian at times, it really masks philosophical doctrines quite alien to popular religion and thought:

"Most majestic of immortals, many-titled, ever omnipotent Zeus, prime mover of nature, who with your law steer all things, hail to you. For it is proper for any mortal to address you: we are your offspring, and alone of all mortal creatures which are alive and tread the earth we bear a likeness to god. Therefore I shall hymn you and sing forever of your might."

"All this cosmos, as it spins around the earth, obeys you, whichever way you lead, and willingly submits to your sway. Such is the double-edged fiery ever-living thunderbolt which you hold at the read in your unvanquished hands. For under its strokes all the works of nature are accomplished. With it you direct the universal reason which runs through all things and inter-mingles with the lights of heaven both great and small . . ."

"No deed is done on earth, god, without your offices, nor in the divine ethereal vault of heaven, nor at sea, save what bad men do in their folly. But you know how to make things crooked straight and to order things disor-derly. You love things unloved. For you have so welded into one all things good and bad that they all share in a single everlasting reason. It is shunned and neglected by the bad among mortal men, the wretched, who ever yearn for the possession of goods yet neither see nor hear god's universal law, by obeying which they could lead a good life in partnership and intelligence.

Instead, devoid of intelligence, they rush into this evil or that, some in their belligerent quest for fame, others with an unbridled bent for acquisition, others for leisure and the pleasurable acts of the body . . . But all that they achieve is evils, despite traveling hither and thither in burning quest of the opposite."

"Bountiful Zeus of the dark clouds and gleaming thunderbolt, protect mankind from its pitiful incompetence. Scatter this from our soul, Father. Let us achieve the power of judgment by trusting in which you steer all things with justice, so that by winning honor we may repay you with honor, forever singing of your works, as it befits mortals to do. For neither men nor gods have any greater privilege than this: to sing forever in righteousness of the universal law."

—Taken from Long & Sedley, *The Hellenistic Philosophers*, vol. 1, pp. 326–7.

CHAPTER FIVE

Poseidon, Ares, Hermes, Hephaestus

POSEIDON

"I sing about Poseidon, the great god, mover of the earth and fruitless sea, god of the deep who is also lord of Helicon and broad Aigai [a town on the Corinthian Gulf sacred to Poseidon]. O you shaker of the earth, the gods have appointed you to be the awful tamer of horses and preserver of ships! Hail, Poseidon holder of the earth, dark-haired lord! O blessed one, bear a benign mind and give aid to sailors!"

—*Homeric Hymn 22 to Poseidon*

The three brothers who were descended from Kronos felt they had the right to rule once they had overthrown their father since they were from the royal line. Instead of coming to blows, they decided to divide up the universe into three parts, with Zeus retaining control over the sky since he was the one brave enough to stand up to Kronos, the savage Poseidon acting as lord of the waters, and the gloomy Hades reigning as king in the underworld.

If it is true that the Greeks originally migrated from the northern regions of Europe and western Asia, Poseidon primarily may have been for them a god who brought water to the crops in streams. In other words, he is not so much the god of the sea as he is the god of the fluid element, the fertilizing moisture (as, in some ways, the god Eros was). By the time the Greeks had settled in Greece, which is surrounded by sea on almost every side, they thought of him mainly as a sea god and the "holder of the earth" (because the sea surrounds the earth), but who still retained ultimate control over all water in all forms. He is usually shown holding a fishing spear, or trident, and is associated with horses. The hymn cited above calls him the "awful tamer," not an indication that he's incompetent but that he deserves reverence for his ability to tame the wild horse, an animal which he himself created as a gift to the inhabitants of Thessaly (remember the Centaurs came from this region as well). He is *Hippios* Poseidon. It was Poseidon who taught men to manage horses by the bridle and he himself is often depicted riding horses on the sea or in a chariot pulled by a team of horses. For this reason he is revered

(CNG 76, Lot: 3251) Sextus Pompey, Silver denarius, c. 42–40 B.C. Uncertain Sicilian mint. Quinquereme adorned with eagle, scepter, and trident sailing left before the lighthouse of Messana, decorated with a statue of Neptune. On the reverse, the monster Scylla, her torso consisting of dogs and fishes, wielding a rudder as a club.

by charioteers and is often worshiped in festivals that include chariot racing. Not surprisingly, when Demeter turned herself into a horse to try to escape Poseidon, he turned himself into a horse and mated with her. With her he sired the horse named Arion. Poseidon also bears the epithet "earth-shaker" not only because he pounds the shores with his waves and uses his trident to create earthquakes (many earthquakes begin in the sea), but because horses hooves thunder as they pound the earth.

Poseidon's wife was Amphitrite, one of the many daughters of the old sea god Nereus (making her a "Nereid") and his wife Doris. At first she rejected Poseidon's attentions, but when he tried to sexually assault her near the island of Naxos, she fled to the Atlantic Ocean. After a long search some dolphins found her, convinced her to return, and escorted her through the Mediterranean to Poseidon to be his bride.

> "Poseidon loves dolphins very much, sinces when he was seeking Amphitrite the dark-eyed daughter of Nereus, who fled from his embraces, the dolphins discovered her hiding in the halls of Oceanos and told Poseidon; and the god of the dark hair straightway carried off the maiden and overcame her against her will. He made her to be his bride, queen of the sea, and for their disclosure of Amphitrite's whereabouts he commended his kindly attendants and bestowed on them a great honor for what they had done."

—Oppian, *Halieutica* 1.38

The couple produced the child Triton, king of the mermaids and mermen, who made his home on the Libyan shores and often blew into a conch shell for a horn.

Poseidon spawned many monstrous children who either took the form of a horse or lived in or near the sea. Typically these creatures were the result of a violent assault by Poseidon on some innocent girl and were themselves indomitable or savage. Polyphemus, the ill-mannered one-eyed giant whom Odysseus met and whom the sea god had sired with the nymph Thoosa, took his temper from his father. By Athena's priestess Medusa he produced Chrysaor, a golden giant who brandished a sword from birth, and Pegasus, the winged horse that Bellerophon eventually captured. Theseus met and destroyed two of Poseidon's inhospitable sons, Cercyon and Sciron, on his way from Troezen to Athens. Poseidon's two sons Otus and Ephialtes, known also as the Aloadae giants, grew so large and fearsome that one day they piled mountain upon mountain in Greece in effort to dislodge the Olympian gods from heaven. Clearly the Greeks endowed Poseidon with the violent and unpredictable nature of the sea itself.

In fact, one can mark this surly nature of Poseidon in all of his myths and in artistic depictions. In the war against the giants, the sea god pursued one certain giant, Polybotes, as far as the Aegean sea and the island of Kos. There Poseidon tore off a huge piece of the island Kos and threw it on top of the giant himself, crushing him. The rock, which stands at the tip of Kos, from then on became separately named Nisyros. At another time, when the mother of Andromeda boasted that her daughter was more beautiful than the Nereids, Poseidon punished her by sending a terrible sea monster named Cetus to ravish the land (perhaps Ethiopia or Joppa). The people of the region were told by an oracle that they had to sacrifice Andromeda to the sea monster in order to remove the danger from themselves. It was during this incident that Perseus showed up and used Medusa's head to turn the monster to stone (see the Perseus chapter below), thereby rescuing the maiden and marrying her. Poseidon also sent a sea monster against the Trojans once when their leader, Laomedon, refused to pay Poseidon for building Troy's walls, along with the help of Apollo. The sea monster was about to devour Laomedon's daughter Hesione (as the other one almost ate Andromeda) when Herakles showed up and killed him. This event is recorded on a famous vase which has made quite a stir in recent years when one scholar noticed that the sea monster depicted there in skeletal form in fact has the exact skull of a creature of the Miocene period known only through the fossil record (at least 5 million years old). The creature is known to us as the Samotherium. Such a discovery has led to a greater interest on the part of scholars as to what the ancients knew of fossils and dinosaurs. At any rate, it should be noted that the reason Poseidon was building walls for the Trojans in the first place was because he had participated in a conspiracy, along with Hera and Athena, to put Zeus in chains. Once defeated in this revolt, Poseidon was forced to work for Laomedon as a common laborer (but not a slave, thus the interest in receiving wages).

All cities of ancient Greece believed that they had a patron god or goddess who watched over them and gave them special protection in return for special recognition, a beautiful temple, and worship. The god or goddess would often represent the character that the citizens wanted to project. When Athens was being formed, they too needed to find a patron to protect their city, and their invitation found two takers: Both Athena and Poseidon wanted to be patron of Athens. As the story goes, the founders of the city held a contest for the two gods to see who could give the greatest gift. They all stood around on the tallest hill in town, called the Acropolis (a word which means "high point in the city"); there Poseidon struck a hole in the ground with his trident and up sprang a stream of water (it happened to be salt water, so not very beneficial). True to his earthquaking character, he caused a rift in the ground.

Athena, in contrast, caused an olive tree to grow, a very useful thing since one can eat olives, trade them, use the oils, enjoy the shade, and so on. So the Athenians chose Athena, and took their name from her.

Poseidon, in his anger, caused the entire area of Athens to flood. Zeus was later able to reconcile the Athenians to Poseidon by convincing them to grant honors, albeit secondary, to him too. On the Acropolis the Athenians built a huge temple to Athena, the Parthenon, one of the grandest buildings in the ancient world. But they also built one to Poseidon, in combination with their founder, and called it the Erechtheum. There they still marked the spot where the trident made a crack in the ground, just as Athena's olive tree still grew next to her temple until 480 B.C. when the attacking Persians uprooted it.

Poseidon's most famous temple in all Greece was on Cape Sounion, what Homer called "the sacred headland." This Doric temple, built around 440 B.C. on the foundations of an even older one, occupied a commanding position overlooking the Aegean Sea at the entrance to the Saronic Gulf. It was from here that Aegeus jumped when he saw Theseus' ship with the black sail still hoisted (see the Theseus story in chapter sixteen). Sailors rounding the cape could look up at the temple of Poseidon and say a prayer or make a vow for a safe passage through these treacherous waters. In ancient times the temple was filled with plaques and trophies of various types given to the god by the grateful mariners. Jason suspended his enormous ship Argo from the ceiling as a thank-offering for a safe voyage through the Black Sea.

ARES

"Ares, exceeding in strength, chariot-rider, golden-helmed, manly in heart, shield-bearer, savior of cities, harnessed in bronze, strong of arm, unwearying, mighty with the spear, O defender of Olympus, father of warlike Nike (Victory), ally of Themis, stern governor of the rebellious, leader of righteous men, sceptered king of manliness, who whirl your fiery sphere [the star Mars] among the planets in their sevenfold courses through the ether wherein your blazing steeds ever bear you above the third firmament of heaven; hear me, helper of men, giver of dauntless youth! Shed down a kindly ray from above upon my life, and strength of war, that I may be able to drive away bitter cowardice from my head and crush down the deceitful impulses of my soul.

—*Homeric Hymn 8 to Ares*

The *Homeric Hymn to Ares* delineates well the credentials of Ares: He is the god who gives manly courage and a zeal for battle to warriors. A child of Zeus and Hera, Ares' personality reflects the tension that existed in the marriage of the king and queen of the gods. He controls strife of every kind, whether citizens are rising up against their leaders, or foot soldiers are clashing armor in the field. He is there among them, rallying the hearts of those whom he supports, bolstering their courage, and striking fear in those whom he does not protect. He can both bring conflict and, when it is time, take it away. But mostly he does not care about the causes of war, or right and wrong, or the best tactics to take. Those are the concerns of Athena. Ares can support both sides of a conflict, whatever allows him to relish the din and confusion and uproar that is associated with warfare.

Ares is said to have had the strength and effectiveness of ten thousand soldiers, but that did not ensure that he would always be victorious in his own battles. Athena was able to strike him down during the Trojan War and to leave his body sprawling before the walls. Herakles defeated him as he defended his son Cycnus at Delphi after the latter had attacked Herakles. The list goes on. Sometimes Ares won his battles, sometimes he did not. Nothing, however, could keep him from joining them.

The ancient authors tell us that Eros (Cupid) caused Ares to fall in love with Aphrodite by handing to him one of his arrows of love. After taking it and holding it in his hands, Ares looked over at Aphrodite and saw her smile. He was hooked. Aphrodite likewise found Ares very handsome, as extreme femininity was attracted to extreme manliness. The two would have been married then and there, but this did not happen. After Hephaestus was booted from heaven by his mother Hera (see below) and subsequently bound her deceitfully to a chair, Dionysus told Hephaestus that he could bargain for the hand of Aphrodite in marriage in exchange for Hera's release. Hephaestus liked the idea and so the other gods had to agree. But this did not stop Ares and Aphrodite from carrying on an affair. A rather elaborate story is told in the *Odyssey* how Hephaestus figured out what was going on and ensnared the two in the embraces of love. The result of this affair was the girl Harmonia, daughter of Ares and the goddess of love. But Aphrodite also cheated on Ares by falling in love with the human Adonis (Aphrodite appears to have taken on some of her father's characteristics in this regard). Ares remedied the situation by morphing into a boar and mortally wounding his rival.

The Greeks believed that Ares was worshiped among especially warlike peoples: The Thracians, just northeast of Greece, whom the Greeks called barbaric savages, are said to house the god in their country. In fact, Ares may have been introduced to Greece from the Thracians. The Amazons were descendants of Ares, so the story went, and carried on nightly rituals to their patron near the Athenian acropolis that terrified her citizens. The Spartans built a temple to Ares outside of their city walls with a statue of the god wrapped in chains as a warning to enemies who approached that they revere the very god of war who never can leave. We hear of human sacrifices made to Ares both at Thebes and Sparta, and a few temples to the god were scattered elsewhere throughout Greece. Clearly, the Greeks admired and coveted the manly courage that the god of war could offer to them, but the destructiveness and confusion of war that he could cause lessened his overall attractiveness to them. He was a god of necessity, not one that they would choose to love for his own sake.

HERMES

"I sing of Hermes of Mt. Cyllene, the Slayer of Argus, lord of Cyllene and Arcadia rich in flocks, luck-bringing, messenger of the deathless gods. He was born of Maia, the daughter of Atlas, when she had made love with Zeus, although she is a shy goddess. She always avoided the throng of the blessed gods and lived in a shadowy cave, and there Zeus used to lie with the rich-tressed Maia in the middle of the night, while white-armed Hera lay bound in sweet sleep. And neither deathless god nor mortal man knew it. And so hail to you, Son of Zeus and Maia; with you I have begun; now I will turn to another song! Hail, Hermes, giver of grace, guide, and giver of good things!"

—*Homeric Hymn 18 to Hermes*

Hermes was the son of Zeus and Maia (daughter of Atlas). He was born in a cave on Mt. Cyllene in southern Arcadia, and, like all babies of the day, wrapped in swaddling clothes. His mother placed him in a basket instead of a crib (or even a manger). According to the Homeric Hymn to Hermes, "the child whom she bore was devious, winning in his cleverness, a robber, a driver of cattle, a guide of dreams, a spy in the night, a watcher at the door who soon was about to make manifest renowned deeds among the immortal gods." His tricky nature derives from the fact that he was conceived in the deep dark night when both gods and men were asleep.

From the very first day the child proved that he was precocious: He began by extricating himself from his swaddling clothes and sneaking off to steal the cattle of Apollo. Some authors say he stole fifty cattle, some say more, but at any rate he compelled the cattle to walk backward so that it would look like they were headed toward the meadow instead of away from it. Furthermore, he later tied a branch to their tails to cover up their tracks. He drove them all the way back to Pylos, near his cave, and sacrificed some of the cattle to the twelve Olympian gods. He also made a sacrifice to himself so that he could enjoy the aroma, which is what the gods most enjoy about sacrifices.

After concealing the rest of the herd, Hermes sneaked by into his cave and hid in his basket. On the way in, however, he found an empty turtle shell which he used to construct the very first lyre (a kind of guitar). But some man had seen Hermes stealing the cattle and he ran off and told Apollo. Enraged, Apollo went to the child's cave and found him in his basket. He grabbed the baby (Hermes was only one day old!) and began threatening him with violence (Hermes suffered from shaken baby syndrome, I suppose). Looking innocent, Hermes retorted, "Do I look like a cattle thief? I'm just a baby! I swear I didn't steal them." Hermes went on to claim that he had never even heard of cows before. The two of them went to Zeus then to plead their cases before his tribunal. Hermes acted pitiful while telling some fairly transparent lies. Zeus, though, rather enjoyed Hermes' storytelling capabilities and just laughed off the whole affair. He ordered Hermes to return the cattle and be done with the whole trick. Hermes was also anxious to win Apollo over in the end, so he offered the lyre to him as a gift. Apollo gratefully accepted it as Hermes' token of apology. From that time on, the lyre became the special instrument of Apollo.

Later, Apollo offered Hermes a gift of a golden crook, which came to be known as the caduceus or herald's wand, a common attribute of him in art, along with the broad-rimmed hat of travelers and the winged shoes. All these objects symbolized the fact that Hermes was the messenger (herald) of both Zeus and Hades. Zeus had been pleased with all of Hermes trickery, which saved him many times during dangerous battles: Hermes knew how to steal from the enemy and gain an advantage; he knew how to slip into difficult places and to emerge safely. Therefore, Zeus chose him as his special emissary and messenger. For example, he was involved in relaying Zeus' commands to the Greek and Trojan heroes during the Trojan War and its aftermath; it was he, in fact, who led Hera, Aphrodite, and Athena to Paris so that the latter could pass judgment on which goddess was the most beautiful. As Hades' messenger, and as the god who watched over travelers in general, Hermes became known as the *psychopompos,* that is, the escort of the souls of the dead to their final home.

In his role as a traveler god, Hermes was in charge of commerce, flight and robbers.

Mostly, though, travelers liked to believe that Hermes was watching over them, and along the roads they would have seen many *Hermae*, that is, statues set up at in honor of Hermes. The statues, usually placed at crossroads, were shaped like a human bust with male organs attached. The Greeks even placed them at crossroads inside the city limits, and as they passed by would give some token of respect to the Herm. Once, in fact, while the Athenians were preparing for war against Sicily, they discovered that someone had disfigured the stone Hermae in Athens. They took the whole affair very seriously as a bad omen, and offered reward money for anyone who came forth with information that led to an arrest and conviction. Sometimes Hermes appears in art carrying a sheep over his shoulders, a sign that shepherds thought of him as their patron god as well.

HEPHAESTUS

"Sing, clear-voiced Muses, of Hephaestus famed for inventions. With bright-eyed Athena he taught men glorious crafts throughout the world, men who before used to dwell in caves in the mountains like wild beasts. But now that they have learned crafts through Hephaestus the famed worker, easily they live a peaceful life in their own houses the whole year round. Be gracious, Hephaistos, and grant me success and prosperity!"

—Homeric Hymn 20 to Hephaestus

Hephaestus was originally a god of fire, both of the earth and in the sky. In myth it is said that Hera produced him unilaterally, without the help of Zeus, because she was jealous that Zeus had produced the beautiful child Athena from his own head (a male giving birth gave concern to Hera, the goddess of childbirth). Hera could only produce an ugly child, in contrast to the usual beauty and symmetry of the other gods, with twisted legs that forced him to hobble when he walked (perhaps Hephaestus' limp symbolized the zig-zag of lightning). According to Homer, as Hephaestus walks around Mt. Olympus during their banquets he cuts such a ridiculous figure that he arouses the "unquenchable laughter of the immortals."

Hera was so ashamed of Hephaestus' ugliness and deformities that she immediately threw him from Mt. Olympus so that he fell into the sea. There he was taken in by Thetis, daughter of Nereus, and Eurynome, daughter of Ocean. For nine years he remained concealed in the ocean depths and became fascinated by all the volcanic activity there. He soon proved skilled in the blacksmith's art and spent his time forging thousands of ingenious objects for the two nymphs who rescued him. He also plotted his revenge.

One day, Hera received a gift from her rejected son, a golden throne so artistically wrought that she could not wait to sit on it. But when she sat down, invisible bonds wrapped around her rendering her immobile. The other immortals tried in vain to extricate her from this clever trap, until they resolved that they must bring Hephaestus himself up to Mt. Olympus to unlock the chair's mysteries. Hephaestus, however, refused to leave his ocean home. Ares tried to drag him up by force, as we would expect of the war god, but Hephaestus put him to flight by throwing firebrands at him. Dionysus was more successful: He made Hephaestus drunk, then attached him to the side of a donkey and drove him back to Olympus.

It was one thing to get Hephaestus to Mt. Olympus, still another to get him to agree to release his mother from the trap. The gods must meet his demands: Hephaestus refused to release Hera unless he could take Aphrodite, loveliest of the immortals, as his bride.

From that time on Hera and her son loved each other. In fact, Hephaestus would often risk his life to break up fights between his mother and her husband Zeus, lest his mother be abused. Once, while attempting to defend his mother as she was being beaten, Hephaestus irritated Zeus greatly. The king of the gods grabbed his son by the foot and flung him from Mt. Olympus once again. He fell for the space of one whole day until at sunset he landed more dead than alive on the island of Lemnos, a barren, volcanic island, which from then on became Hephaestus' favorite forge. Every night he went to work at his furnace with the assistance of the Cyclopes. There he made all kinds of amazing objects: the palaces of Mt. Olympus, Zeus' throne and thunderbolts, weapons for famous heroes, Demeter's sickle, Artemis' arrows, various cups, vases, shields, and even Pandora. He also made artificial beings to serve him in the forge. Homer refers to them in a striking passage about the visit by Thetis to the forge to procure new armor for her son Achilles:

"Thetis found Hephaestus sweating as he turned here and there to his bellows busily, since he was working on twenty tripods at once. Hephaestus took the huge blower off from the block of the anvil while limping; and yet his withered legs moved lightly and nimbly beneath him. He set the bellows away from the fire, and gathered and put away all the tools with which he worked in a silver toolbox. Then with a sponge he wiped clean his forehead and both hands, and likewise he cleaned his massive neck and hairy chest, and put on a tunic, and took up a heavy stick in his hand, and went to the doorway limping. And in support of their master moved his attendants. These attendants are golden, and in appearance like living young women. There hearts possess some form of intelligence, and they have the ability to speak and strength, and from the immortal gods they have learned how to do things. These stirred nimbly in support of their master."

—Homer, *Iliad* 18.136

Thetis, it should be emphasized, has come here to this sooty, grimy place seeking from a lame, dirty god magnificent new weaponry for her son. It is ironic that the ugliest of the gods is the very one who brought so much beauty into the lives of the gods.

CHAPTER SIX

Artemis, Protectress of the Young and Athena, Goddess of Crafts

ARTEMIS

"I don't care what city you assign to me. To the cities Artemis does not often come down. I will visit them only when women, vexed by the sharp pang of childbirth, call me to their aid—even in the hour when I was born the Moirai (Fates) ordained that I should be their helper, forasmuch as my mother suffered no pain either when she gave me birth or when she carried me in her womb, but without travail put me from her body."

—Callimachus, *Hymn 3* (Artemis addressing her father Zeus)

Ancient writers from Homer to Ovid consistently describe Artemis as an impressive figure who towers head and shoulders over her companion nymphs and outstrips them in loveliness. She lives among the hills, streams, and glens, not in the cities, content to pursue the wild animals with hunting dogs and her fearsome arrows. She knows the use of nets and snares. Apollonius of Rhodes tells us that the fawning wild beasts whimper in homage and tremble in awe as she passes by. The mountains themselves quake and groan. Deer humbly take on the yoke to pull her chariot. For good reason all of nature fears Artemis, because to her alone did her father Zeus give the power to slaughter animals at will. She is *Potnia Therōn* ("mistress of the wild animals"), stag hunter, lynx slayer, queen of birds, fish, and beasts. The ancient travel writer, Pausanias, describes a relief that he saw at Olympia showing Artemis with wings on her shoulders and gripping a leopard and a lion in her hands. Another statue he saw elsewhere depicted Artemis wrapped in the skin of a deer and accompanied by a hunting dog. The quiver on her shoulders was full of arrows. She wore boots and a tunic girt up for hunting. We know from other sources that the goddess also liked to fish. The temple of Artemis at Syracuse in Sicily contained a pond with large fish sacred to the goddess and untouched by humans. Her sanctuaries often contained wells or were built on the shores of lakes or rivers. Her influence stretched over all living things, whether on the mountains, in the air, or in the water.

(CNG 76, Lot: 78.) Lucania, Thourioi, a silver double nomos, c. 350–300 B.C. Helmeted head of Athena; helmet decorated with Scylla holding trident. On the reverse, a bull butting right.

The *Homeric Hymn to Artemis* 2.1-10 rehearses succinctly many of the important elements of her character:

> "I sing of the brilliant Artemis with her golden arrows, the venerated virgin, the archeress who strikes deer with her arrows, the sister of Apollo with his golden sword, she who, in the shadows of mountains and on the mountaintops whipped by the winds, stretches her bow of pure gold, and, for the joy of the hunt, shoots the arrows that make her victims groan. The peaks of great mountains tremble. The forest in its darkness screams with the frightened clamor of the animals of the woods. The earth trembles, as does the fish-filled sea. The goddess of valiant heart runs and leaps, appearing everywhere, sowing death among the race of wild animals."

But the ancients did not think of Artemis simply as a killer. She was the protectress and nourisher of the young in particular. Women invoked Artemis at childbirth, along with other goddesses, because they knew she would ease their pain in labor and ensure the safety of the infant as it exited the birth canal. Children, especially girls, remained in the care of Artemis until they reached the age of marrying and adulthood, at which time they dedicated their childhood toys and virginal lingerie in her temple as a sign that they had matured from their state of innocence. The girls were grateful that Artemis had guarded their chastity until this time when it was proper to relinquish it to the male. This act of relinquishment was viewed by the ancients as a death of sorts, a threshold from one state of being to another. The maiden dies, the childhood ends, the girl is stripped from her mother's protective arms and given over by the father to the husband and to the city. She is now wife, mother, citizen-bearer, something new from something old. This act of transformation is sometimes represented or symbolized by the sacrifice of an animal, such as a deer or a bear. Both of these animals undergo major, visible transformations (the deer grows antlers, the bear emerges from the cave) that mark a new stage in their life.

This imagery is what stands behind the bizarre story of the sacrifice of Iphigenia, the daughter of Agamemnon, who was set to lead the Greek troops against the Trojans. After

Helen was stolen by Paris and taken to Troy, Greeks from all over Greece gathered at the harbor Aulis to prepare an expedition against Troy. While the huge army gathered, Agamemnon had the problem that he had to feed all these hungry mouths. Food was becoming scarce, so much so that on one hunt Agamemnon struck and killed a young deer (so young that normal hunting laws would forbid such a slaughter); Artemis, who protects the young animals, became angry, and caused an opposing wind to blow against the Greek fleet. Since the Greeks had not yet mastered the art of sailing *into* the wind, there was no hope that their expedition would ever leave Aulis until the goddess was appeased in some way. As it turns out, she demanded that Agamemnon sacrifice to her his firstborn daughter (Iphigenia, who was right at the proper age for marrying) before the winds would stop blowing against them. Agamemnon was so anxious to sail to Troy and get on with the fighting, that he complied with the goddess' command: He invited Iphigenia to come from Mycene to Aulis on the pretext that she would be marrying Achilles, the great hero. When Iphigenia came to Aulis and was led to what she thought was the wedding altar, she sank in fear as the attendants at the altar pulled out a knife and pushed her onto the altar for sacrifice.

Now to everyone watching, it looked as if Iphigenia was killed right then and there, and maybe she was, but some mythographers and artists relate that at the last minute Artemis substituted a deer for Iphigenia and whisked the maiden away in a mist to a place called Tauris on the Black Sea. There, Artemis set her up as a priestess in her temple. Years later, when her brother Orestes comes to that place, he finds her there attending the strange rites of Artemis that take place in Tauris, including the sacrifice of all foreigners who come to shore. Orestes rescues her from the Taurians and brings her back to Greece, where she spent the rest of her life as a priestess at Artemis' temple in Brauron near Athens and Sounion. It is at this very sanctuary at Brauron that the young girls of the region of Attica (around Athens) gathered each year to prepare themselves to enter the next stage of their lives.

These are the words of Athena, spoken in Euripides' play *Iphigenia in Tauris*: "And let this be the law. When they observe Artemis' festival, the priest shall hold, in memory of you, the sharp blade of his knife against a human throat and draw one drop of blood, then stop— this in no disrespect, but a grave reminder of her former ways. Iphigenia! Steps are cut in rock at Brauron for a shrine to Artemis. You shall reside as keeper of the keys there and at your death you shall be buried there and honored in your tomb with spotless gifts, garments unworn, woven by hands of women who honorably died in giving birth."

The story has many twists and turns, but several important elements emerge as particularly significant: The young girl who thought she was heading to a marriage is in fact sacrificed at the altar. Although no one sees it happen, a deer serves as a substitution and, after a time of separation from society and reintegration, Iphigenia becomes a priestess who guides other girls through a similar ritual of self-sacrifice, separation, and reintegration.

Thus, it is important that Artemis herself remain forever chaste. No male ever touches her, and the one male who sees her naked soon is torn apart by his own dogs (see the Actaeon story below). This makes sense if we remember that Artemis is keeping young girls sacrosanct and unviolated in their youth. It also makes sense that Artemis remain at odds with the less discriminate Aphrodite, who is driven by desire and the laws of attraction without regard for the proper stages of life. In the Hippolytus story (also below), Artemis' desire to nurture and protect conflicts with Aphrodite's pull on the young son of Theseus.

ORIGINS

Hesiod says that early on in the generation of the gods, Leto was joined in love with aegis-bearing Zeus and gave birth to golden Apollo and arrow-delighting Artemis, who were more beautiful than any other children in heaven. Now Leto was an ancient Titaness, whose iconography (in particular the veil) suggests that she was a goddess who urged on young girls modesty and demure. This modesty both protected the young girl from entering into a sexual state too soon, and demanded the respect of young men while at the same time provoking their curiosity. Leto was also connected to darkness, and in that regard may have stood as a symbol of the passage from darkness (the womb) into the light. At any rate, Hera was jealous of the union between Zeus and Leto. As often, the chronology is fuzzy. Was Hera pursuing Zeus for a future marriage with herself or was she already his wife? Was Leto a wife or a concubine? Regardless, Hera dogged and harassed Leto all over the earth, denying her refuge and aid in childbirth, until the floating island of Delos gave her refuge. The other gods, feeling sorry for Leto, convinced Eileithyia, daughter of Hera and goddess of childbirth, to go to her aid. Thus Leto gave birth to the twins Apollo and Artemis while clasping two palm trees (the trees later become a symbol of Artemis and the pangs of childbirth). Apollo (or perhaps Leto herself) fixed the floating island of Delos in place near modern Mykonos and both he and his sister enjoyed major cults there.

Cult and Meaning

Devotees set up cults to Artemis throughout ancient Greece, primarily in the countryside, though gradually shrines in her honor appeared in the cities as well. The best attested cult center was in Brauron, some miles from Athens and Marathon along the seashore in eastern Greece. An old wooden statue stood there which the ancients believed Iphigenia brought with her from Tauris on the Black Sea when she returned from that region with her brother Orestes. Because of an unfortunate incident at the site involving the death of a she-bear who was just reaching adulthood, young girls were sent to Brauron each year to appease the goddess by "playing the she-bear." The rituals that these girls performed, though our evidence for the details is rather sketchy, indicate that the act of "playing the she-bear" was a rite of passage into womanhood. This is true for Artemis shrines all over Greece, where some sort "putting to death" of the old self manifested itself in various symbolic rituals.

The goddess worshiped at Ephesus of Ionia (western Turkey) in the famous temple there, one of the seven wonders of the ancient world, may not have been Artemis at all, at least not in the beginning. Legend had it that the Amazons had built the temple there and had established the cult. The statue of the goddess at Ephesus was unlike any Greek statue of Artemis. Instead of being a young girl dressed in hunting clothes, with boots and quiver, the Ephesian statue is *polymastos* ("having many breasts"), indicating her nourishing nature, and surmounted by a mural crown (a high-walled crown) that identifies her with the protective mother earth. The lower part of her body looked like an upside-down pyramid decorated with mystical animals. Her priests were Eunuchs, men who had devoted their sexuality to the goddess.

In general, the cults of Artemis throughout Greece involved dances performed by women in rural sanctuaries. The women dance in honor of the goddess, but the dance itself may have been a re-enactment of some transformation in nature or the slaying of a wild animal. The dancing is likely to have been a means of separating the most nimble, healthy girls, from the lesser girls—we know from pottery depictions that the girls engaged in athletic contests for this reason—and there may have been a seductive element as well. The girls were exercising and moving their bodies in anticipation of giving it to their husbands.

Major Myths

In all of these myths, one must keep in mind the character and concerns of Artemis herself. These are not just random stories. Each one illustrates Artemis' fierce devotion to certain principles that govern human life. If humans want to be happy, the Greeks thought, they should learn the goddess' nature through these stories and align themselves to the eternal truths that she upholds with her power.

Actaeon

The well-known story of Actaeon's encounter with Artemis is best told through Ovid's version in book 3 of the *Metamorphoses* (this is Rolfe Humphries' translation):

> "One of these grandsons was the lad Actaeon, first cause of Cadmus' sorrow. On his forehead horns sprouted, and his hound-dogs came to drink the blood of their young master. In the story you will find Actaeon guiltless; put the blame on luck, not crime: what crime is there in error?
>
> There was a mountain, on whose slopes had fallen the blood of many kinds of game: high noon, short shadows, and Actaeon, at ease, and friendly telling his company: "Our nets and spears drip with the blood of our successful hunting. Today has brought us luck enough; tomorrow we try again. The Sun god, hot and burning, is halfway up his course. Give up the labor, bring home the nets." And they obeyed his orders.
>
> There was a valley there, all dark and shaded with pine and cypress, sacred to Diana, Gargaphie, its name was, and it held deep in its inner shade a secret grotto made by no art, unless you think of Nature as being an artist. Out of rock and tufa she had formed an archway, where the shining water made slender watery sound, and soon subsided into a pool, and grassy banks around it. The goddess of the woods, when tired from hunting, came here to bathe her limbs in the cool crystal. She gave her armor-bearer spear and quiver and loosened bow; another's arm received the robe, laid off; two nymphs unbound her sandals, and one, Crocale, defter than the others, knotted the flowing hair; others brought water, Pescas, Phyale, Nephele, and Rhanis, pouring it out from good-sized urns, as always.
>
> But look! While she was bathing there, all naked, Actaeon came, with no more thought of hunting till the next day, wandering, far from certain, through unfamiliar woodland till

he entered Diana's grove, as fate seemed bound to have it. And when he entered the cool dripping grotto, the nymphs, all naked, saw him, saw a man, and beat their breasts and screamed, and all together gathered around their goddess, tried to hide her with their own bodies, but she stood above them, taller by head and shoulders. As the clouds grow red at sunset, as the daybreak reddens, Diana blushed at being seen, and turned aside a little from her close companions, looked quickly for her arrows, found no weapon except the water, but scooped up a handful and flung it in the young man's face, and over the young man's hair. Those drops had vengeance in them. She told him so: "Tell people you have seen me, Diana, naked! Tell them if you can!"

She said no more, but on the sprinkled forehead horns of the long-lived stag began to sprout, the neck stretched out, the ears were long and pointed, the arms were legs, the hands were feet, the skin a dappled hide, and the hunter's heart was fearful. Away in flight he goes, and, going, marvels at his own speed, and finally sees, reflected, his features in a quiet pool. "Alas!" he tries to say, but has no words. He groans, the only speech he has, and the tears run down cheeks that are not his own. There is one thing only left him, his former mind.

What should he do? Where should he go—back to the royal palace or find some place of refuge in the forest? Fear argues against one, and shame the other. And while he hesitates, he sees his hounds, Blackfoot, Trailchaser, Hungry, Hurricane, Gazelle and Mountain-Ranger, Spot and Sylvan, Swift Wingfoot, Glen, wolf-sired, and the bitch Harpy with her two pups, half-grown, ranging beside her, Tigress, another bitch, Hunter, and Lanky, Chop-jaws, and Soot, and Wolf, and the shite marking on his black muzzle, Mountaineer, and Power, the Killer, Whirlwind, Whitey, Blackskin, Grabber, and others it would take too long to mention, Arcadian hounds, and Cretan-bred, and Spartan. The whole pack, with the lust of blood upon them, come baying over cliffs and crags and ledges where no trail runs: Actaeon, once pursuer over this very ground, is now pursued, fleeing his old companions.

He would cry "I am Actaeon: recognize your master!" But the words fail, and nobody could hear him so full the air of baying. First of all the Killer fastens on him, then the Grabber, then Mountaineer gets hold of him by a shoulder. These three had started last, but beat the others by a short-cut through the mountains. So they run him to stand at bay until the whole pack gathers and all together nip and slash and fasten till there is no more room for wounds. He groans, making a sound not human, but a sound no stag could utter either, and the ridges are filled with that heart-breaking kind of moaning. Actaeon goes to his knees, like a man praying, faces them all in his silence, with his eyes in mute appeal, having no arms to plead with, to stretch to them for mercy. His companions, the other hunting lads, urge on the pack with shouts as they did always, and not knowing what has become of him, they call *Actaeon! Actaeon!* each one louder than the others, as if they thought him miles away. He answers, hearing his name, by turning his head toward them, and hears them growl and grumble at his absence, calling him lazy, missing the good show of quarry brought to bay. Absence, for certain, he would prefer, but he is there; and surely he would rather see and hear the dogs than feel them. They circle him, dash in, and nip, and mangle and lacerate and tear their prey, not master, no master whom they know, only a deer.

And so he died, and so Diana's anger was satisfied at last."

Callisto

The story of Callisto is one of the best for understanding Artemis' function as a goddess of the rites of passage (especially female transitions). Callisto was a nymph who dedicated her life to virginity and to association with Artemis. She accompanied the goddess on her hunts and spent her life in her company. But one day Zeus saw her, and, falling in love with her, disguised himself as Artemis and lured her into a sexual relationship. Callisto, although she shunned all men, didn't think there was any harm in having a relationship with Artemis herself. But through this union she became pregnant. Then, once while bathing with Artemis and the other nymphs, her offence became known to the other virgins: She was no longer a virgin. She fled, but Artemis hunted her until she finally trapped her and slew her. Most mythographers say that Zeus had transformed Callisto into a she-bear before Artemis struck her in the hope that he could conceal what was happening from his jealous wife Hera. But Hera understood the ruse, and persuaded Artemis to pierce the bear with her arrow, the nymph's punishment for losing her virginity. Before she was killed, however, she gave birth to Arcas, from whom the region of Arcadia takes its name, and, according to some, a twin brother who eventually became the god Pan. Zeus pitied her, and transformed her into the constellation of the Great Bear.

Hippolytus

Hippolytus was a child of Theseus and the Amazon Hippolyta. When Hippolytus was still a teenager, Theseus had taken for himself a young wife named Phaedra, whom he had met long before in Crete while fighting the Minotaur there. Once, while Theseus was away for a time (probably in the underworld trying to help his friend kidnap Persephone, the queen of the underworld), Hippolytus continued doing what he loved best, honoring Artemis by devoting himself to her worship and especially to the hunt, together with his hunting buddies. In devoting so much attention to Artemis, however, he was at the same time scorning Aphrodite, since Artemis demanded virginity, and Aphrodite sex. Phaedra, on the other hand, although she honored all the gods and goddesses, cared most about Aphrodite. Cruelly, then, Aphrodite saw Phaedra as a fitting tool to take revenge on Hippolytus, so she caused her devotee to fall in love with the young man in the hope that it would ruin him. Phaedra was torn with passion for Hippolytus, and eventually the boy found out about it. When he refused to have sex with her, she became ashamed, and killed herself. Before she committed suicide, unfortunately, she tore her clothes and trashed her bedroom, then wrote a note to Theseus that Hippolytus had tried to rape her (this is Potiphar's wife story from the Bible, in case you don't recognize it). When Theseus returned, he found the note and his dead wife, and became enraged at Hippolytus. But Theseus did not want to kill his own son, so he sent him off into exile. As Hippolytus was driving away, Theseus could not control his anger, so he called on his half-father Poseidon to help him punish Hippolytus. Poseidon sent a sea monster up from the sea, which frightened the horses of Hippolytus' chariot, causing Hippolytus to fall out and be drug across rocks while tangled in the reins. Some versions of the myth say that Artemis had Asclepius, son of Apollo and god of medicine, bring Hippolytus back to life, after which Artemis took him to Italy to serve in her temple.

The story of Hippolytus is remarkable for its portrayal of the rivalry between Aphrodite, who represents indiscriminate lust, and Artemis, who wants sex only to be a part of adulthood and proper marriage. In his play *Hippolytus*, Euripides has Artemis utter these words to the dying Hippolytus: "Hush, that is enough! You will not be unavenged, for Aphrodite will find the angry shafts she hurled against you for your piety and innocence will cost her dearly. I'll wait until she loves a mortal next time, and with this hand—with these unerring arrows I'll punish him." That mortal lover turned out to be Adonis.

ATHENA

"I begin to sing of Pallas Athena, the glorious goddess, bright-eyed, inventive, unbending of heart, pure virgin, savior of cities, courageous, Tritogeneia. From his awful head wise Zeus himself bore her arrayed in warlike arms of flashing gold, and awe seized all the gods as they gazed. But Athena sprang quickly from the immortal head and stood before Zeus who holds the aegis, shaking a sharp spear; great Olympus began to reel horribly at the might of the grey-eyed goddess, and earth round about cried fearfully, and the sea was moved and tossed with dark waves, while foam burst forth suddenly; the bright sun stopped his swift-footed horses a long while, until the maiden Pallas Athena had stripped the heavenly armor from her immortal shoulders. And wise Zeus was glad. Hail to you, daughter of Zeus who holds the aegis!"

—*Homeric Hymn 29 to Athena*

Overview

We can say with great probability that "Athena" is an eponym of the city of Athens. In other words, the city predates the existence of the goddess and lends her its name. Even if prototypes of the goddess predated the rise of Athens, she becomes very early on a unique and divine projection of the corporate personality of the city itself. The Athenians wanted to be known for their wisdom, their excellence, and their talents in various crafts, all of which the goddess embodied. Thus they used Athena as a kind of symbol or mascot on their coins and in images throughout their city. Their foundation myth, that is, the story that tells how their city came to be, includes the dominating presence of Athena. They were, for all intents and purposes, the children of Athena, a difficult feat that only myth could accomplish, given that she had never been touched by a male.

The Athenians used the epithet "Parthenos" to describe their goddess. This means that she was a virgin goddess, eternally so because she sprang from Zeus' head, not a woman's womb, and so in a sense rejected womanly ways. Her unusual birth appears to have taken place at Lake Tritonis in Libya, thus we see her called "Tritogeneia," that is, "born at Tritonis," in the *Homeric Hymn*. As a result of the birth itself, she often, as noted, exhibited traits that were more typically male than female, even though she was often depicted as a beautiful woman. Her temple on the acropolis at Athens took the name "Parthenon," and here the Athenians worshiped her in the form of a gigantic statue some 40 ft. tall and made of gold and ivory. They also called Athena "Promachos," that is, "fore-fighter," because she stands on the front lines to defend her favorites in battle. Thus, another statue on the acropolis showed her in a defensive posture, wielding a spear and looking fierce.

She receives the epithet Pallas, and often is called simply "Pallas," perhaps because during the gigantomachy she defeated a snaky giant named Pallas, whom she flayed and turned into a breastplate. The breastplate itself contains snakes on its border. Other ancient mythographers say that "Pallas" was from the name of a small girl, the daughter of Triton, who had become a ward of Athena. The two quarreled one day, or were just pretending at war, when Pallas struck at Athena with a spear, which Zeus warded off with his aegis. Athena struck back in anger and killed Pallas. Because she felt such regret for her actions, she took on the girl's name, and thus became known as Pallas Athena. Athena made a statue of the girl and put armor on it, calling it the Palladium, which fell from heaven into Troy. As long as it was in the city Troy was invincible, thus it became the focus of much intrigue among the Greeks and the Trojans toward the end of the war, and eventually brought about the ruin of the city.

It was also at a shrine to Athena in Troy that a terrible act happened. Once the Greeks were inside the city and were ransacking it, a fellow named Ajax raped the Trojan princess Cassandra at the foot of the shrine where she had run for protection. Temples and altars of the gods were supposed to serve as an indisputable safe haven for the helpless. It is said that during their struggle they knocked over the statue of Athena in the temple, and as it fell it turned its eyes away from the outrageous act. For this sacrilege and disregard for divine laws, Athena punished many Greeks on their way home from Troy.

In the story of the contest or *agon* between Poseidon and Athena for patronage of Athens, Athena gave the valuable and well-received gift of the olive tree. The olive was the source of wealth and power for Athens, providing, as it did, oil, food, shade, wood, a commodity for trade. This showed just what Athena could bring to the table. In fact, Athena had only begun to give gifts to Athens. Athena with her clever mind was particularly skilled in taking raw materials and untamed elements and exploiting them for social use. She taught the art of weaving; she turned iron into the plough and developed the yoke and bridle for animals; she helped the Athenians develop wartime tactics and technologies, and she built up the defenses of the city. She inspired art, literature, philosophy, and statecraft. As we shall see in a later chapter, it was Athena who set up the first trial by jury and introduced the idea of mitigating and extenuating circumstances in judging the accused. In short, she provided everything needed for high civilization, and in doing so propelled Athens to the forefront of the Greek city-states.

The many epithets of Athena speak to her technical skills and wisdom. She has clear vision, thus she is "bright-eyed" or "owl-eyed" Athena (owls have distinct eyes, thus the bird often appears with the goddess). She is sharp-witted. She also has a fierce, warlike character, because, as the Greeks recognized, civilization has to be defended in order to thrive. Thus Athena is known as the goddess who fights on the front lines, who defends the citadel, and who holds up the shield for the city. Her statues most often show her wearing a helmet richly decorated with mythical monsters, wielding a spear and a shield, decked out with a breast-plate mounted by the horrific head of Medusa, her former priestess. In her hand sometimes she holds Nike, the goddess of victory, while a serpent slithers at her feet, a sign that this land belongs to her. Many heroes depended on her craftiness and intelligence to carry out their endeavors. Athena particularly supported wily Odysseus, the man of many turns, who depended on his wits to help him navigate a world filled with violence and brute force. Perseus could not have accomplished the insurmountable task of beheading Medusa without the assistance and advice of Athena.

Origins

We have already seen that Athena sprang fully armed from the head of Zeus while, as the ancient poet Pindar puts it, "pealing the sky with her clarion war cry." The event of the birth of Athena was so startling and significant that the Athenians depicted it on the pediment of Athena's temple on the acropolis, which is called the Parthenon. Athena herself is often referred to as the daughter of Zeus without any mention of a mother, as if Zeus unilaterally produced her. Such unilateral birthing caused a crisis for Hera, the patron of wives and mothers, but the birth of Athena was not without feminine influence. Zeus gave birth to Athena after swallowing the Titaness Metis, whose very name means "intelligence." Athena sprang notably from the *head* of Zeus, that is to say from his brain, after Hephaestus split Zeus' skull with an ax. The connection between Hephaestus and Athena, who both promote crafts and handiwork, is a natural in and of itself. It is clear that Athena possesses the traits of the goddess whom Zeus swallowed, and that by virtue of her origin Athena can contribute *metis* to the health of the city and to the endeavors of the heroes.

Cult and Meaning

Athena was not only worshiped in Athens. She had temples and sanctuaries dedicated to her throughout Greece. But it was in Athens, on the high hill in the center of the city called the acropolis, where the Parthenon stood, a magnificent temple to Athena, that the celebration of the goddess reached its acme. One of the most popular and spectacular events in Athens was the Panathenaea, the birthday of Athena. The civic festival was especially grand every fourth year, when a procession of noble youths and maids carried sacred implements, led sacrificial animals, and rode in chariots up to the Acropolis, bearing a freshly woven and embroidered robe (peplos) for the statue of Athena. The famous friezes of the Parthenon, over which Greece and Great Britain are currently disputing, depict this very event. We can see young girls carrying baskets of gifts for the goddess, city magistrates, young men on horseback, old men with olive branches, and of course the peplos. These friezes occupy a special room today in the British Museum. The statue that was cleaned and given a new robe in this festival was not the large statue in the Parthenon itself, but a smaller, olive-wood statue that stood in the sanctuary of the Erechtheum (or Erechtheion), the other temple on the Acropolis. This temple is easily recognizable for its "Porch of the Caryatids," six columns in the shape of women who seem to hold up the roof on their heads.

Clearly, Athena received worship in Athens as a form of respect and special petition. The Athenians were requesting that the goddess continue to protect their city from enemy occupiers and to enrich it with the highest expressions of human achievement. The Parthenon itself, in fact, was a testament to the engineering and artistic brilliance of her people.

Major Myths

The primary stories surrounding Athena have already been touched upon. The manner of her birth and the way in which she won patronage over Athens occupied ancient writers and artists the most. Athena was also involved greatly in the war with the Titans and the Giants, and so can be seen as one of the great defenders of the Olympian world order. Only she and Zeus were brave enough to defend the world order from the usurper Typhon, a monstrous, fire-breathing son of Gea who is said to have had an outlandish appearance, with many strange-shaped heads and hands and snakes extending from his thigh. When the other Olympians fled and concealed themselves in Egypt, but Athena and Zeus hunted him and cut him down in Syria. They then drug him across the sea to be buried under Mt. Aetna in Sicily as a volcanic god and source of the fire in the forge of Hephaestus. A similar story is told about Athena's encounter with another Giant in the work of the ancient Greek mythographer Apollodorus (*The Library* 1.35):

> "As Enceladus was fleeing, Athena threw the island of Sicily in his direction. She stripped
> off the skin of the Giant Pallas and used it to protect her own body during the battle."

It is important to note in all of these stories that the Giants, under the direction of Gea, the mother of the Titans, wanted to reestablish the reign of terror and violence that had characterized earlier generations of the gods. Athena shows herself to be a champion of Zeus civilized, intelligent rule and, by extension, progress and civilization in the society of men.

Athena assisted the Greeks during the closing years of the Trojan War when not all the gods did, though the presence of a major shrine for her in the city of Troy did complicate matters. In the end, however, she helped Odysseus design and create the wooden horse that brought down the city and won the day for the Greeks. Again, this should be interpreted in terms of the march of civilization. In the Greek view, Troy represented the East, with all its decadence and strange world-view. In other words, Troy stood for another direction that mankind could take in its progress, a direction that challenged the Greek (and therefore Western) vision for what mankind should be. The struggle was great, but in the end Greeks defeat the Trojans and secure, with the help of Athena, a social order molded in their image.

Other myths, including those that involve the origins of the early kings of Athens, also depend on Athena. These are myths that tie Athenians to the land around their acropolis and explain, if not encourage, the drive towards innovation and skill within the city. The story of Arachne should be understood in this regard. Arachne was a Lydian girl who bragged excessively about her skill in weaving, and so was challenged by Athena to a contest. Athena wove a tapestry showing her contest with Poseidon for lordship of Athens, plus punishments that the gods impose on presumptuous mortals. Arachne wove a tapestry that depicted the sexual escapades of the gods. No one could find any fault with what Arachne had done. So Athena, in typical god fashion, picked up the shuttle of boxwood, and beat her over the head. Arachne would not be shamed, though, and hung herself with her thread. Athena felt sorry for her, and said she could live, but had to hang forever. She kept her old occupation, but was turned into a spider.

CHAPTER SEVEN
Cybele, The Great Mother

"Please, o clear-voiced Muse, daughter of mighty Zeus, sing of the Mother of the gods and men. She delights in the clangor of castanets and drums, the roar of flutes, the clamoring of wolves and bright-eyed lions, with echoing hills and wooded valleys."

—*Homeric Hymn to Cybele*

Students of myth who are already familiar with the names and stories of the major gods in the Greek pantheon may find it odd that an entire chapter here is devoted to an obscure goddess whose name few even recognize. Yet for the ancient Greeks and Romans, Cybele held a prominent place among the other gods, both in myth and in art. Her cult, with its unique emphasis on resurrection and salvation, thrived long after those of the major divinities had fallen into neglect and for a time stood side by side with Christianity in the Roman empire. This longevity and preeminence may owe to the goddess' important function and status: She represents the mysteriously constant life principle or potency that exists unmoved at the center of the cycle of birth, growth, death, and renewal. In this regard she was seen as the "Mother of the Gods" or the "Great Mother." Since she is a personification of the earth itself, naturally in worship and iconography the ancients connected her with Demeter and Rhea, and her ritual processions often included a representation of the globe. As a goddess of permanent vitality, she could heal the sick and even resurrect the dead. She could even give oracles, probably because she had a timeless quality about her. As a goddess of the earth, she not only promoted fertility in general, she dominated and subdued wild nature to her commands, while her mountains (she is closely connected to Mt. Dindymene in Bithynia and Mt. Ida in Phrygia) and natural defenses gave cities protection in times of war.

Typically in art Cybele is depicted wearing a turreted crown, i.e., a crown fitted with city gates and walls, and attended by lions. She is often seated on a throne, indicating that she is queen of the earth, and sometimes (in Roman art) that throne is being pulled along in a

(CNG 76, Lot: 3327.) Faustina Junior. Gold aureus. Struck under Marcus Aurelius, A.D. 161–176. Cybele seated, holding drum on knee; a seated lion at feet on either side.

biga (a chariot or wagon pulled by two animals) by two yoked lions. She often holds an enormous drum, called a tympanum, while standing next to her consort, Attis. She is attended by eunuch priests, called Galli, who play raucous, loud, and booming music while shouting and generally acting berserk. She is the one, in fact, who taught Dionysus the ecstatic rites that he would employ in his own cult, and because of that the two sometimes throw parties for the gods together. Such is the idea behind an interesting passage from the ancient Greek poet Pindar in his *Dithyrambs to Herakles the Bold*:

> Wise men know the sort of festivals the Heavenly Gods hold on Mt. Olympus for Thundering Dionysus. There, close to the throne of Zeus and in the adorable presence of the mighty Mother of the Gods, they begin with the whirling of timbrels; there is also the ringing of rattles, and the torch that blazes beneath the glowing pine-trees.

> There, too, are the loudly sounding laments of the Naides, and there the frenzied shouts of dancers are aroused, with the throng that tosses the neck on high; there too has been brandished the almighty fire-breathing thunderbolt of Zeus, and the spear of Ares, while the war-like aegis of Pallas Athena resounds with the hissings of countless serpents.

> Meanwhile, lightly cometh the lone huntress Artemis, who in Bacchic revels has yoked the brood of savage lions for Thundering Dionysus, who is enchanted even by the dancing herds of wild beasts."

Even though this is properly a party of Dionysus, the Mother Cybele receives prominent mention and particularly enjoys the details of what is happening. In Greek myth, it was said that Dionysus had been cured of his madness by Cybele, who taught the young god how to perform tension-releasing ecstatic rites once while he was in Phrygia. Thus, many features of their rites are held in common. Notice the noise level throughout the passage. Dionysus thunders; the music shakes and rattles and whirls; Naides lament; dancers shout while snakes hiss. Here too we read about lions, and not just lions alone, but *yoked* lions. The wild beasts' savagery is brought under the domination of the great gods, Dionysus and Cybele both, because within the context of their cult does all the frenzied energy of animals and worshipers find controlled release. The necks tossed back suggest the ecstasy of the revelers, while the mention of the snakes, part of the worship of Dionysus, shows the extraordinary state of mind that could be achieved. To know the Great Mother, the Mother of the Mountains, Cybele, was to experience firsthand within oneself the incredible vitality of nature.

Similarly, in Euripides' passage from his play *The Bacchae* that follows, we can see just how closely connected the two cults are as a leader of the chorus chants a song to Dionysus:

"Let every mouth be hushed. Let no ill-omened words profane your tongues. Make way! Fall back! Hush. For now I raise the old, old hymn to Dionysus. Blessed, blessed are those who know the mysteries of god. Blessed is he who hallows his life in the worship of god, he whom the spirit of god possesseth, who is one with those who belong to the holy body of god. Blessed are the dancers and those who are purified, who dance on the hill in the holy dance of god. Blessed are they who keep the rite of Cybele the Mother. Blessed are the thyrsus-bearers, those who wield in their hands the holy want of god. Blessed are those who wear the crown of the ivy of god. Blessed, blessed are they: Dionysus is their god!"

—transl. by William Arrowsmith

Sometimes Dionysus is invoked during the worship of Cybele under the guise of his Phrygian name Sabazios or by his cultic title Bacchus. Attis is also addressed when the devotees are shouting out names.

THE MYTH

There are variations of the bizarre story of the relationship between the Great Mother Cybele and her consort Attis, but basically it runs as follows (as taken from (Pausanias 7.17.9–12; Arnobius 5.5–8): Cybele was born from a great rock in Phrygia on Mt. Ida (this is possibly one of the rocks that Deucalion and Pyrrha threw behind their backs in the flood story). Zeus saw her asleep on the rock and approached her in a blaze of lust. She resisted him until he prematurely ejaculated his seed onto the rock. Because of the divine power and effectiveness of Zeus' seed, the rock itself became pregnant from this incident, and eventually gave birth to a son, Agdistis. Agdistis' strength and violence were so great that they could not be resisted; even the gods in Olympus shuddered at his power and fled before him. Furthermore, his bestial lust raged crazily and indiscriminantly toward both sexes, so that the whole universe felt threatened by his presence.

The gods knew that they had to subdue Agdistis, but none of them were willing to face Agdistis in combat. They turned instead to their old standby, Dionysus, the god of wine. Dionysus, it has been said, has "drowned more men than Neptune," a reference to the deleterious effects of excessive drinking. The gods hoped that Agdistis would also succumb to the effects of wine (Odysseus pulls the same trick on Polyphemus the Cyclops). Dionysus went to a fountain where Agdistis was known to drink, and he poured in a powerful dose of wine. Agdistis came to the fountain and guzzled massive quantities of water without realizing that wine had been mixed in. Soon he passed out in a drunken stupor. Dionysus then made a noose of braided hair from his own head and slipped one end over Agdestis' feet, and the other end he attached to his genitals.

Eventually Agdistis recovered from his drunkeness and awoke from his deep sleep. He did what most people do first thing in the morning, he stretched a long, lazy stretch. In doing so, though, he ripped his own genitals from his body, and screamed in agony as blood spurted onto the earth. From the spurted blood miraculously a pomegranate tree grew.

The story only becomes more bizarre. It seems that a certain girl named Nana, daughter of a local king, was walking by and stopped in amazement at the tree growing from the blood. She plucked a pomegranate from it, slipped the fruit into her dress, and soon found herself pregnant. Her father was disgraced (not believing the whole pomegranate story, of course), so he locked her up in a prison in the expectation that she would die from starvation. Cybele, however, kept her alive with fruit and grain that she would sneak to her in her prison cell. In time Nana gave birth to a boy named Attis.

Now Cybele doted on Attis because he was extremely handsome, while Agdistis, now castrated and subdued, became the boy's companion in hunting. As the years went by, Midas, another local king (later of the "golden touch" fame), arranged for Attis to marry his own daughter, Ia. To keep away ill-wishers, he walled off his town. But Agdistis was furious that the boy had been taken from him, and on the wedding day he showed up and drove all the wedding guests mad.

A man named Gallus (probably the new father-in-law of Attis) grew so crazed that he sliced off his own genitals, while some of the girls cut off their own breasts. Attis went crazy, too; he cursed Agdistis, then flung himself at the foot of a pine tree, and ripped off his own genitals.

Cybele took up the organs of Attis, washed them, and buried them under a pine tree. From the blood grew violets which wreathed the tree. Meanwhile, his bride (not to be forgotten) killed herself over his body, and Cybele buried them in a common grave. Up grew an almond tree on the spot. Cybele and Agdistis begged Zeus to return Attis to life, but he would only grant that Attis' body would not decay, that his hair continue to grow, and that he could move his little finger.

ON THE WORSHIP OF CYBELE

The cult of Cybele came to Greece by way of Phrygia in Asia Minor (modern Turkey). The cult must have first been picked up by Greeks living on the Ionian coast of Asia Minor. Plenty of evidence point to a relatively early acceptance of the goddess' worship on the Greek island of Samothrace. We do not have enough reliable information on the worship of Cybele during the classical Greek period. The few images and passages that relate to the cult hint that the goddess' image remained in her temple (not paraded about as in the Roman version of the cult) while worshipers approached her with sacrificial gifts and the banging of metal objects, recalling the Corybantes. We read of the typical timbrels, castanets, drums, flutes, and shouting of the participants. There is talk of the "Corybantic" dances and prayers. But it does not seem likely that the Greeks adopted some of the more frenzied aspects of the cult, including the self-flagellating and castrating priests whom the

Phyrgians called Galli. One author mentions that the Greeks in Athens threw a Phrygian priest into a chasm in the earth because they thought he had gone mad, though we have no indication of a date when this happened. But one must be cautious in making any pronouncement about the worship of this goddess in the ancient world. The cross-influences and reverse-influences are so complex between Mediterranean cultures that often it is impossible to disentangle them.

For the Roman worship of Cybele we have more evidence. One valuable piece comes from Lucretius, an Epicurean Roman poet who lived in the time of Julius Caesar and Cicero. He wrote a lengthy didactic epic called *On the Nature of the Universe* in which he tries to dissuade Romans from fearing the mythological gods and urge more reliance on scientific enquiry. In the following passage, Lucretius gives us an indication of how the Romans practiced the cult of Cybele during the late Republic (1st Century B.C.). Attis is not mentioned, and does not appear to have been part of the public cult, though recently uncovered archaeological evidence reveals that worshipers did come to Cybele's temple on the Palatine Hill and offer her small gift statues of Attis. You will notice in this passage as well in this passage a growing interest in allegorical interpretations of myths and cults among the Greeks and the Romans.

"In this connection you should also keep in mind one other fact, sealed and treasured in your memory; there is nothing, whose nature is clearly visible to us, that consists of one type of element only; and nothing that is not formed from a mixture of different kinds of particle; and the more powers and qualities any particular substance has, so it shows us that there are within it elements of very many different types and shapes.

First the earth contains the primordial matter from which the springs, rolling down their coolness, constantly replenish the vast sea; and it possesses the matter that gives birth to fire. For in many places the earth's surface smoulders and burns, and from its depths the eruptions of Etna blaze furiously.

Then too it has the capacity to bring forth shining crops and bounteous orchards for the races of men, and to furnish rivers and leaves and bounteous pastures for the breed of wild beasts that roams the mountains. That is why this one thing has been called the Great Mother of the Gods, Mother of the Beasts, and creator of the human body.

She it is whom the ancient and learned poets of Greece celebrated, as a goddess seated in her chariot, driving her twin-yoked lions; and so they taught us that the great world hangs in spacious air, and that the earth cannot rest on earth. They gave her wild beasts in her yoke—because children, however fierce, are necessarily tamed and subdued by the devotion they owe to their parents. And they surrounded her head with a turreted crown, because the earth, fortified in chosen places, upholds cities.

So adorned with this emblem, the image of the divine mother is carried through the wide world with terrifying effect. She it is whom the different nations, by their ancient religious custom, hail as the "Idaean Mother," and they give her a retinue of Phrygians as her escort, because they claim that corn was first created in those parts and spread from there over the whole world. They assign her eunuchs as priests, because they want to show that those who have defied the power of their mother and have been found ungrateful to their parents must be thought unworthy to bring forth living offspring into the realms of light. Taut drums thunder beneath their palms, and round about the curved cymbals crash; and horns blast in a raucous strain, while the hollow pipe stirs the heart with its Phrygian tune. And they carry before them weapons, symbols of their mad frenzy, to strike awe into the ungrateful hearts and impious minds of the rabble with dread for the goddess' majesty. So, when first she rides through mighty cities, silently bestowing wordless benefaction on the human race, they strew every path of her route with copper and silver, pouring out riches in extravagant largess; and overshadowing the Mother and her retinue of attendants, they shower her with rose blossoms."

—transl. taken from Beard, North, Price, *Religions of Rome*, vol. 2, A Sourcebook
(Cambridge 1998), 48–49.

Although Lucretius fails to mention Attis in his description, he does paint a picture of a eunuch (castrated) priesthood whose members show their devotion to the goddess through rather bizarre and frightening behavior. They were reflecting the behavior of Cybele's consort Attis, who was coming to be known in Rome at this time through the importation of Greek literature and ideas. The Great Mother's priesthood must have seemed to the Romans a scary representation of the Attis side of the goddess' myth. We know that when the goddess was first introduced into Rome, the aristocracy had attempted to suppress some of these unnerving aspects of the cult. While they could appreciate the natural vitality that Cybele embodied, they weren't so sure that they wanted their citizens losing control for her.

This fear culminates in a poem (*carmen* 63) written by Catullus, a talented poet living at the same time as Lucretius. Here, Attis is a Greek who in a fit of religious fanaticism castrates himself, only to regret this impulsive act when he comes to his senses. Nevertheless, he must serve Cybele forever as her slave and priest(ess). Note how the gender of Attis changes after he cuts off his genitals. Notice, too, the typical Roman disdain for extreme emotionalism and zealotism, the fear of losing one's home and place in society, and the apotropaic prayer at the conclusion of the poem.

"Attis was carried above the high seas in a swift skiff, when frantically he touched the Phrygian grove with his lithe foot and approached the goddess' shady grove encircled with trees. There, goaded by a raging madness, ecstatic and delirious, he sliced off the load of his genitals with a sharp flint. And then when he, now a she, realized that her groins were stripped of their manhood as she stained the ground with her fresh blood, she quickly took up the light tympanum in her snowy white hands, your tympanum, Cybele, your rites, mother. And thumping the hollow bull's hide with her tender fingers, she began to sing these trembling words to her companions:

'Up! Come to the high groves of Cybele, womanly priests, come at once, wandering herds of Lady Dindymus. You followed my lead as my companions, like exiles seeking a foreign land, and you endured the salt sea and its storm-tossed waves, and you emasculated your body with total disregard for your sexuality. Gladden your heart with the excited movements of the mistress. Don't let your mind be sluggish! Come, at once, follow me to the Phrygian home of Cybele, to the Phrygian grove of the goddess, where the sound of cymbals resound, where tympana echo, and the Phrygian piper plays a heavy tune on a curved reed, where the ivy-clad Maenads toss their heads violently, and sing their sacred songs with ear-piercing howling, where that wandering band of the goddess usually flits about. We should hasten there with our swift dance steps.'

As soon as Attis, a pseudo-woman, chanted these things to his friends, suddenly as a dancing troupe they howl with warbling tongues, the light tympanum booms, the hollow cymbals clang, and the quick chorus approaches Ida with hasty step. Mad, panting, gasping, Attis, a leader accompanied by his tympanum, goes through the shady grove, like an untamed bullock trying to avoid the burden of a yoke, and the womanly priests quickly follow their swift-footed leader. And so when wearily they reach the home of Cybele, they fall to sleep, tired from their labor, before they have a chance to eat. A slow numbness closes their eyes with drooping exhaustion. The mad fury of their minds subsides in gentle rest. But when the golden-face sun illuminates the white ether with its radiant eyes, and the hard ground, the wild sea, and drives away the shadows of night with its lively horses, then quick-fleeing Sleep departs from the awakened Attis, and his graceful wife takes her in her trembling bosom. So as soon as from gentle rest without the crazy madness Attis recalls in her heart what she has done, and sees with a clear mind what she must live without, and where she will be, she returns again to the seashore in confusion. There, as she looks out over the vast seas with tears in her eyes, pitifully, with sadness in her voice, she addresses her native land:

'Homeland, you who created me, my parent, whom I left behind like refugee slaves flee their master, I have borne my foot to the groves of Ida, so that in the snow and chilly dens of wild beasts I might live, and so that I might enter their shady haunts in my ecstatic state—where or how shall I find you? The pupil of my eye longs to direct its sight to you, now in this brief time while the mind is free from this raging madness. Will I be borne from my home into these remote groves? Will I be absent from my homeland, my property, my friends, my parents? Will I be absent from the forum, the wrestling mat, the stadium, and the gym? Poor ah poor me. Heart, you must complain over and over again. What gender have I not experienced? I've been a woman, a teenager, a young man, a boy. I was the flower of the gym, I was the glory of the contests. My doors were full of visitors, and many suitors sat in the hallway. My house, where once I used to awake in my bed at the sun's rising, was covered in flowery garlands. Will I now be carried off as a attendant of the gods and a handmaid to Cybele? Will I be a Maenad, a part of my former self, a sterile man? Will I inhabit the chilly places of snow-clad Mt. Ida? Will I lead my life under the high cliffs of Phrygia, where the wood-dwelling deer and the brush hog dwells? Now, now I am sorry for what I have done, now I repent.'

As the swift sound departed from his rosy lips, bringing the news to the ears of the gods, Cybele there loosened the yokes from her lions and, goading the king of the beasts on the left, she said,

'Up, come on, go, strike madness in that one again, cause a blow of madness to drive him back to my grove: he is too eager to escape my power. Come, strike your back with your tail, endure your blows, make everywhere echo with your roars, and ferociously shake the ruddy mane on your back.'

This is what she said, and the menacing goddess dropped the rein from her hand. The wild beast whipped himself up into a frenzy, then went roaring and breaking branches with his careless steps. But when he reached the wet and sandy shore, and saw the tender Attis near the smooth sea, he attacked. She fled, now half out of her mind, into the wild groves. There she was a handmaid all the days of her life.

Goddess, Great Goddess, Cybele, Lady Dindymus, may all your madness stay far away from my house: make others frenzied, drive others mad."

—transl. by Kirk M. Summers

Dionysius of Halicarnassus 2.19.3–5: Here, a Greek writer from the late 1st Century B.C., also comments on the fact that the Romans, at least those of the Republican period, resisted ecstatic practices and frenzied religion. Even though Cybele was introduced to Rome from Phrygia in 204 B.C., at the prompting of an oracle, the Romans adapted the cult according to their own temperament, as we have already noted, leaving the ecstatic practices to imported Phrygian priests.

"And one will not see among them [sc. the Romans]—even though now their manners are corrupted—ecstatic processions, Corybantic frenzies, begging under the guise of religion, bacchanals or secret mysteries, no all-night vigils of men and women together in the temples, nor any other such antics; rather, they act piously and with restraint in all their words and actions in respect to the gods, unlike the Greeks or barbarians. And what amazes me the most, although there has been a great influx of nations into the city, nations who feel the need to worship their ancestral gods in their traditional ways, still the city has never officially adopted any of these foreign practices, as has been the experience of many cities in the past. But even though Rome has, at the bidding of oracles, introduced certain rites from abroad, she observes them in accordance with her own traditions, after casting off all the mythical nonsense, as in the case of the rites of Cybele. Every year the aediles perform sacrifices and put on games in her honor according to

Roman customs, but it is Phrygian men and women who carry out the actual rites and lead her image throughout the city in procession, begging alms according to their custom, and wearing images around their necks, striking their timbrels while their followers play tunes upon their flutes in honor of the Great Mother. But by a law and decree of the senate no native Roman walks in procession through the city decked in flamboyant robes, begging alms or escorted by flute players, or worships the goddess with the Phrygian ceremonies."

—transl. by Kirk M. Summers

It is very important to note that *no Roman citizen* participated in an official role within the cult of Cybele during the Republican period, even though her temple stood prominently on the Palatine Hill. The Romans were still holding ecstatic religion at arms length, a fact that would not change until after the introduction of Christianity into the empire.

We should backtrack at this point. I have mentioned several times that the cult of Cybele was introduced into Rome at some historical point. We know many of the details of its introduction from a passage of the Roman poet Ovid, who, writing in a work entitled *Fasti* (*Religious Calendar*) during the reign of Augustus, tells the story of the introduction of the cult into Rome in the year 205 B.C. The situation was as follows (with some details supplied by the ancient Roman historian Livy): Hannibal has been in Italy ransacking the countryside and controlling it, defeating Roman armies, for some 13 years. The disastrous defeat at Cannae in 216 B.C. had nearly wiped out the Roman army; the money was debased, food was short, the people were exhausted in every way. Livy tells us that the religious leaders had begun to lose control of the people, who were increasingly ignoring traditional religion and turning to foreign gods, carrying out sacrifices and prayers in foreign ways.

The matter was soon referred to the senate. They scolded the town supervisors for not controlling the people, and they had the city praetor read out a resolution in a town meeting: all books and manuals of foreign rites had to be turned over to city officials, and no one could sacrifice in public or in a sacred place in a "new" foreign rite.

So, undesirable characters had come to disturb the Roman religion, and the traditionalists had to do something about it. If there was going to be the introduction of foreign cults, and if that was what the people were clamoring for (their gods didn't seem to care about them anymore), then, by golly, they were going to be in charge of it. The senators got the clever idea to play on the Trojan connection (many Roman families prided themselves on the fact that they had descended from Trojans) and an interest in Asia Minor in general.

It was decided that some prophetic books that the senators had in their possession, called the Sibylline books, should be consulted, and the excuse was that there had been unusual "showers of stone" over the course of the year. Now, according to Livy, the Sibylline books declared that "whenever a foreign enemy has invaded Italy, he can be driven away and vanquished, if the Mother of Mount Ida is transferred from Pessinus to Rome."

Simultaneously, a report came from a legation that had been to Delphi that the Sibyl had spoken to them, and that they would win a great victory soon. This coincided, by the way, with the eagerness of the Roman general Scipio to depart with the army from Italy and to attack North Africa in hopes of drawing Hannibal away.

The Romans' only ally in Asia Minor was King Attalus of Pergamum (Phrygia), whom the Romans had helped against the Macedonians, and who was friendly toward them because of it. Five nobles, selected by the people, went to Pergamum, after receiving further instructions from Delphi, saying that Attalus would aid them, and that they should have only the "best" man in Rome receive the goddess on behalf of the State.

When they arrived, the king received them, and cordially, according to Livy at least, handed over a black stone (a rough, jagged, meteorite) that represented the mother goddess Cybele, the Idaean mother. Vergil says that originally, when the Trojan Aeneas fled to Aeneid, Cybele had wanted to come with the Trojans, but the Fates denied her, so she gave her trees instead so that they could make ships.

Ovid says that Attalus at first refused to give her up, but the legation pleads their kinship with Aeneas, and then the earth trembles and rumbles, and she herself speaks (*Fasti* 4.267–270).

Back home, the "best" man is chosen to receive the black stone, and after some wrangling, the people agree that the best man is Publius Scipio Nasica, the nephew of Scipio (Africanus). Women were also chosen, Vestals, and noble matrons, and in particular Claudia Quinta, to assist Scipio, but people began to whisper behind her back and her reputation became sullied.

After Scipio received the stone (probably placed in the face of a big statue) from those who brought it from Pessinus (near Pergamum), it was taken from Ostia up river to the gates of Rome on a boat pulled by cables from shore. But the statue was heavy, and the boat became mired in the shallows and couldn't be moved. Confusion seizes the crowd since this is a bad omen.

Now supposedly Claudia steps out of the crowd, prays that the god will vindicate her and her purity, then with almost no effort pulls the ship up the stream, while the crowds shout joyfully.

When they come to the Almo, a tributary that flows into the Tiber near Rome, they stop and bathe the statue and her utensils, while the attendants utter wild cries and play frenzied music and beat the tympanum. Then the goddess is placed in a chariot, decked with flowers, and carried into Rome, where Scipio receives her.

Here the goddess is at last "at home"; enthusiastically Ovid exclaims: Rome is traced back to its Phrygian ancestors. Preparations were made to build a temple for her close to the site of the huts of the early settlers on the Palatine, the founders of Rome. She rested in the temple of Victory until then. Thirteen years later she was moved to her own temple, the temple of the Great Mother, sometimes called the Metroon. Festivities were established in her honor, the Megalensia in April, and included feasting and a rather bizarre procession of the goddess on a lion biga.

During the Empire, when among the Romans Attis begins to play a more prominent role, Cybele's cult becomes very complicated. With ritual additions such as the taurobolium and the annual Roman celebrations, the cult takes on definite theological characteristics. Like Christianity, the emphasis in the worship tends to the creating of a mysterious connection or communion with Cybele's life-giving power and to the delivering of a message of salvation.

During the Republic, there were two special days, April 4th, when she arrived and the order was given to build her a temple on the Palatine, and when the temple was completed, April 10th. The feasts on these two days were national, consisting of sacrifices, banquets, games and plays in the circus and the theater, under the supervision of the curule aediles (secular magistrates). There also seems to have been a procession (pompa) of the statue through the city along with her lions. There was a common meal too, and the goddess herself was given a special couch to sit on, while fraternities were created whereby people invited each other to dinner. In particular, they ate *moretum*, cheese mixed with the strongest herbs, to show that Cybele kept primitive man alive with herbs (as opposed to Ceres), and then gave them grain (Ceres is her subordinate). The Ludi Megalenses were circus games and theatrical productions performed in front of her temple. Christians later complained of the lewd mimes that took place before her temple, while she watched, especially reenacting the love story between Cybele and Attis.

CHAPTER EIGHT
Aphrodite

"The Horae (Hours) clothed Aphrodite with celestial garments: on her head they put a fine, well-wrought crown of gold, and in her pierced ears they hung ornaments of amber and precious gold, and adorned her with golden necklaces over her soft neck and snow-white breasts, jewels which the gold-filleted Horae wear themselves."

—*Homeric Hymn 6 to Aphrodite*

Aphrodite appears in ancient art with certain recognizable attributes. She often wears elaborate, Eastern-style clothing, holds doves or sparrows in her hands (these birds are known for their affectionate ways), or a mirror in which she vainly admires her own beauty. She is attended by one or more Erotes (Eros or Cupid) who, some scholars believe, symbolize the primal moisture that is an essential ingredient of all procreation. At times Aphrodite is depicted naked in an effort to emphasize her voluptuousness. The poets call her "golden" Aphrodite and attribute to her the power to stir up sweet passion in gods and mortals.

Ancient authors describe the birth of Aphrodite in various ways. Most say that she was born from the severed genitals of Ouranos (Uranus), the sky god whom Kronos (Cronus) deposed. When his genitals fell into the sea, Aphrodite sprang from his seed and arose from the foam of the sea at Cytherea, a small Ionian island on the southwest tip of the Peloponnesus. From there the west winds carried her off to Cyprus to be cared for by the Horae, who dressed her in exotic clothing and taught her seductive ways (see the passage above). As a result, she became the glamorous goddess of sensual love and allurement, and, as such, she took on the Graces as her companions. The magical girdle that she wore was said to inspire love in human hearts, probably because, by its very positioning, it absorbed the warmth of her sexuality.

"Entwine around your neck love's very essence, a girdle warm from the bosom of Venus."

—Martial (writing around c. 85 A.D.)

Cn. Egnatius, 75 B.C. Silver denarius. Diademed head of Libertas with a liberty-cap behind. On the reverse, Roma (personified Rome) standing and holding scepter and sword; she places her left foot on a wolf's head; Venus stands on her right holding a scepter; Cupid flies near Venus.

Her beauty was unsurpassed, but her power knows no bounds, neither in heaven nor earth, and ignores all propriety. Her only concern is to strike passion into the hearts of gods, men, and animals alike, regardless of the cost to the parties concerned. Because she was born on Cytherea and reared on Cyprus, she retains two epithets: Cytherean and Cyprian Aphrodite.

In stark contrast to Aphrodite's origins, her sisters the Furies sprang from Ouranos' blood that dripped to the earth after he was attacked. They represent everything that Aphrodite is not. Horrific looking women with snakes for hair, sharp fangs and the smell of rotting flesh in their mouth, blood-shot eyes and dog-like faces, the Furies see to it that murders are avenged. When someone is murdered, they goad family members of the victim to pursue the perpetrator and retaliate. If no family member remains to do the job, the Furies themselves will chase the murderer and drive him mad until he kills himself.

Numerous fascinating and scandalous stories surround Aphrodite. Her exploits, as one might expect, are always erotic in nature. Homer tells how she carried on a nighttime affair with Ares (Mars) while her husband, Hephaestus (Vulcan) was away at his forge at work. Hephaestus had won Aphrodite as his bride as terms for the release of his mother Hera from the trap he had set for her. But Aphrodite, the goddess of love and beauty, held her husband in disdain, and much preferred the handsome and impulsive god of war Ares. To conduct the affair in perfect secrecy, the two had employed a sentry named Alectryon (the Greek word for "rooster"), who was supposed to warn them when the day was breaking. One morning, however, Alectryon fell into a deep slumber and failed to sound the warning. The sun god Helios, who sees everything beneath him, caught the two in embrace, and immediately told what he knew to Hephaestus. The blacksmith god then set a trap for the couple, a kind of invisible net that ensnared them as they lay in bed together. The next morning, Hephaestus called the other gods to come see his wife and Ares in this compromising position and to witness his wife's infidelity. The Olympian gods laughed heartily, and Mercury exclaimed to Apollo, "I wish I could get caught in such a trap!"

Such was the character of Aphrodite: always passionate, always indiscrete. Still, the powers that Aphrodite embodied are an omnipresent component of our existence. The following poem was written by Sappho of Lesbos, a female poet of the seventh century B.C.

Notice how the poet thinks it fitting to invoke Aphrodite for aid in her time of desperate, emotional love. You will notice, too, that her love interest appears to be another female. In fact, the English word "Lesbian" comes from the name of Sappho's island.

> "Undying Aphrodite on your caparisoned throne,
> Daughter of Zeus and weaver of ruses—
> Now I address you:
>
> Queen, do not hurt my heart, do not harry it
> But come as before when you heard and you hearkened
> A long way away,
>
> And leaving behind the house of your father,
> Harnessed a golden chariot winged
> By your beautiful sparrows,[1]
>
> Beating and whirring across the sky,
> Bringing you down to the unbright earth—
> So suddenly there:
>
> Mistress, the smile on your undying features
> Asking me what was it troubled me this time?
> What made me call you
>
> This time? What was my desperate heart wanting done?
> And your: 'Whom shall I this time bend to your love?
> Who is it Sappho
>
> That's doing you wrong? For if she's escaping
> Soon she'll be chasing; if she's refusing
> your gifts, she shall give them.
>
> And if she's not loving, soon shall she love you,
> Like it or no.' Oh, come again now:
> Let me go loose from this merciless craving.
> Do what I long to have done: be my own
> Helper in Battle.

—transl. by Paul Roche

Many of the myths of Aphrodite illustrate the complexity of love, how it brings beauty to our lives, but also how it causes confusion and distress. Love is indiscriminate, touching gods

---

[1] I have substituted the more accurate and usual rendering "sparrows" for the translator's "swans."

and humans alike; it comes unexpectedly and leaves as quickly as it came; its power knows no limits. The following story from Ovid's *Metamorphoses* 10 brings together all these elements into one story that itself has served as the inspiration for many modern tales (such as "My Fair Lady"). Cyprus, the island where traditions say that Aphrodite spent her early days, became an island full of whores, so Ovid says, the first ever such women to sell their bodies. This is Pygmalion's reaction to them:

The Story of Pygmalion

"One man, Pygmalion, who had seen these women leading their shameful lives, shocked at the vices Nature has given the female disposition only too often, chose to live alone, to have no woman in his bed. But meanwhile he made, with marvelous art, an ivory statue as white as snow, and gave it greater beauty than any girl could have and fell in love with his own workmanship. The image seemed that of a virgin, truly, almost living, and willing, save that modesty prevented, to take on movement. The best art, they say, is that which conceals art, and so Pygmalion marvels, and loves the body he has fashioned. He would often move his hands to test and touch it, could this be flesh, or was it ivory only? No, it could not be ivory. He kisses, he fancies, she returns; he speaks to her, holds her, believes his fingers almost leave an imprint on her limbs, and fears to bruise her. He pays her compliments, and brings her presents such as girls love, smooth pebbles, winding shells, little pet birds, flowers with a thousand colors, lilies, and painted balls, and lumps of amber. He decks her limbs with dresses, and her fingers wear rings which he puts on, and he brings a necklace, and earrings, and a ribbon for her bosom, and all of these become her, but she seems even more lovely naked, and he spreads a crimson coverlet for her to lie on, takes her to bed, puts a soft pillow under her head, as if she felt it, calls her *Darling, my darling love!*

And Venus' holiday came round, and all the people of the island were holding a festival, and snow-white heifers, their horns all tipped with gold, stood at the altars where incense burned, and timidly, Pygmalion made offering, and prayed: 'If you can give all things, O gods, I pray my wife may be—(He almost said, *My ivory girl*, but dared not)—one like my ivory girl.' And golden Venus was there and understood the prayer's intention, and showed her presence, with the bright flame leaping thrice on the altar, and Pygmalion came back where the maiden lay, and lay beside her, and kissed her, and she seemed to glow, and kissed her, and stroked her breast, and felt the ivory soften under his fingers, as wax grows soft in sunshine, made pliable by handling. And Pygmalion wonders, and doubts, is dubious and happy, plays lover again, and over and over touches the body with his hand. It is a body! The veins throb under the thumb. And oh, Pygmalion is lavish in his prayer and praise to Venus, no words are good enough. The lips he kisses are real indeed, the ivory girl can feel them, and blushes and responds, and the eyes open at once on lover and heaven, and Venus blesses the marriage she has made. The crescent moon fills to full orb, nine times, and wanes again, and then a daughter is born, a girl named Paphos, from whom the island later takes its name."

—transl. by Rolfe Humphries

There is another story involving Aphrodite, this time with the goddess herself falling in love. The story links Aphrodite with many of the other female goddesses as a divinity representing fertility, and, in particular, the principle that life and death work in a kind of cyclical tandem, each dependent upon the other. Life is not a race to a finish line, but a continuous and never-ending circle of life, death, and rebirth, best seen in the life cycle of plants.

The story goes that a certain king of Syria, named Theias, had a daughter named Myrrha who was very beautiful. Because Myrrha's mother boasted that she was more beautiful than Aphrodite herself, the goddess took revenge by stirring up an incestuous love within the girl for her father. With the help of her nurse, Myrrha managed to deceive her father, who had a mistress that he visited almost every night anyway. Instead of visiting his mistress, however, now Theias, who seems to have liked to operate in the dark, visited his daughter in bed, so that on twelve successive nights the two were lovers. On the last night, Theias discovered the trick and was so filled with anger and hate that he began to pursue his own daughter with a knife to kill her. The gods took pity on Myrrha, though, and transformed her into a myrrh tree. Ten months after the transformation, the bark of the tree split open and out plopped a marvelous baby who received the name Adonis. Aphrodite loved the child, secretly giving it to her Persephone for care and safe-keeping. Persephone was likewise moved by Adonis, and did not want to give the child back. Aphrodite and Persephone then wrangled over the child as if the two were vying for a lover, and the fight that ensued threatened to disrupt the peace of the gods themselves. Zeus intervened, saying that Adonis could spend one-third of the year with Persephone and two-thirds of the year with Aphrodite. Aphrodite fell in love with Adonis, but Adonis cared more about hunting than love. The goddess warned him against pursuing big game, fearing that something bad would happen to him, but Adonis ignored her advice, until one day a boar gouged him in the groin area (hunting boars was a rite of passage in ancient Greece), causing him to bleed to death. From the blood of the wound sprouted the blood-red anemone, a plant that holds its seeds inside a pliant outer rind. The poet Ovid notes that "even this protection soon passes; the light seeds soon fall away and are blown away by the breezes from which they receive their name."

To celebrate the beautiful Adonis as a dying god of vegetation, the women of ancient Greece (particularly the region of Adonia) would plant seeds in a shallow tray, adding warm water to make the seeds develop quickly. Soon after the seeds sprouted in this way, they would die, to which the women tore their hair, struck their breasts, and wandered about, lamenting the death of Adonis.

> There he lies, the delicate Adonis, in purple wrappings, and the weeping Erotes lift up their voices in lamentation; they have shorn their locks for Adonis' sake. One flings upon him arrows, another a bow, this one a feather, that one a quiver. One has untied Adonis' shoe, others fetch water in a golden basin, another washes his thighs, and again another stands behind and fans him with his wings.
>
> The Erotes cry woe again saying, "Woe unto Cytherean Aphrodite!"
>
> —Bion, writing a funeral dirge for Adonis' rites

THE CULT OF APHRODITE

Although it is true that some Greeks treated Aphrodite as a goddess of the sea (she was born from the sea) or, through her connection with Ares, as an armed goddess of war (as was the case of Sparta and Thebes), in general, as we have seen, Aphrodite promotes fertility, and so most of her rites focus on that aspect of her power. On the island of Paphos, for example, she was worshiped in a Near-Eastern style sanctuary in the form of a conical stone, a fertility image found on many Roman coins, and the votive offerings found there connect her to the Semitic (and Cyprian) goddess Astarte or the Babylonian Ishtar. The Greek writer Strabo tells us that on the acropolis of Corinth the Greeks worshiped her with temple prostitutes, though some have doubted it. If he is to be believed, however, perhaps as many as one thousand prostitutes worked the temple in its heyday. Certainly the foundations of her temple are still visible on the acropolis. We do know that in both Greece and Rome, prostitutes looked to Aphrodite as their patron goddess. The Athenians worshiped Aphrodite as a goddess "in the gardens," that is, she makes the ground fertile for herbs and flowers. They also worshiped her in a festival called the Arrephoria, which involved young girls between the ages of seven and eleven, and so may have been a kind of initiation rite illustrating citizen-girls' entry into puberty and their child-bearing period. We know from votive offerings from sanctuaries all over Greece that women viewed Aphrodite as the goddess responsible for stimulating their sexual powers. These votive offerings were often figurines of birds, fruit, or phalluses.

PRIAPUS

Some legends say that Aphrodite also had an affair with Dionysus, and the union produced the phallic child Priapus, who was especially revered in the Asia Minor town Lampsacus (said to be his birthplace). Priapus was a symbol of the male erection, and thus fertility. His image was often placed in gardens to ward off anything that could damage the growth of the plants; some ancients even wore an image of Priapus (or a phallus) around their neck to ward off the "evil eye," that is, the glare of any ill-wishers. Priapus is often accompanied by a donkey, because once the bray of a donkey of Dionysus' friend Silenus woke Hestia at the very moment Priapus was trying to rape her. This incident embarrassed the god, so he demanded that donkeys be sacrificed to him.

Besides her relationship with Dionysus, Aphrodite also consummated a relationship with a Trojan shepherd named Anchises, by whom she eventually bore the child Aeneas, who founded the Roman race. It was Zeus, ironically, who put the desire into her heart for this Trojan who herded cattle around Mt. Ida and had the looks of a god. When Aphrodite spied him, she burned so with desire, desire that she so often enflames in others, that she flew immediately to her temples to adorn her body with all kinds of perfumes and jewelry. Then she appeared to Anchises radiating with lust and sexuality.

"Aphrodite, the daughter of Zeus stood before Anchises, being like a pure maiden in height and bearing, that he should not be frightened when he took heed of her with his eyes. Now when Anchises saw her, he looked her over well and wondered at her bearing and height and shining garments. For she was wearing a robe out-shining the brightness of fire, a splendid robe of gold, enriched with all manner of needlework, which shimmered like the moon over her tender breasts, a marvel to see. Also she wore twisted brooches and shining earrings in the form of flowers; and encircling her soft throat were lovely necklaces. And Anchises was seized with love . . . Aphrodite's head reached to the well-hewn roof-tree; from her cheeks shone unearthly beauty such as belongs to rich-crowned Cythereia . . . and when Anchises saw the neck and lovely eyes of Aphrodite, he was afraid and turned his eyes aside another way, hiding his comely face with his cloak."

—Homeric Hymn 5 to Aphrodite

Perhaps the affair between the goddess of love and a human male is supposed to symbolize the utter weakness of a male during the very apex of passion with a woman. Certainly, Anchises was overcome with the sight of this ultimate woman's beauty and had to submit himself to its demands. The result was the birth of Aeneas, Trojan hero and eventually the father of the Roman race.

CHAPTER NINE
Demeter and Persephone

"Then Demeter went, and to the just kings Triptolemos and Diocles, the horse-driver, and to manly Eumolpus and Celeus, leader of the people, she showed the conduct of her rites and taught them all her Mysteries, awe-inspiring mysteries that no one may in any way transgress or pry into or utter, for deep awe of the gods checks the voice. Happy is he among men upon earth who has seen these mysteries; but he who is not initiated and who has no part in them, does not ever share in such good things once he is dead, down in the darkness and gloom."

—*Homeric Hymn 2 to Demeter*

The story of Demeter and Persephone, her daughter with Zeus, is told in the *Homeric Hymn to Demeter*, a lengthy poem dating to around 650 B.C., the contents of which are summarized below. Generally speaking, though, one can say that Demeter, in conjunction with her daughter Persephone, oversees the fertility of the earth, the growth of the crops, and the activities of agriculture. Her cult, the Eleusinian Mysteries, was one of the major celebrations in the ancient Greek world, attracting potential initiates from all over, mainly because it reassured participants that life has meaning and promised happiness in the hereafter. The story of Demeter and Persephone also is remarkable for the central position it gives the mother/daughter relationship in interpreting human experience.

Demeter is always depicted as tall and radiant, with long flowing clothes and an iconography that suggests both her function as the goddess of agriculture and as the queen of the Mysteries that took place at Eleusis. We recognize her by the ears of barley and poppy that she holds in her hand or wraps around her head as a garland. She often carries a torch and the mystic basket (the basket that holds her sacred objects), both of which remind us of the cult. Sometimes she holds a scepter or wears a crown.

ORIGINS

Demeter was one of the original children whom Cronus swallowed upon presentation by Rhea. She was freed by Zeus with the help of Metis and the emetic drug, but did not play a

Lucania, Metapontum, Silver stater, c. 330 B.C. Head of Demeter wearing corn-wreath in her hair; the head is lightly veiled with cloth falling behind and in front of head. On the reverse appears a barley ear with a mouse on leaf to left.

major role in the battle with the Titans. She does appear on Greek vases holding a golden sword (Homer sometimes refers to the sword of Demeter as well) or spear and torch fighting in the battle against the Giants. Even so, Demeter did not distinguish herself in the various early clashes of the gods in the way that Athena did. She was much more concerned with the fertility of the earth. The name of Demeter has in it the obvious root "-meter," indicating plainly that she is a mother, in the way that the earth itself is the mother and nourisher of all things. The meaning of the initial word element, however, is not as clear. Perhaps it comes from the same root as the name of Gea, so that she is to be understood as the "Earth Mother." But there is another similar Indo-European root that means "barley," which fits well with the central role that barley plays in her cult and the fact that she is the one who promotes the growth of grains and taught the arts of agriculture.

Persephone herself was born from a union between Demeter and her brother Zeus. On the details of how this came about we do not have much information. Hesiod quite plainly says, "Also Zeus came to the bed of all-nourishing Demeter, and she gave birth to white-armed Persephone whom Hades carried off from her mother; but wise Zeus gave her to him." (*Theogony* 912f.) In Homer's *Iliad* (14.326) Zeus claims Demeter "of the fine-tresses" as one of his memorable lovers. The union of the weather god Zeus and the goddess responsible for agriculture is natural enough and does not need elaboration. Zeus' affairs with various divinities were gifts to mankind and contributions to the natural order of the universe. What does stand out from the Hesiod passage, however, is that the story of the rape of Persephone at the hands of Hades comprises the defining myth of Demeter.

CULT AND MEANING

There was scarcely a city in ancient Greece where sanctuaries did not exist for Demeter, and the sacrifice of pigs and the offerings of fruits were not part of her rites. The rites at Eleusis, however, gained worldwide fame. Eleusis is now essentially a suburb of Athens, but in ancient times it was a great city lying some 14 miles or so west of the Athenian agora, and connected to it by the "Sacred Way." By the time of Solon in the 6th Century B.C., Eleusis had become the location of the panhellenic cult of Demeter. The sanctuary of Demeter and Persephone was situated on the acropolis overlooking the city. Within the sanctuary one finds the Telesterion, or Hall of Mysteries, an enormous structure used in the ceremony of the mysteries. It housed a kind of large theater that could seat about 3,000 initiates. The Telesterion and sacred precinct contained several sacred areas, including the spot where Demeter supposedly wept for her daughter (the Mirthless Rock), a sacred well where dances were performed in honor of the goddess (supposedly this is where the goddess first rested when she came to Eleusis), and the Anaktoron, a kind of holy of holies where the climax of the mysteries occurred. Also, at the nearby cave of Pluto, Persephone was believed to make her annual return to the earth.

A visit to the sanctuary today can be confusing, since the site is an archaeological mess. The temple was rebuilt some nine times at different stages in the city's history, from 750 B.C. up to and including the period of Roman domination. Invading Visigoths destroyed the temple in 396 A.D. When the English scholar Edward Clarke visited the site in the 18th Century, he found the inhabitants there still worshiping the statue (probably as a version of Mary, mother of Jesus) as a source of fertility for their crops.

The Mysteries performed at Eleusis were perhaps so successful because the priests there treated the agricultural cycle as a metaphor for the human experience. Everything in the ceremony seems to have been designed to draw the attention of the initiates to one major principle within nature: Death precedes life. Plants must flourish, spread their seeds, and die. The seeds themselves lie dormant, buried in the ground through the bleak winter. With the care and favor of Demeter, spring comes and the seeds become new plants with new seeds. The cycle continues.

The Greeks in the Peloponnese tended to emphasize the darker character of Demeter. The Arcadians, for example, referred to her as Melaina (Black) Demeter and Demeter Erinys (Avenger, or Fury). Various stories explain her origin, but in each case, Demeter is angry at Poseidon, who, as the god of moisture, is naturally associated with the goddess of the crops. In one well-known story told by the people of Thelpousa and Phigalia, with some discrepancies between them, Poseidon saw Demeter as she wandered looking for her daughter, and conceived a terrible lust for her. To avoid his advances, Demeter turned herself into a mare, but Poseidon was undeterred. He changed himself into a stallion and mated with her all the same. From this union Demeter produced a child whose name was kept secret from the uninitiated (she was simply called "Despoina," a common name for underworld divinities) and a horse named Arion, who served many masters, including Herakles. In response to her rape at the hands of Poseidon, and still distraught over the loss of Persephone, she retired into a cave, withdrawing with her the power of growth. In this cave, the Arcadians worshiped a black-clad image of Demeter, fitted with the head and mane of a horse, and decked out with snakes and other wild beasts. The horse's head makes us think of Poseidon, of course, whose fertilizing power had provoked anger in Demeter and made her withdraw into the darkness of the cave. It was the Arcadian divinity Pan who eventually discovered her in the cave and reported her whereabouts to Zeus, and he, with the help of the Fates, convinced her to set aside her anger. In this scheme of things, therefore, we can see that

Demeter's time of productivity and growth is her most vulnerable, submissive time, to which she responds with fury—quite the opposite of the version at Eleusis.[1]

MAJOR MYTHS

One day, while Demeter's daughter Persephone was gathering flowers with her companions in the fields of Sicily around Mt. Etna (some authors speak of the "plains of Nysa," but the location is vague in any case), she noticed a narcissus flower of striking beauty by the edge of the meadow. As she wandered away from the group, drawn by the flower, a terrible thing happened: Suddenly the earth opened up, and Hades (Pluto), riding in a golden chariot, swooped up from the underworld and grabbed her. She let out a shriek, she wept and she struggled, but in the end was unable to resist the king of the underworld as he took her down to his abode. Now no mortal or even immortal heard her cry for help, except for Helios, the sun god who sees everything, Hekate, the mysterious goddess of black nights (the dark side of the moon) and evil magic, and her mother, Demeter, who faintly heard her voice echoing from the mountains—that only these three could hear her emphasizes the inaccessibility of the realms below. Persephone is lost, an unwilling bride to the very personification of death.

The hymn describes Demeter's reaction like this: "Then bitter sorrow seized her heart, and she tore the veil on her ambrosial hair with her own hands. Over her shoulders she threw a somber cloak and flew like a bird over land and sea, seeking here, seeking there."

For nine days she roamed the earth, carrying torches in her hand (torches are a symbol of both funerals and mystery rites), until finally she consulted Hekate herself, who admitted that she had heard Persephone's cry, but did not know who took her. Together the goddesses went then to consult Helios to hear what he had seen. He told them this: "No other god is guilty but Zeus himself, who awarded your daughter to his brother Hades so that he might call her his flowering bride."

This revelation overwhelmed Demeter, who withdrew from Mt. Olympus, shunned the other gods, and disguised herself as an old woman. She took refuge among the cities of men, the poet tells us, as she wandered aimlessly about the earth in despair over her lost daughter.

By chance she wandered near the city of Eleusis, which at that time was ruled by the wise king Celeus (Keleos). She stopped to rest at a popular watering hole called the Maiden's Well that was shaded by a large olive tree. As the despondent goddess sat by the well, the daughters of the king happened upon her. They pitied the old woman, not recognizing her as a divinity, of course, and offered her a job back at the palace as a nurse and caretaker for the king's son Demophon.

When Demeter, still disguised as an old woman, entered into the palace, she found it difficult to conceal her divinity. Her head nearly struck the ceiling, she loomed so large, and a

---

[1]Information about Black Demeter comes primarily from Pausanias 8.25.4–5, 37.9–10, and 42.1–2; archaeological evidence points to a similar cult at Mycenae. At Hermione in Argolis, Demeter had her own temple where she was perceived of as an *underworld* (or "chthonic") divinity. In the local tradition, Persephone was abducted here, and so the villagers had to appease her irate mother by a special festival (Chthonia) during which several old women would sacrifice a cow.

kind of divine light filled the throne room. When the queen saw the old woman, she leapt from her throne and immediately offered it to the old woman the girls had found.

> "Demeter walked behind the girls with her head veiled and wearing a dark cloak which waved about her slender feet. Soon they came to the house of heaven-nurtured Celeus and went through the portico; the goddess walked to the threshold. Her head reached the roof and she filled the doorway with a heavenly radiance. Then awe and reverence and pale fear took hold of the queen, and she rose up from her couch to give way before Demeter."

(Homeric Hymn to Demeter)

Demeter refused, and for a long time stared at the ground with the veil hanging over her face. None of the girls were able to cheer her up or please her in any way. One of the girls in the house, named Iambe (from whose name we have the term "iambic" poetry), found a stool for Demeter to sit on, and then tried with buffoonery, lewd jokes, and even obscene gestures, to lighten the old woman's spirits. She even went so far as to expose her private parts to her in a kind of vulgar way. She even gave Demeter a special drink, called *kykeon*, made of water, barley, and mint. These efforts of Iambe did the trick, making the old woman (Demeter) finally crack a smile. Now she was ready to take up the task of watching over the young child Demophon, much to the delight of the queen, at least initially.

It's not that Demeter was a bad babysitter; she simply could not resist trying to make the baby special in some way. Every night, when the rest of the house was asleep, Demeter would take the child, smear him with ambrosia (the food of the gods), breathe on him with her divine breath, then hold him in the fire of the hearth in an attempt to burn off his mortal parts so that he would be immortal. These mysterious rites went on for several nights until finally the queen became suspicious. One night, she crept up on Demeter and Demophon and burst into the room at the very moment the goddess had the baby in the flames. The queen shrieked, as one would expect, but Demeter reacted badly: She threw the baby across the room and cursed at the queen, telling her that mortals have to die because of their own foolishness. She then revealed herself as a goddess and demanded that the Eleusinians build her a grand temple on their acropolis. When it was complete, Demeter withdrew into the temple to sulk and bemoan the loss of Persephone. Meanwhile, she refused to allow the earth to bring forth crops of any kind, so human beings everywhere were starving.

Zeus finally became concerned with the very existence of mankind, so he sent the gods to placate her. She always retorted one thing to their pleading, however, that she wanted her daughter back. Nothing else would do. So Zeus was forced to give in, and he ordered his brother Hades to return Persephone to Demeter. But before Hades permitted Persephone to leave, he tricked her into eating the seeds of a pomegranate (probably 4 seeds). This fruit was a symbol of the marriage union, that is, of sexual intercourse between man and wife, so that her ingesting of the seeds made their marriage indissoluble and tied Persephone to the underworld forever. Zeus, therefore, had to compromise: since she had eaten 4 seeds, he decided that she had to stay with Hades in the underworld for 4 months out of the year (some authors say 6), and the remaining 8 she could be with her mother in the world above.

When Persephone is in the underworld, Demeter is in mourning, and the earth is plunged into winter. As the daughter returns, however, springtime returns to the world, and everything is in bloom. As time wears on, and Demeter thinks of her daughter's departure, the resulting depression causes fall to come and eventually the return of winter.

In repayment to the Eleusinians for their kindness to her when she wandered the earth, she taught them certain mysteries about the cycle of life (the Eleusinian Mysteries), and she also taught one of the king's children, Triptolemus, the secrets of agriculture, and charged him with spreading that information throughout the whole world (some authors treat Triptolemus and Demophoön as one and the same, some consider Triptolemus a citizen of Athens):

> "Bounteous Ceres [Demeter] yoked her twin snakes to her chariot, and fixed the curbing bits and made her way between the earth and sky to Athens, and brought the flying chariot to Triptolemus. She gave him seed and commanded him to scatter it, partly in untilled earth and part in fields long fallow. Rising up high the young prince rode through Europe and the realms of Asia, and with every people he met, he declared: 'I come from Athens. I bring the gifts of Ceres [Demeter]. If you sow them wide over your ploughland, they will give you back bountiful harvests, gentle nourishment.'"

(Ovid, *Metamorphoses* 5.354)

In this way, Athens (and Eleusis), at least in the minds of its citizens, became the source of agricultural knowledge for the whole world.

CHAPTER TEN

Apollo

"I won't fail to sing a hymn for far-shooting Apollo as well. When he comes to Mt. Olympus, to the house of Zeus, the gods there tremble, and all spring from their seats as he approaches, stringing his splendid bow. Leto alone sits with thunder-loving Zeus, and she alone unstrings her son's bow and fastens up the quiver. She takes the bow from his sinewy shoulders and hangs it on a golden peg on the paternal pillar, then leads him to his seat."

—*Homeric Hymn 3 to Pythian Apollo*

Although the Greeks believed in the existence of many divinities and that these divine beings often interacted with humankind, they were also keenly aware of the transcendence of the gods. In other words, the Greeks understood that they themselves were tied to the earth, sharing in common many characteristics with the brute animals, and that the gods were lofty and hard to know. Earthbound mortal creatures could hardly expect to comprehend beings that never die, who have the universe as their playground, who comprehend the inner workings of nature and even control it. The immortal gods are transcendent, mysterious, and magnificent. Even so, the Greeks also noticed that human beings differ from other animals in some ways, since they have rational powers and the ability to speak and create tools and walk on two legs. Therefore, they posited the idea of the divine spark, inserted into every person at birth, that allows them a connection, albeit faint, with their heavenly counterparts.

One divinity, a child of Zeus, has it as his role to exploit this spark. Apollo, the god of reason, prophecy, music and poetry, medicine, and the like, offers to mankind the chance to gain understanding of the nature of the gods through his gifts. Poetry and music elevate the mind to a new way of thinking, using words and sounds and combinations that stir up our imagination in ways that plain language cannot. For this reason, poetry, according to ancient writers, depends on the inspiration of the gods, the Muses, in particular, and their leader Apollo, since the language itself is divine. Medicine is a secret of the gods, derived from their understanding of how nature is intertwined, of causes and effects, and of how the body functions in all of its parts. Prophecy speaks to the will of Zeus himself. All the gifts

Macedon, Chalcidean League (Olynthus). Silver tetrobol, c. 427–421 B.C. Laureate head of Apollo and Lyre.

that Apollo gives to humans, and all the functions that he is responsible for, separate them from the animals and draw them closer to the ethereal gods. Yet even this is limited, since humans often misinterpret the oracles (they seem obscure to those who receive them), can't understand the language of poetry, and do harm with medicine instead of good.

One of the earliest literary references to Apollo refers to his function as a god of medicine: At the beginning of the *Iliad* we are told the story of how, in the ninth year of the Trojan War, a priest of Apollo came to the Greek camp to ransom back his daughter who had been seized from a nearby town during Greek raiding. It so happened that Agamemnon, the chief on the Greek side, was holding the priest's daughter as part of his "loot." Agamemnon rejected the priest's ransom and entreaties, then rebuked him and sent him on his way harshly. He said, "Don't let me catch you around here again or nothing will be able to save you. I'm going to take your daughter home with me and she's going to do my housework and share my bed with me and grow old in my house back in Greece."

The priest went away in sorrow, and appealed to Apollo for help: "If I have been a loyal priest to you, let the Greeks pay for this!" he said. Apollo heard his prayers, and descended from the heavens with his quiver and arrows clanging around his shoulders. He sat on a hill across from the Greek camp and let his arrows rain on their camp for nine days. First the mules fall, then the dogs, and then the men. It was like, and in fact it was, a plague raging through the camp. "Day and night the funeral pyres were kept busy burning the corpses of Greek soldiers." It was not until the Greeks returned the girl to her father and sacrificed 100 oxen (the so-called "Hecatomb") to Apollo that the god ceased raining the plague (symbolized by the arrows) on the camp.

ORIGINS

Leto, a minor divinity, had an affair with Zeus and become pregnant. As time drew near to give birth, Hera learned what had happened, and so decided to make things difficult for Leto. She sent out warning to all the lands of the earth that she (Hera) would punish any people who gave Leto refuge so that she could give birth to her child(ren). Leto wandered the earth, suffering from labor pains, but could find no one who would help her and no place where she could rest and give birth. Finally, the inhabitants of the island of Delos, a floating, relatively barren island in the Aegean (near modern Mykonos), agreed to take her in after Leto made this plea:

"Delos, would you want to be the abode of my son,
Phoibos Apollon, and to house him in an opulent temple?
For it cannot escape you that no other will touch you
since I think you shall never be rich in oxen or sheep
and shall never produce vintage nor grown an abundance of plants.
If you have a temple for Apollon who shoots from afar,
than all men shall gather here and bring
hecatombs, and the ineffably rich savor of burning fat
shall always rise, and you shall feed your dwellers
from the hands of strangers, since your soil is barren."

—Homeric Hymn 2 to Apollo, 51 ff., transl. by A. N. Athanassakis

For several days Leto tried to give birth, but without the aid of Eileithyia, goddess of childbirth and daughter of Hera, she could not. Her labor was intense and wouldn't end. Finally, the other Olympian gods felt so sorry for Leto that they insisted that Eileithyia attend her and help alleviate her suffering. As soon as the goddess arrived, Leto gave birth to twins, Apollo and Artemis. From then on, Delos became special to Apollo: He anchored the island into place and had a temple built there for himself. Delos exulted in the deed and covered herself in golden flowers, which now have the name "Delosperma," from the name of the island itself. In fact, even today on the island of Delos one can see a huge statue of Apollo dating from the 6th Century B.C., surrounded by a field of yellow Delosperma flowers.

When Apollo was still a baby, he was fed nectar and ambrosia instead of milk, given to him by Themis, so he grew rapidly into a strapping young man. In fact, he grew in just one day, and demanded for himself a lyre and a bow (with which he intended to capture some land), and declared that he would reveal the will of Zeus to mankind. Zeus told him to establish an oracle at Delphi and gave him a chariot drawn by white swans to help him get there. Delphi, west of Athens, on the steep slopes of Mt. Parnassus, was already sacred as a place of prophecy. Themis, a primordial goddess, had long ruled over the place and advised Zeus from it. A dragon called the Python guarded the place, and everything in the area feared him. The oracle had warned the dragon that one day a son of Leto would come and slay him. So, when the dragon saw Apollo coming he unleashed his fury, spitting venom and fire at the god, while the god shot him with a thousand arrows. A great struggle ensued, until finally the venom flowed down the mountain in torrents and the dragon lay dead. Apollo allowed his body to rot on the spot (this detail probably developed from a play on the Greek word "pytho," which means "to rot"). From then on, Delphi belonged to him.

Apollo wished to cleanse himself from the guilt of having murdered the Python, which led him to visit the river Peneios in the Vale of Tempe near Mt. Olympus. During that time of ritual cleansing, Apollo chased his first love, Daphne, from whom he would eventually take the laurel branch as his symbol. Afterwards, Apollo established the Pythian games at Delphi, which were second only to the Olympian games in prestige. Often the name "Delphi" is explained from the following story: Once Apollo appeared to some Cretan sailors by leaping aboard their vessel as they sailed. He guided the terrified sailors to a port at the foot of the mountain beneath Delphi, and, transformed into a handsome youth, he appointed the sailors as priests of his temple. This etymology for the word "Delphi" as coming from the Greek word "Delphis" (= dolphin) is certainly a late addition to explain the name of the town and Apollo's epithet "delphinios." It is more likely that Apollo's function of bringing young men into society reminded the Greeks of the social habits of dolphins. But dolphins are so-called because the root meaning of "delphis" in Greek is "womb," since they among the fish of the sea are mammals and have a womb. If that is the real origin of "Delphi" and "delphinios," then perhaps the words recall Delphi's designation as the center or "omphalos" (= navel) of the world.

CULT AND MEANING

The ancient Greek author Plutarch tells us that the day of Apollo's birth was the seventh of the month, from which he takes the epithet "seventh-born." From then on, the number seven was sacred to Apollo. He demands sacrifices on the seventh of each month, and his festivals tend to fall on the seventh as well. Cult centers of Apollo were scattered throughout the ancient Greek world and most contained an oracle of some sort. It is to these institutions that Greeks looked for advice, both corporately in times of national crisis and war, and individually, when personal problems and decisions were the issue. Socrates started his long and well-documented quest for someone in Athens smarter than himself after the oracle proclaimed him the wisest man in that city. Oedipus came here looking for information about the true identify of his parents. The Romans are said to have sent to Apollo for advice as to whether they should expel their kings in 508 B.C., though we know that the cult of Apollo was not introduced into Rome until 430 B.C., when the Romans needed to avert a plague.

In fact, it is in this latter function, as one who averts evil (Alexikakos), that we mostly find Apollo being worshiped. He drives the blight away from the crops, if only he is properly appeased. He sends away disease from both humans and animals, and keeps them safe from wild beasts. He protects children from the burdens and evils that plague adults until they are ready to fend for themselves. He strengthens men so they can ward off enemies who wish to do them harm. He can even drive the stain of murder from a man with his rites of purification. Thus the sacrifices (typically a hundred oxen, if an entire body of people are involved) and votive offerings had as their aim the procurement of Apollo's protection from various types of evil. It should be noted, however, that Apollo's greatest skill was seen to be in the area of medicine, and for this reason his temples and those of his son Asclepius were often places of healing. Still, the oracle was always central to Apollo's sanctuaries: The god preferred to tell humans directly how to take care of their own problems.

The Romans had an interesting additional take on the role of Apollo in the health of the State. After enduring decades of civil war and social unrest, the Romans under Augustus finally began to see a period of renewal and peace. Augustus directed the building of a temple to Apollo on the Palatine that was meant to signal the coming of this new period of respite. The temple was a thanksgiving offering to the god who brought Rome into a golden age of prosperity, intellectual growth (a library was attached to the temple and many public records and great books were housed there), and concord (for the first time in a long stretch, Rome was not at war anywhere). The temple also stood as a symbol of just vengeance, for Apollo could not renew Rome without first justly punishing the evils that had gone on before. Sins had to be paid for, as Apollo himself demonstrated whenever he went astray. Augustus, in that regard, had killed the assassins of his uncle Julius Caesar. He had also defeated Mark Antony and the rebellious queen Cleopatra in a remarkable naval battle near Actium. Priesthoods had been reestablished and crumbling temples restored. All these things Apollo demanded by the very nature of his personality.

MAJOR MYTHS

There are many myths surrounding the figure of Apollo. Most of them reflect his many spheres of influence (medicine and plagues, the sun, the arts, intellectual activity, music, rites of passage and so on) and show that Apollo had become a symbol for the exemplary, well-rounded Greek youth. Some of the myths tell of Apollo's failed love affairs with various divine and mortal women (Cassandra, Daphne, Marpessa, Sinope); occasionally, Apollo even shows an interest in young boys (Hyacinthus, Cyparissus). This may seem odd to us, but we should remember that to the Greeks, the love between a man and a young boy, whom he trains in the ways of warfare and manly responsibility, was often viewed as more intense and pure than the love between a man and a woman. Two of the stories of Apollo's failed love affairs are told below.

Sibyl

Sibyl was a mythical female who lived near Troy. Apollo was attracted to her and spent much of his time trying to woo and court her. As often happened, Apollo tried to win her over by offering some spectacular gift that would melt her heart. At a loss for how to bend her, Apollo finally told her that he would give to her anything her heart desired. With that, Sibyl finally responded. She reached down into the sand at her feet where she stood and brought up a handful of it. She showed her fistful of sand to Apollo and proclaimed, "I want one year of life for every grain of sand in her hand." Immediately Apollo granted it. Still, Sibyl was not won over, and this frustrated Apollo to no end. He could not take back what he had already given to her, but he needed some way to punish her for refusing him. But suddenly he realized that Sibyl had made a crucial mistake: She had gained for herself a life of a thousand years, for so many grains of sand had been in her hand, but she had forgotten to also ask for perpetual youth. Apollo only had to let age take its course, and after the years went by Sibyl found herself withered and frail, but unable to die. Petronius, a late Roman author, reports that this same Sibyl ended up at Cumae, in Italy, where Apollo had a temple carved into a vast cave. There, her body all withered and faded, she remained simply as a weak voice, kept in a box that hanged from the temple ceiling. As the wind blew through the holes in the box, Sibyl's voice could be heard to groan from within. Children used to like to go there to play, and ask of the Sibyl, "What is it you want, Sibyl?" Invariably the sad response would be, "I want to die, I want to die."

Sibyl was the name given to the specific girl whom Apollo courted, but it was also used for all prophetesses of Apollo, generally speaking. As we have noted, one of the sibyls, maybe the original, was said to live in Italy at Cumae, where Apollo had a temple. Apollo was said to visit her in the vast cave, overcome her, and speak through her words that would echo from the many mouths of the cave. The description of his speaking through her sounds something like demon possession, or, as Vergil describes it in the passage that follows, like a wild horse trying to throw a rider:

> "The vast end of the temple built in Euboean stone is cut out into a cavern; here are a hundred perforations in the rock, a hundred mouths from which the many utterances rush, the answers of the Sibyl. They had come to the threshold, when the virgin cried: 'Now is the time to demand the oracles, the god, behold, the god!' She spoke these words in front of the doors and her countenance and color changed; her hair shook free, her bosom heaved, and her heart swelled in wild fury; she seemed of greater stature and her cries were no mortal as she was inspired by the breath of the god drawning nearer . . . Not yet willing to endure Apollo, the prophetess raged within the cavern in her frenzy, trying to shake the mighty god from her breast; all the more he wore out her ravings, mastering her wild heart and fashioning her to his will by constraint. Now the hundred mouths of the cavern opened wide of their own accord and bore the responses of the phrophetess to the breezes . . . [then, after her prophecies are given] With such words the Cumaean Sibyl chants her terrifying riddles and from the innermost shrine of the cavern truth resounded enveloped in obscurity, as Apollo applied the reins to her raving and twisted the goad in her breast."

Clearly, the Greeks and the Romans believed that the Sibyl would enter some sort of ecstatic trance and wildly babble the prophecies and admonishes of the god.

Coronis

Coronis was a lovely maiden from Larissa in Thessaly. Apollo loved her and successfully courted her. Eventually, she became pregnant with his child. Even so, she did not really love Apollo, and while pregnant she began having an affair. The raven, Apollo's bird, saw her and reported all her actions to Apollo. The poet Ovid tells the terrific tale of what happened next:

> "When Apollo heard this charge against Coronis, the laurel wreath slipped from his head, his expression changed, and the color drained from his cheeks. As his heart burned with swollen rage, he took up his usual weapons and bent his bow to string it; with his unerring arrow he pierced the breast that he had so often embraced. She gave a groan as she was struck; and when she drew the shaft from her body, red blood welled up over her white limbs. She spoke: 'You could have exacted this punishment and I have paid with my life, after I had borne your child; as it is, two of us die in one.' With these words her life drained away with her blood; the chill of death crept over her lifeless corpse."

Apollo, the story goes, was sorry for what he had done, and snatched the child from her body before it was burned on the funeral pyre.

Like many other heroes, Asclepius, the child, was trained by the wise and gentle Chiron, a centaur who happened to be friendlier than most. Asclepius learned his lessons well, particularly in the field of medicine. When he grew up, he refined this science and raised it by transforming it into a high and noble art. Asclepius married and had several children, most importantly Hygeia (Health).

So skilled a physician was Asclepius (he was worshiped as both a hero and a god) that when Artemis' devotee Hippolytus (see the Theseus story) died, Artemis appealed to him to restore her beloved follower to life. Asclepius agreed and succeeded in his attempt. In doing so, however, he incurred the wrath of Zeus, who hurled him into the lower world with a thunderbolt for such a disruption of nature. As with all branches of knowledge and advancement, the Greeks felt a tension between medicine and the will of the gods. Medicine allowed people to take problems into their own hands and solve them, and so alienated them from the gods. Apollo retaliated by killing the Cyclopes who forge Zeus' thunderbolts, and for this Zeus made Apollo serve as a human slave to Admetus and Alcestis in Thessaly for ten years.

The Story of Marsyas

Marsyas was a satyr, a half goat, half human figure who roamed the forests of ancient Greece. One day he came upon a flute that had been invented and discarded by Athena when she became frustrated that she couldn't play it. He picked it up, and Athena then gave him a sound thrashing for doing so. He was not deterred, however, and became so proficient that he dared to challenge Apollo himself to a contest. The condition imposed by the god was that the victor could do what he liked to the vanquished. Apollo won, of course, because in the art of music everyone was inferior to him. So he decided to flay Marsyas alive. Ovid describes the anguish of the satyr:

> "Marsyas cried out, 'Why are you stripping me of my very self? Oh no, I am sorry; the flute is not worth this torture!' As he screamed, his skin was ripped off all his body and he was nothing but a gaping wound. Blood ran everywhere, his nerves were laid bare and exposed, and the pulse of his veins throbbed without any covering. One could make out clearly his pulsating entrails and the vital organs in his chest that lay revealed. The whole forest wept a river of tears."

CHAPTER ELEVEN

Dionysus

"But girlish Dionysus does not blush to sprinkle with perfume his flowing locks, nor in his soft hand to shake the slender thyrsus, when with dainty gait he trails his robe richly decked out with Eastern gold."

—Seneca, *Hercules Furens* 472ff.

The passage cited above emphasizes one of the oddest and striking characteristics of Dionysus: In his dress, gait, appearance, manner, and style he is an effeminate deity. He has golden curls sprinkled with perfume. His features are round and soft. His skin is white, unaccustomed to the sun, and his cheeks are flush. But why? We immediately think of how his aunt had to dress him as a girl in order to fool Hera as she sought him in a jealous rage. But mostly his effeminate nature must relate somehow to the power of nature which he represents and probably also to the way in which he was worshiped. Some divinities are *ethical* in nature, that is, they concern themselves primarily with human endeavors (art, intellect, etc.), societal issues, and life stages (rites of passage, marriage, etc.). Dionysus stands for the enviable vital force in nature apparent in everything that is young, fruitful, and full of the energy of life. The Greeks noticed this power in nature and recognized that it was almost always sexual, aggressive, and loud. Thus Dionysus manifests himself in humans in an emotional way (the Greeks considered emotionalism a feminine quality), characterized by the loss of self-control, a sense of danger, and the presence of much noise and ululation. In fact, his cultic name "Bacchus," used primarily as a way to invoke his presence, refers to the riotous, orgiastic uproar of his worship; similarly, his epithet "Bromius" means "thundering." In short, he is *noisy* Dionysus.

The followers of Dionysus are also noisy and sexually aroused. The Maenads, nymphs who once nursed Dionysus on Mt. Nysa, accompany him in his travels with ululations and abandonment. They twirl the thyrsus, a kind of baton representing the male phallus. They are chased constantly by other more animalistic followers of Dionysus, the satyrs and the

Macedon, Mende. Silver tetradrachm, c. 460–423 B.C. Bearded Dionysus facing, nude to waist, reclining on a donkey; he holds a kantharos in his right hand and thrysus in his left hand. On the reverse, a grape vine.

sileni, as objects of their passion. In a frantic drunken swirl of resisting and teasing and relenting, the mythic followers of Dionysus carry on a constant orgiastic festival of carnival fun:

> "In the mountains the leader of the dance is Bromius, evoē! [a shout of excitement typical in the worship of Dionysus] The plain flows with milk, it flows with wine, it flows with the honey from the bees. Bacchus, raising the flaming torch of pine on his thyrsus, like the smoke of Syrian frankincense, darts about, arousing the wanderers with his racing and dancing, agitating them with his shouts, tossing his rich tresses into the air. And amid the Maenad's cries his voice rings deep."

> —Euripides, *Bacchae* 135ff

It's no wonder that Dionysus' intoxicating ways led to his connection with the vine and the grape. In fact, as Dionysus traveled the world, introducing various cities and peoples to his divinity and his rites of worship, he rewarded those who received him kindly with the knowledge of the vine's cultivation. Anyone who refused to acknowledge his divine status he either flayed alive, as was the case of a certain man named Damascus in Syria, or he drove them to madness, as happened at Thebes with his cousin Pentheus. In his mad wanderings, Dionysus also drove his band as far east as India, where many received him, but three powerful kings resisted him with their armies. In a furious battle, Dionysus, the satyrs, sileni, and Maenads brought them to submission and introduced cultivation to the Indians. While there, Dionysus established many towns and left behind numerous monuments that would one day inspire Alexander the Great to try to surpass him. The god returned from the East in a glorious triumphal parade that made all the gods and nations stop and take notice. Dionysus was not to be denied.

ORIGINS

Dionysus was born from a relationship between Zeus and Semele, a human female from Thebes, daughter of the founder of Thebes, Cadmus. As a result of a trick by the jealous Hera, Semele was consumed in a ball of fire and destroyed. Zeus realized that Semele was pregnant, though, and from the gulf of flames he snatched out the fetus, cut open his thigh, and inserted the child (from which he takes the name "Insewn" in hymns). Several months later, Dionysus was born from the thigh of Zeus, and so received the epithet "Twice-born." In order to hide the baby from Hera, Dionysus was entrusted to King Athamas of Orchemenos (a town near Thebes) and his wife Ino (sister of Semele, along with Agave and Autonoe), and they were told to disguise the child as a girl. Hera soon discovered the trick, however, and in her anger made both Athamas and Ino mad. Ino ended up throwing one of her children into a caldron of boiling water, while Athamas speared another thinking he was a deer. Ino then jumped off a cliff into the sea, where the sea-gods, out of their pity, transformed her into Leucothea, goddess of the sea spray, who one day would rescue Odysseus after a shipwreck. Also, it should be noted that Semele's sister had been spreading vicious rumors that Zeus was not the father of Dionysus, and that she had only fantasized the whole affair.

Afterwards, Dionysus was taken from Ino, transformed into a kid, and given to the nymphs of Mt. Nysa, where they nursed him as a goat-child. Mt. Nysa is usually placed in Asia Minor, in modern day Turkey, but another strong tradition places Dionysus in Thrace in the mountains near Philippi (now Greece). Either way, when he was returned to human form, his nurses became his followers, the Maenads. The name Dionysus, in fact, means "Zeus of Nysa," but it is hard to know whether he is a god who came from that region in Asia Minor or whether the story was invented to explain his name. Some say these nymphs transformed Dionysus into a kid (the animal) so that Hera wouldn't recognize him, which explains why sometimes in cultic ritual Dionysus is represented by a kid.

CULT AND MEANING

Dionysus was worshiped in several festivals of the wildest sort around Greece, including the City Dionysia at Athens, in which he was celebrated as the lord of indestructible life. Drunken bands of cross-dressed men and women roamed the streets wearing masks and exaggerated make-up, while obscenities and role reversals were widespread. Decorated phalluses were escorted into the city on wagons and paraded through the streets. The City Dionysia, as well as another festival called Lenaea, featured performances of tragedies and comedies in honor of Dionysus. The choral songs of these dramas appear to have their origins in the cultic songs themselves. One of the hymns (dithyrambs) sung to him at the festival went as follows:

> "Who is this one? What is His name? A Wanderer from exotic lands? Of iron heart, invincible, who checks the strength of every foe. Bright flames leap from His shining eyes like Lemnos-fire. With hunting boots and deerskin clad, His staff held high, He comes to us.

He marches through our noble town. A God has come, who forges laws to rid the land of monstrous things. Every outrage will be answered! The flow of Time ends everything."

—Bacchylides

These tragedies further clarified the role of the god Dionysus in the city: Bringing together the populace into an otherwise unprecedented assembly of men, women, children, slave, aristocrat, and worker, they could evoke laughter or horror, they could reverse or subvert, and even call into question the very structures that brought them into being.

MAJOR MYTHS

Dionysus one day was on the islands of Icaria or Chios, both famous for their wine. There he attempted to hire some sailors for a ride to Naxos, where certain nurses were waiting to take care of him (these nurses represent a divergent tradition with the Mt. Nysa myth told above). The sailors turned out really to be pirates from the Tyrrhenian Sea, and figured that any small boy trying to get onto a boat by himself hailed from wealthy parents. Therefore, they seized him, hoping to kidnap him and get a ransom, or to sail him into slavery. For this purpose they steered off course and headed towards Asia instead of the island Naxos. Some of the pirates even found him so handsome they plotted to rape him.

The young boy Dionysus understand their intentions. Suddenly, in spite of a breeze, the ship stood still. The sound of flutes filled the air. Ivy and grapevines twined themselves about the oars and masts, or the oars, some say, turned into snakes. The sailors were at first astonished, then terrified, because wild beasts appeared on board, including panthers, lions, bears. The captain was eaten by a lion, while the rest of the sailors jumped into the sea, but then Dionysus turned them into dolphins, which remain somewhat humanlike. At any rate, Dionysus sailed on to Naxos by himself. There he met his future wife, Ariadne, who was passing through by chance with Theseus back from his defeat of the Minotaur in Crete.

At length, Dionysus came to Phrygia. There Cybele purified him and presumably cured him of his madness. It was while he was in Phrygia that he adopted the oriental costume that he and his followers wore; there also he instituted many of his own rites, some of which resemble those of Cybele. It is generally understood that Dionysus learned the mysteries from Cybele *before* he began his journey to India and the rest of the world. In fact, these were the rites that Dionysus was encouraging the people whom he met to take up.

There are some odd tales floating around that say Dionysus was eventually caught by Hera and torn apart, and that the other gods gathered up all the parts and put him together again. This, too, could explain the epithet "twice-born." These stories also add the detail that Hera, frustrated by the reconstruction of the god, drove him mad and caused his wanderings about the earth.

It is clear from these cursory descriptions of the myth and cult of Dionysus that he stands in sharp contrast to all the other Olympian gods. He was born of a human mother, for example, and his worship takes place, not in the traditional sanctuaries and temples that adorn the cities of Greece, but wherever the god's wandering band or *thiasos* of followers stops to revel. When his image appears it is often merely a stake driven into the ground and deco-rated with a mask and effeminate clothing. Instead of the normal kind of sacrifice and feast-ing, his followers engaged in violent, wild rituals that preferred the unexpected and perverted. If rituals for other gods involved roasting and eating meat, Dionysus wanted his worshipers to tear into raw flesh. The other gods demanded solemnity and respect in their worship, Dionysus asked for unrestrained revelry. The unorthodox form of piety that he demanded appealed, not just to men, as was the case with many other cults of Greece, but also to women and slaves. But Dionysus was not a "foreign" god, as some have suggested in the past. Many myths portray Dionysus as a divinity who comes from overseas and tries to impose his exotic, irrational brand of religion on the relatively rational cities of Greece. The discovery of Dionysus' name in the most archaic records of the Mycenean Greeks (dated to about 1250 B.C.), however, causes us to rethink his status as an outsider who imposed him-self on Greek order. It seems likely that the Greeks played up the "otherness" of Dionysus precisely because of the ecstatic effects of his power: He removes men and women from their conventional roles, subverting their traditions and forcing them to take the point of view of the stranger. The norms of society are called into question and even broken in his cult, men brought together with women, slaves with citizens, in wild abandonment and euphoria. The fresh perspective, the irrational point of view, served to rejuvenate the populace.

CHAPTER TWELVE
The Topography of Hell

"Plouton holds a key, and with it he has locked up that place called Hades, and they say that nobody will return back again there from."

—Pausanias, *Guide to Greece* 5.20.2–3

The term "Hades" is both the name of the god who rules in the underworld and the name of the place itself. The name "Hades" likely comes from a root that means "unseen" and refers to the fact that Hades is a dark, mysterious god whom people do not usually see. For this reason he was thought to possess a cap of invisibility given to him by the Cyclopes that other gods and heroes borrow from time to time during their adventures. Some believed his name derived from another root meaning "all-receiver," because, as the god of the realm below, he received all souls of the dead. The cap and the unseen nature of the god and place coupled with the idea that he devours souls made this name, Hades, a holy and awesome name. The average person was afraid to even utter it. It evoked images of confusion and sadness and isolation. They preferred another name, Plouton (the Romans often called him Pluto), which refers to the wealth that lies buried in the earth: gold, silver, bronze, marble, and so on. From Pluto's domain come the minerals that men mine and the cash crops that feed the farmers' families. The Greeks believed that the planting of seeds in the earth has an affinity with the practice of burial and that it is the business of Hades and his wife Persephone to nurture the seeds so that the process of birth, maturity and death remain reliable. Many images on vases show him holding a cornucopia full of the bounty of the earth that he is ready to poor out for human benefit. Thus in a positive way Pluto was seen as a provider of wealth.

Hades won control of the underworld when he and his brothers, Zeus and Poseidon, drew lots after the defeat of the Titans. Upon his request, Zeus awarded him Persephone, his daughter with Demeter, to be his bride. Both Zeus and Hades realized that Persephone would never consent to enter the realm of the dead to be queen, so they contrived a plan where Hades would take his bride by force. This set off the chain of events that are described

A bronze semiunca dating to 211 B.C., showing Herakles on the obverse and Cerberus on the reverse.

in the chapter on Demeter elsewhere in this book. Suffice it to say here that Persephone became a part-time bride of Hades, spending some of her time with her mother making the crops grow and the rest of her time with her husband in the underworld, ruling over the souls of the departed and nurturing the buried seeds.

When the ancients worshiped Hades, they did so with rites that were often the opposite those offered to other divinities. They poured out blood, wine, or oil onto the ground or into a pit instead of onto an altar. The victims sacrificed were black, typically sheep or in many cases pigs, and the sacrificer often had to turn away his face from the act. Men pounded the earth and sent their curses or oaths down to Hades in the hope that he or his minions would see to their fulfillment. They tried to win the favor of Hades' ghosts through necromancy in the hope of gaining otherwise hidden information or punishing their enemies.

As for the place Hades, the ancient poets had a saying that the descent to the underworld is easy, but the way back up is difficult. In fact, in Greek and Roman myth, only heroes who have in them some measure of divine blood in their veins ever entered and returned. Vergil, the Roman poet and author of the *Aeneid,* gives a very detailed description of the underworld, its major features, and its inhabitants as he tells the story of Aeneas' journey there. Aeneas, a son of Aphrodite, was a Trojan hero who had escaped the city of Troy as it fell to the Greeks and who had made his way to Italy by the commands and fates of the gods with the goal to establish a new race (the Romans). When Aeneas landed at Cumae he met the Sibyl, prophetess of Apollo, who served a shrine there and attended the entrance of the underworld. Aeneas had been told by the gods to use her as his guide into the underworld so that he could see again his dead father. His father, Anchises, had information to give him about the future of the Roman race and could instill courage in him to face the many trials and hardships that lay before him.

Aeneas begins his journey into the underworld accompanied by the Sibyl. He carries two items, his sword and the golden bough to give to Persephone (Roman Proserpina). The bough would guarantee that he could gain admittance into the realm of the dead. He had been ordered by the Sibyl to find the bough in a nearby Grove of Hecate, but only those who are approved by the gods to enter the underworld could find and pluck the bough in the forest.

Aeneas and the Sibyl found the entrance to the underworld near Lake Avernus, a rancid, foul lake whose stench was so bad that birds flying overhead would fall dead into the water ("Avernus," according to Vergil, means "birdless"). Passing alongside the lake, the two entered into the Jaws of Orcus, the threshold of the underworld. Here at the entrance are personified evils and discomforts of life, such as Old Age, Death, Discord, Hunger, diseases, and so on, anything, that is, that could lead to the death of someone (thus they are at the entrance). All kinds of monsters live here too, including Briareus, the hundred-handed giant, centaurs, harpies, and gorgons. Yet they do not have real forms, and pose no real threat, since everything in the underworld is a mere phantom or shadow, without bodily substance. Aeneas also sees an elm tree from which false and scary dreams hang, like bats in a tree.

From the Jaws of Orcus the road winds downward to the river Acheron, thick, muddy, swampy, sometimes thought of as a lake fed by the river Styx, and connected, likewise, to the rivers Cocytus and Pyriphlegethon. There thousands of men and women throng as they try to secure a ride on the boat that crosses the lake, piloted by the ferryman of hell, Charon, with his matted hair and protruding eyes. The ferryman, however, does not let everyone board his boat. Those who have not had a proper burial in the world above have to wait, homeless, until 100 years have passed before they can finally find rest in the underworld. And certainly those who are not dead cannot board the creaky boat, since the underworld is not for them. Charon has regretted letting a few living people enter the underworld, because when they arrive, they always carry out some mischief. Herakles entered, for example, and proceeded to drag off Cerberus, the guard dog of the underworld. Theseus and Pirithous came, but only to attempt a rape of Persephone. Aeneas and the Sibyl gain entrance to his boat, however, by showing him the golden bough, a sign that the gods have foreordained this journey.

The boat ferries the two travelers to the other side to what is called the Far Margin, and there they disembark. The soil is gray sedge and dark-brown ooze, drab and shapeless. From there they take the path into the heart of the underworld, past the cavern of Cerberus, the hell hound, who keeps the living from entering the infernal regions, and also keeps the dead from escaping their confinement. The Romans depicted him as having three heads, with serpents bristling along them, and a bellowing bark. It should be noted here that traditionally the ancients believed that ghosts are afraid of loud noises. So while a dog could do no actual physical harm to insubstantial shades, the very sound of his bark keeps them back. That is why, also, loud noises were used in any event someone wanted to keep spirits away, such as at a wedding or a banquet. The Sibyl came prepared, throwing him a sop soaked in honey and a drug that put him to sleep immediately. Thus the hero enters live into the realm of the dead with the hope of returning to the world above again, thereby conquering death on our behalf.

Just beyond Cerberus lies an area for those who die too young or unjustly. This includes infants and suicides, who have learned that even a sorrowful life is better than death. Achilles once lamented that fact to Odysseus when the latter visited the underworld. When Odysseus saw him and exclaimed that he must enjoy being like a king among the dead, Achilles replied, poignantly, that it is better to be the slave of a poor man in the world of light than ruler in the world below. At any rate, here are also people who were judged unjustly and put to death. King Minos, a famous and wise king of Crete, sits here on a bench giving them a second trial and reviewing the facts of their case again. Injustices can never stand forever.

Nearby stretch the Fields of Mourning for those who pined away their life in love, or committed suicide because of love. One of Aeneas' former girlfriends is here, the Carthaginian (North African) queen Dido, a Phoenician whom Aeneas had to abandon because the Fates had other plans for him. She was there with her former husband Sychaeus, but was unwilling to speak to Aeneas. Here is Vergil's description of their meeting:

> "And here, new come from her own wound, was Dido,
> wandering in the wood. The Trojan hero,
> standing near by, saw her, or thought he saw her,
> dim in the shadows, like the slender crescent
> of moon when cloud drifts over. Weeping, he greets
> her: —
> 'Unhappy Dido, so they told me truly
> that your own hand had brought you death. Was I—
> Alas!—the cause? I swear by all the stars,
> by the world above, by everything held sacred
> here under the earth, unwillingly, o queen,
> I left your kingdom. But the gods' commands,
> driving me now through these forsaken places,
> this utter night, compelled me on. I could not
> believe my loss would cause so great a sorrow.
> Linger a moment, do not leave me; whither,
> whom, are you fleeing? I am permitted only
> this last word with you.'
> But the queen, unmoving
> as flint or marble, turned away, her eyes
> fixed on the ground: the tears were vain, the words,
> meant to be soothing, foolish; she turned away,
> his enemy forever, to the shadows
> where Sychaeus, her former husband, took her
> with love for love, and sorrow for her sorrow.
> And still Aeneas wept for her, being troubled
> by the injustice of her doom; his pity
> followed her going."

Next the two come to the Field of the Warriors, the place where warriors go who have died in battle and still carry their arms. In a sense, they too have died before their time, and so belong here near the others who died too soon. Many of the Greeks and Trojans were there fresh from the war, including the good friend of Aeneas, Deiphobus. Helen killed him during the fall of Troy as she was trying to convince her husband that she did not like being taken captive at Troy and that she really wanted to go back with him. After ten years there was some doubt among the Greek warriors, who knew that Helen had a chance to escape from Troy several times. Helen, in fact, had willingly married Deiphobus after Paris was killed during a battle. When Aeneas sees him in the underworld, Deiphobus is mutilated in the worst possible way, with his nose and ears cut off, his face slashed everywhere. Even in the afterlife he bears the marks of his horrible death (compare Jesus, who still had the marks of his crucifixion when he arose from the dead, though in his case it was a mark of his glory rather than a mark of shame).

After the Field of the Warriors, our intrepid travelers come to a crossroads where stands the palace of Hades and Persephone. Aeneas places the golden bough at the doorstep for Persephone without trying to enter. To the left the road leads down to Tartarus, surrounded by a fiery river and protected by a gate made of adamantine steel (from which we get the word adamant), a mythical metal that even the gods could not break. Monsters guard the gate, and Furies leap about, whip in hand, striking prisoners. Here are housed the worst criminals from the world above, people who have insulted the gods, betrayed their country, or done harm to their own family members. People who have broken faith and cheated others are also here. Rhadamanthus, brother of King Minos, rules over this region, torturing the criminals and trying to force each one of them to acknowledge their sins. Despite the torture, they are reluctant to admit that they committed any wrong: They are habitual sinners. Tartarus is a horrible, pitch black place with horrible sounds issuing forth, shouts of pain, cracking whips, dragging chains, and grinding bones. (Note: In Greek literature, Rhadamanthus is king over Elysium, a much happier place).

To the right the road leads to the Elysian Fields, a blessed place where most people go. It is full of greenery and music, and even has light. There everybody can do their favorite thing all day long, such as engaging in sports or reading books. There Aeneas finally meets his father Anchises, whom the hero tries to touch, but he is like the other "shades," just a phantom. Anchises shows Aeneas the spirits of the men and women who are awaiting to be reborn. He explains that for a thousand years they drink from the river Lethe ("Forgetfulness") until they have forgotten their former selves, and are ready to be take on a new life in the world above. Aeneas sees the great leaders of future Rome, and catches a glimpse of the glory that will be Rome. A Roman reading this in Vergil's time would marvel at how long before the grandeur of Rome has been fated and how many difficult struggles the Roman race had to go through to get to where it is. He would feel that Rome itself exists as the fulfillment of destiny. So Aeneas sees many great future Romans (none, obviously, who lived after Vergil's time), men such as Romulus, the founder of Rome, Augustus Caesar who ruled Rome while the poem was being written, and even Marcellus, Augustus' first son-in-law, who died while the poem was less than half finished.

Aeneas sees, therefore, the vision of future Rome, and feels emboldened to continue his task. He bids farewell to his father, and we are told of this strange exit by the hero and Sibyl into the world above:

> "There are two portals,
> twin gates of Sleep, one made of horn, where easy
> release is given true shades, the other gleaming
> white ivory, whereby the false dreams issue
> to the upper air. Aeneas and the Sibyl
> part from Anchises at the second portal."

How odd it is that doubt is cast on Aeneas' enterprise when he exits through the gate of false dreams!

It should be noted that Vergil's vision of the underworld is much more optimistic than that of Homer seven hundred years before. In Homer's vision, the shades are all gathered into one place, a dark place, gloomy, and they themselves cannot speak and in fact barely exist. To be able to communicate with anyone or show any sign of life someone must give them blood to drink. Odysseus does just that when he goes to the entrance of the underworld and calls out for the old seer Teiresias. Only a few of the greatest heroes could make it into a better place, usually called the Isles of the Blessed or the Plains of Asphodel (sometimes Elysian Fields or Elysium). The much more hopeful attitude of Vergil may be explained by the growth in popularity of the Mystery Religions (including the worship of Cybele, Demeter, Dionysus, and the cult of Orphism), and mystical philosophies such as Pythagoreanism, all of which taught that death is not final, that human beings reincarnate, and that, not only do punishments exist after death, rewards do as well.

MANES

In Roman religious formulas, that is, in prayers and invocations, we often find reference to the Manes, or Di Manes. Originally, the terms seem to be euphemistic expressions applied to the infernal gods as a whole in an effort to gain their favor. In two instances, for example, Roman nobles who were sacrificing their lives to save their country prayed to the Manes to receive their body as an offering of appeasement. One, the consul Decius, consecrated himself and the enemy army to the gods below as he rode alone headlong into their midst; the other, M. Curtius, devoted himself to the Di Manes when, after a terrifying earthquake that struck the heart of Rome, he leapt along with his horse into a chasm that opened up in the forum. Eventually, though, during the period of the empire, the expression "Di Manes" becomes a part of the cult of dead ancestors. The Romans had long worshiped their ancestors in a February festival called the Parentalia, but inscriptions on tombstones from this later period indicate that the ancestors themselves receive the title Manes. Clearly the Romans felt that their relatives exist after their death and that some degree of communication between their world and the world of the living continued. Still, we are left to wonder what Vergil meant when he writes in his *Aeneid* the following enigmatic verse at 6.743: "quisque suos patimur Manes" ("each of us suffers our own Manes"). Ancient commentators thought that Vergil was speaking of the judgment and punishment that we must each endure, and some modern scholars have accepted this interpretation with some modification. In the context, however, Virgil appears to be alluding to the fact that in the underworld each of us must undergo a process of purification. At the very least, his words reflect a growing sense of individualized (rather than corporate) immortality among the Romans.

CHAPTER THIRTEEN

Orpheus

"And right away, when the poet was still a baby, he gurgled and with earliest accents sweetly whimpered, Calliope took him to her loving bosom. Then finally did she lay aside her grief and cease her long lament for her dead son Orpheus, and said: 'Child, consecrate yourself to the art of poetry. You are destined to outmatch soon the bards of old, and you will not be stirring rivers or wild herds of Thracian ash-trees with your music, but with eloquent song will draw after you the seven hills of the Martian Tiber [Rome].'"

—Statius, *Silvae* 2.7.36

The myth of the hero Orpheus stretches back to earliest recorded history. Throughout the long span of years it accrued numerous variations in its details at the hands of diverse groups of people. In particular, the imagery of the story of this musical hero (he played the lyre and the cithara, which he invented) with all its symbolism was used by esoteric religious movements to advance their doctrines and by poets to claim a certain religious authority. As an allegory, it even makes its way into early Christian iconography. In the catacombs, for example, Christ appears at times in the guise of Orpheus with the lyre. In some Christian tombs Orpheus is depicted delivering the Sermon on the Mount or acting as "The Good Shepherd." Music has a mystical quality to the extent that it can hold sway over the soul and purify it of its disturbing elements, even resurrect it when it is at the point of death. Orpheus had used his celestial harmonies to try to raise his dead wife and to exert influence over the shades of the underworld, which makes us think of Jesus' harrowing of Hell and conquest of death as well. Among the Jews, Orpheus appears, not surprisingly, as king David, the forerunner of the anointed one who would bring salvation and eternal life. David, as you recall, played the lyre too and wrote psalms. Today we still believe in the healing power of music. At many universities there exists a separate field of study called "music therapy," which acknowledges that music can effect the human psyche in some profound way.

Antoninus Pius, 142 A.D. Bronze drachm showing Orpheus on the reverse, seated on a rock and playing a lyre while the charmed animals listen intently.

Orpheus was the son of Oeagrus, a river god and son of Ares, and of Calliope, one of the nine muses (later attached to epic poetry):

> "Orpheus, borne, so the story goes, by Kalliope herself to her Thracian lover Oeagrus near the heights of Pimplea. They say that with the music of his voice he enchanted stubborn mountain rocks and rushing streams."

—Apollonius of Rhodes, *Argonautica* 1.24

In the remarkable vase painting that depicts Orpheus' head being fished out of the waters of Lesbos, Calliope can be seen there, resting on her lyre, watching the rescue of her son. Orpheus was a pupil of Apollo, though, but also a devotee of Dionysus and his worship. He comes from Thrace in northern Greece, and thus is often depicted wearing the more exotic clothes of that people. According to the traditional stories, he was so marvelous a musician that when he sang and played his lyre, the whole of nature would listen entranced. Creatures would follow him, the wild Thracians became gentle as they listened to him, and even trees and stones came to hear his music. It is said that Linus, the music teacher whom Herakles slew, was his brother as well, and some ancient authors even suggest that Apollo was the father of both and not Oeagrus.

Orpheus had many adventures in his early days. In particular, he joined the Argonauts on their Voyage to retrieve the golden fleece, and supposedly he was able to calm the waves in a storm, drown out the songs of the sirens who were trying to ensnare the Argonauts, or calm the crew when they became unruly. Some versions of the Jason and the Argonauts myths say that it was Orpheus who lulled the dragon to sleep so that Jason could grab the golden fleece. And when the Argonauts were sailing passed the Sirens, whose beautiful voices were luring the Argonauts into a trap, Orpheus sang even more beautifully, thus keeping the men at their oars.

On his return to Greece, or Thrace, really, he lived in a cave and spent his time taming the countryside with his music (this shows that the Greeks connected a knowledge of music with the very existence of social order: It controls the passions, pleases the gods, requires discipline, and therefore was a fitting pursuit for young men in the city). He was set to marry a girl whom he loved passionately, whose name was Eurydice. But when the wedding day came, many dreadful things happened. Although the god Hymen came to the wedding, always a good sign, he couldn't keep his sacred wedding torch lit. No matter how much he was shaking it, it just produced a smoke that irritated the eyes of the guests and made them cry. This was ominous, for on that very day, Eurydice was assaulted and pursued through the meadows by Aristaeus, who lusted after her greatly. He was the husband of Autonoe, sister of Semele, the mother of Dionysus. He was also Actaeon's father (Actaeon is the one that Artemis had to turn into a deer). The family connections of Aristaeus, it should be noted, bring Orpheus into even closer contact with the stories of Dionysus.

At any rate, in Eurydice's haste to escape Aristaeus, she stepped on a snake, which bit her on the leg so badly that she died. Overwhelmed with inconsolable grief, Orpheus ceased to sing and play, but moped around in silence. Finally he got the idea to wander around looking for the entrance to the underworld, which he found in southern Italy, and he made his way into the passage leading down. Once down there, he began to play his lyre, and so charmed Charon and Cerberus, the guard dog, that they let him pass. All the shades of the underworld were entranced by his music, so much so that even the tortures of Tartarus stopped. The power of music to save men from the black dank realm of hopelessness and death inspired many poets to linger over this part of the story. Ovid hints that the music can even release the guilty from the punishment of their sins: "Tantalus stopped reaching for the receding waters, the wheel of Ixion stopped in wonder, the vultures ceased tearing at the liver of Tityos, the Danaid sisters left their urns empty, and Sisyphus sat on his throne to listen." Vergil extends this, making every corner of Hell respond to Orpheus' song:

> "Assuaging his bitter love with a hollow tortoise-shell, he sang of you, his sweet wife, he sang of you to himself on the lonely shore, he sang of you at the day's coming and at its departing. He entered the Taenarian jaws, the lofty portals of Dis, and the grove shadowed in black dread and approached the souls of the dead, their fearful king, and hearts not known to soften at human entreaty. But moved by his song there came from the deepest regions of Erebus flitting shades and spectral images of those who have departed from the light, in number like many thousands of birds who seek cover in the leaves of the trees when evening or a winter rain drives them from the mountains. There were mothers and husbands and the bodies of great-souled heroes which had departed from life, boys and unmarried girls, youths who were placed on the pyre before the eyes of their parents. And around these the black muck, the unsightly reed of the Cocytus, and the hateful swamp with its sluggish water binds, and the Styx, circling nine times around hems them in. Yes, the palace itself was dumbstruck, so too the inmost Tartarean reaches of death, and the Furies, their hair plaited with dark green snakes. Gaping Cerberus held his jaws tight, and even the turning of Ixion's wheel had ceased with a breeze."

—Vergil, *Georgics* 4.464–484

Even the gods Hades and Persephone were softened. Orpheus told them how Eurydice died before her time, how they would have her one day, and that he wouldn't return without her. They granted him the favor of recovering Eurydice and taking her back, but with one condition: Orpheus must lead the way out of the underworld and *not* look back at her until they reached the upper air. Thus he departed, his wife behind him, his eyes fixed ahead. But while he was leading her up through the steep path and black vapors, just as the end of the passage was in sight and the light was visible ahead, he could not refrain from turning and gazing at his wife's face—he was worried whether she was safe, or really there; perhaps he heard her stumble. At that very moment, she turned into a mist, a shade of her former self again, and though he grabbed at her, she was sucked back down into the underworld. He tried to follow, but this time all the music failed.

Orpheus became like a lost soul on earth, wandering here and there, living life like a recluse, avoiding the company, above all, of women. He would sing, but songs of mourning and lament. The women resented this utter devotion to a wife that had passed away, because he was so handsome. He was so distraught about women, in fact, that the Greeks believed that Orpheus originated the practice of older men having relations with younger men: He was "enjoying" as the ancient writers say, "the brief spring of their youth and plucking its first flowers." Remember Persephone was picking flowers when she was dragged off by Hades.

One day he stumbled upon a group of women who were performing the rites in honor of Dionysus. When they saw him, they went into a frenzy and flew after him. Their weapons, however, fell to the ground around him, charmed by his music. The women grew more hostile and bold, abandoning all restraint. As they began to play their Dionysiac music, the curved pipes, the pounding drums, the whooping and shrieking eventually drowned out his lyre.

So they caught him, and tore him to shreds. In fact, there seems to be some confusion between this story and that of Pentheus, who saw the rites of Dionysus and was torn apart. Some authors have Dionysus angry at Orpheus as well, first for rejecting him and then for spying on his worshipers, but others have him punishing the Maenaeds (Bacchants) for harming his devotee. In either case, as the Maenads tore him apart, his head rolled down the hill into the River Hebrus, and was washed down to the sea, rolling this way and that and constantly crying "Eurydice!" Eventually it came ashore on the island Lesbos, where the people buried it, erecting a shrine and an oracle to this detached talking head. The Lesbians became great poets (remember Sappho). The Muses are said to have gathered his fragments and buried them near Mt. Olympus, where a nightingale sang over his tomb; his lyre was placed in heaven by Zeus as a constellation as a favor to Calliope.

There are many ways to understand and interpret the Orpheus story. One part of the story that especially drew attention was his exit from the underworld, when he lost his wife for a second time. The following comes from Boethius, an early Christian writer who included this insight into the story in his composition, *The Consolation of Philosophy*:

> "Long ago the singer of Thrace lamented his dead wife, and by his tearful strains he made the trees follow him, and caused the flowing streams to stand still. For him the hind would fearlessly go side by side with fiercest lions, and the hare would look upon the hound, nor be afraid, for he was gentle under the music's power. But when the hot flame of love consumed him deep in his soul, even his own strains, which had subdued all other things,

could not soothe the singer's mind. Complaining of the hard hearts of the gods above, he dared approach the realms below. There he tuned his songs to soothing tones, and sang the ballads he had drawn from his mother's[1] fount of excellence. His unrestrained grief did give him power, his love redoubled his grief's power; his mourning moved the depths of hell. He prayed to the lords of the shades for grace with the gentlest of prayers. The three-headed guardian[2] was captivated with amazement at his fresh songs. The avenging goddesses,[3] who haunt with fear the guilty, poured out sad tears. Ixion's[4] wheel no longer turned swiftly. Tantalus,[5] so long abandoned to thirst, suddenly could ignore the flowing stream. The vulture, satisfied by his strains, stopped tearing at Tityos'[6] heart. At last the lord of the shades[7] in pity cried: 'We are conquered; take your bride with you, bought by your song; but we set one condition on this gift: Until she has left these dark abodes, do not gaze upon her with your eyes.' Who can impose rules on lovers? Love does whatever it pleases. Oh my! at the very bounds of darkness Orpheus looked upon his Eurydice; looked, and lost her, and was lost himself.

Here is the moral you, who seek to lead your thoughts to the light above, should draw from this tale: Whosoever is overcome by desire, and turns his gaze upon the darkness underneath the earth, at that very moment, as he looks on hell, he loses the prize he carried off."

---

[1] Orpheus's mother was the Muse Calliope, mistress of the Castalian fount.
[2] The dog Cerberus.
[3] The Furies.
[4] Ixion for his crimes was bound upon a rolling wheel.
[5] Tantalus for his crimes was condemned to perpetual hunger and thirst though surrounded by fruits and water which ever eluded his grasp.
[6] Tityos for his crimes was for ever fastened to the ground while a vulture devoured his entrails.
[7] Pluto.

CHAPTER FOURTEEN
Herakles

"I know that Bacchus and Perseus have already reached the gods' abode as their reward; but Dionysus only conquered a small tract of earth in the east, and Perseus only took as his meager spoil the head of the Gorgon! I am your son, Zeus, and the son of your lover, and look at what I have done to merit the stars! I seek the skies which I myself have borne on my shoulders."

—Seneca, *Hercules Oetaeus*

Of all the heroes, Herakles, or Hercules as he was known to the Romans, receives the most attention, both from the ancients and from moderns. He was a "panhellenic" hero, meaning that his deeds benefitted *all* of Greece rather than just one particular region or city. All Greeks were eager to lay claim to him as their benefactor, and, indeed, his exploits take place over an enormous geographical area. It is not easy to describe his accomplishments in a few pages, first, since the chronology of his life is jumbled, and, second, since the number of deeds attributed to him are endless. He is best known for his twelve labors, but before, during, and after those labors he had many sub-adventures, some of which are important for understanding his character.

Typically in Greek art Herakles is holding a club, sometimes a bow, and wearing a lion skin with the head of the lion still attached. Numerous kings, emperors, and generals attempted to attach Herakles' iconography to themselves, thus claiming his power. For example, the coins of Alexander the Great show him dressed as Herakles on the obverse, with a picture of Zeus seated on his throne and holding an eagle on the reverse. Also, many Christian churches from the earliest times through the Renaissance employed his image in their murals as a way of indicating that Jesus has become the new Herakles.

THE MYTH

Herakles was born from a union between Alkmene and Zeus. Although Alkmene was married to Amphitryon, the latter was away at war when Zeus took a fancy to her. He came to her disguised as her own husband, and in order to fulfill his lust for her, caused the night to

C. Poblicius, 80 B.C. Silver serrated denarius, with a draped and helmeted bust of Roma on the front and on the reverse Heracles fighting the Nemean lion.

stretch out three times its normal length. Then, soon after he departed, Amphitryon returned from his expedition, and much to the puzzlement of Alkmene, wanted to have sex with his wife. Now through the union with Zeus, Alkmene gave birth to Herakles, while through her union with Amphitryon, she gave birth to Iphikles, Herakles' weaker twin brother. Some mythographers say that "Herakles" was not his original name (the patronym "Alcides" was, since his grandfather was named Alceus), but that Apollo had given it to him as a mystical, euphemistic name to avert the wrath of Hera. "Herakles" means "glory of Hera," an ironic name given the fact that Hera was jealous of any child that Zeus had through another female. It was Hera, in fact, who caused Herakles most of his troubles in life. Herakles' family was centered in Argos and he himself was a descendant of Perseus through his mother. Even so, most ancient writers say that Herakles was born at Thebes because of his father's family.

Hera was jealous of Alkmene and Herakles even before the baby was born. Zeus had foolishly boasted that the next child born in the line of Perseus would rule over Argos; Hera, therefore, induced her daughter Eilithyia, the goddess of childbirth, to delay the birth of Herakles so that Herakles' cousin, Eurystheus, could be born first (and prematurely). Herakles' mother carried her child for a painful 10 months.

There are several stories about Hera suckling the child when he was still an infant, unaware that this was the very child that she hated. Either because Alkmene had exposed her baby on the mountainside, or because the gods were trying to trick Hera, Athena and Hera came across the abandoned baby one day while taking a walk through the mountains. Hera was struck by his handsome features and decided to take him in to nurse him herself. Nursing on the breast milk of Hera would insure that the child attains immortality, and as such, it was a mark of divine favor from the gods. But as Herakles nursed, his enormous strength, even as a baby, caused him to clamp down too hard on the nipple of Hera. The goddess screamed, pulling him away with a start, with the result that milk spurted across the night sky and formed the Milky Way. Athena then returned the child to Alkmene and told her to rear him from then on.

When Herakles was still a baby in his crib, Hera sent serpents into his nursery to try to kill him. Since she was unsure which child belonged to Zeus, she sent in two snakes to kill both children (Herakles and Iphikles). Iphikles, a mere mortal, began to cry when he saw the snakes, but Herakles grabbed up both snakes in his hands and strangled them. The parents were shocked when they rushed into the room to see such a feat. They knew then that they had on their hands a super-child (cf. the story of the youth of Clark Kent), fed on special milk and possessing fantastic strength. They knew that he deserved a special educational experience from the best teachers, one of whom was Linus, a great musician and educator. While Herakles excelled in the more physically demanding arts, such as archery and wrestling, he failed miserably at music, Linus' specialty. Linus, in fact, was the child of one of the Muses, and it was he who supposedly invented rhyme and melody. One day, when Linus was ridiculing Herakles for being so clumsy and incompetent, Herakles picked up the instrument that he was playing and struck Linus over the head, killing him. He later argued that he killed Linus in self-defense, since music was going to be the death of him.

Herakles' parents feared his temper and his strength, so they sent him off into the country to shepherd the flocks on Mt. Cithaeron, between Thebes and Thespiae (ruled by Thespius). While there, the boy grew tall, and continued to show signs of exceptional athleticism. For example, with his bare hands he killed a ferocious, seemingly invincible lion that was devastating the flocks. This so impressed King Thespius that he invited Herakles to stay in his palace and dine with him. Thespius and the Thespians, meanwhile, were suffering at the hands of Erginus, king of nearby Orchomenos, who was demanding from them a burdensome tribute. Thespius was secretly hoping to beef up his power and his kingdom by having the powerful Herakles produce children with his fifty daughters. At the dinner party, Thespius got Herakles drunk on wine, then sent him in to his fifty daughters. Herakles then proceeded to have intercourse with all fifty daughters in one night, producing a child through each union. Soon thereafter, when the envoys from King Erginus came to Thespiae to exact their tribute, Herakles audaciously lopped off their ears and noses, hung them around their necks, and sent them packing to Orchomenos. This quite naturally started a war, but with Herakles fighting on the side of the Thespians and rearming them with weapons stored in a temple, the Thespians prevailed and began to exact a tribute from the Minyans of Orchomenos in turn.

Soon Herakles married Megara of Thebes, and by her had several children, all of whom he loved very much. Hera, however, was not content to let the hero lead a happy life. She sent a fit of madness on him, and he began to slay everyone in his family (though, by some accounts, Megara survived), either by throwing them into a fire, or by shooting them with arrows. The only way that Herakles could expiate these murders was to submit himself to Eurystheus, who would impose upon him a series of ten tasks whereby he could atone for his sins (later, because Herakles cheated on two tasks, the number was increased to 12).

THE LABORS

"See the neck-breaking hand that Herakles, descended from Perseus, places with every imaginable maneuver on the flesh-eating lion; for the gleaming man-mastering bronze refuses to pierce the beast's impenetrable body: his sword was bent back."

—Bacchylides, Frag. 13

The **first labor** set by Eurystheus was to kill the Nemean lion, not a normal lion, but one born from monstrous parents and brother to the Sphinx of Thebes. Hera, angry at Zeus for his affair, trained it and set it to ravaging the land around Nemea in the Peloponnesus, where it lived in a cave with two exits. Because its hide was invulnerable, Herakles could not harm it with his arrows. After failing to break the hide, he then fashioned a club for himself, used it to drive the lion into his own cave, where he had blocked up one of the exits, and then strangled the lion with his arms and hands. He then used the lion's own claws to flay its skin, which from then on he wore as a distinctive coat and helmet. The club also became an important attribute of Herakles from this point on.

> "And Echidna bore a third monster, the grisly-minded Lernaian Hydra, whom the goddess white-armed Hera nourished because of her quenchless grudge against the strong Herakles. Yet Herakles, son of Zeus, descended from Amphitryon, from the schemes of Athena the spoiler and with help from warlike Iolaus, killed this beast with the merciless bronze sword."

> —Hesiod, *Theogony* 313

Eurystheus did not like Herakles, and his conquest of the Nemean lion only made him fear and loathe him more. Eurystheus, with each labor, hoped to rid himself of Herakles forever. The **second labor** that he imposed on Herakles was the Lernaean Hydra. Lerna was a swampy area in the Peloponnesus inhabited by a multi-headed snake creature who spewed venom from its mouth. Even the breath that issued from its mouth during sleep was poisonous enough to kill anyone nearby. Herakles discovered that every time he cut off one of the Hydra's heads, two would grow back in its place. He then engaged his nephew Iolaus to sear the neck-stumps whenever he cut off a head, so that new ones would not be able to grow back. After successfully beheading the monster of its many heads, Herakles learned that the middle head was immortal. Therefore, he took a huge rock and buried the head immobilized underneath it, after which he dipped his arrows into the Hydra's venomous blood. Because Herakles used the services of his nephew Iolaus, this labor did not count toward the ten that he needed to complete.

> "The hero lifted him from the dust as he still breathed and returned with the foaming beast on his left shoulder, staining his back with blood from the stricken wound. Like this did Herakles return from the Arcadian lair, bringing home to the applause of Argos the captive boar."

> —Statius, *Thebaid* 8.746ff.

Next, as a **third labor,** Eurystheus ordered Herakles to bring back alive the monstrous Erymanthian boar. The boar haunted the slopes of Mount Erymanthus and was causing considerable havoc in the countryside. Boars in myth often symbolize the passage of young boys into manhood, since it was often on boar hunts that a new status was achieved for males. Compare, for example, the stories of Odysseus and of Meleager. Odysseus' nurse was able to recognize him on his return to Ithaka because of a scar he had received on his thigh during his initiation boar hunt. Meleager led the famous hunt for the boar that Artemis had sent to menace the country around Calydon. Herakles managed to drive the Erymanthian boar into deep snow, throw a net over it, and carry it back to Eurystheus. The king, terrified by the sight of the boar, hid in a huge pot in the ground until the danger passed.

> "The nimble hind of Mt. Maenalus, raising her head so gloriously adorned with gold, was caught by Hercules' long pursuit."

> —Seneca, *Hercules Furens* 222ff.

The **fourth labor** involved capturing the stag of Ceryneia. Reportedly this stag was extremely swift, though larger than a bull with a head of golden horns. It wore a collar around its neck that said it was dedicated to Artemis, meaning that it would be an act of great impiety to hunt it. As in the case of the boar, Artemis' deer often symbolizes the rite of passage from childhood to adulthood, even for girls (cf. the story of Iphigenia at Aulis). Herakles chased the stag for a full year until he finally was able to get close enough to it to wound it, then catch it. On his way back to Argos, Artemis and her brother Apollo stopped him and tried to wrestle the animal away from him. Herakles explained to them that he was only following the orders of Eurystheus, and that he would not harm the deer. In a sense, though, we are to understand that Herakles conquered the ultimate rite of passage on behalf of all mankind.

> "When Herakles came to Arcadia, he was unable to drive away the birds that swam on the Stymphalian Lake with bow and arrow. I [Amphidamas son of King Aleus] saw the thing myself. What he did was to take his stand on a height and make a loud racket by shaking a bronze rattle; and the astounded birds flew off into the distance screeching for fear."

> —Apollonius of Rhodes, *Argonautica* 2.1052ff.

The **fifth labor** that Eurystheus imposed on Herakles was to rid Lake Symphalus of certain annoying birds who were devouring everything in sight and making excessive noise. Some ancient authors say that their droppings were acidic and that their feathers were metal-tipped, which they could shoot at the unsuspecting. The ancient traveler Pausanias claimed that they were from Arabia and were particularly aggressive against people who came their way. Herakles used castanets to drive them from hiding and then he downed them with his arrows. Since castanets normally are used for initiations into ecstatic mystery religions, it could be that by this labor Herakles is achieving a measure of emotional well-being for mankind.

> "The Augean stables contained an enormous mass of dung which had accumulated over a great period, and it was a spirit of insult that induced Eurystheus to lay upon Herakles the command to clean out this dung. Heracles declined, saying this is an unworthy task

for him to undertake, because he knew it was an insult. And so, turning the course of the Alpheius river, as it is called, into the stables and cleansing them by means of the stream, he accomplished the labor in a single day, and without suffering any insult."

—Diodorus Siculus, *Library* 4.13

As a **sixth labor,** Eurystheus ordered Herakles to clean the stables of Augeas, the king of Elis on the western side of the Peloponnesus. Augeas' father had blessed him with great herds of cattle, but Augeas had failed to keep the dung cleaned up, and, in fact, the countryside was being deprived of fertilizer and therefore becoming sterile. Herakles went to Augeas and arranged some sort of deal whereby he would be paid for cleaning out all the dung. He then diverted a nearby river to run through the stable and thereby cleaned it thoroughly. When Herakles approached Augeas for his money, Augeas refused on the grounds that the river had done the work, not Herakles. Eurystheus was unwilling to count this as one of the originally imposed ten labors, since Herakles had asked for money. Later, Herakles returned to punish Augeas, whom he eventually killed. During that adventure, near Elis, at Olympia, Herakles founded the Olympian games.

"Elsewhere portrayed [on the shield of Eurypylos, son of Herakles] was the fire-breathing bull of Crete: Herakles' grip on his strong horns wrenched around the massive neck; the straining muscles on his arm stood out; the huge beast seemed to bellow."

—Quintus Smyrnaeus, *Fall of Troy* 6.236

For his **seventh labor,** Herakles was ordered to bring back alive to Eurystheus the bull of Crete. This is the beautiful white bull that Poseidon had sent to Minos but which Minos had failed to sacrifice to him in return. Later, with Minos' wife Pasiphae, this bull fathered the Minotaur. Some ancient authors say that the bull could breathe fire through its nostrils. Herakles was able to capture the bull and swim with it from Crete to Greece. After showing it to Eurystheus, he tried to dedicate it to Hera, but she refused any gifts from him. The bull then wandered throughout Greece, ending up in Marathon, where Theseus later captured it and sacrificed it to Apollo.

"The feeding-troughs of those horses were of brass because the steeds were so savage, and they were fastened by iron chains because of their strength, and the food they ate was not the natural produce of the soil but they tore apart the limbs of strangers and so got their food from the ill lot of hapless men."

—Diodorus Siculus, *Library* 4.15

Eurystheus then told Herakles for his **eighth labor** to capture the mares of Diomedes, king of the savage Thracians, and bring them back alive to him. The four mares were unique in that they lived on human flesh. Herakles was able to tame the animals by giving Diomedes himself to them to eat. After that it was no problem to lead them back to Argos. This myth, as the previous one, shows that now Herakles is subduing the closest, most fearsome enemies of the Greeks. It was during this labor that Herakles met up with Admetus and Alkestis. Admetus had convinced his devoted wife Alkestis to die in his place on his fated day, and when Herakles arrived at Pheres in Thessaly, she had just died. Herakles wrestled Thanatos (Death) and stole the girl back, returning her to the selfish and now embarrassed Admetus.

> "And first of all he demanded of them the girdle which he had been commanded to get; but when they would pay no heed to him, he joined battle with them. Now the general mass of the Amazons were arrayed against he main body of the followers of Heracles, but the most honoured of the women were drawn up opposite Heracles himself and put up a stubborn battle."

—Diodorus Siculus, *Library* 4.16

The **ninth labor** of Herakles involved stealing the girdle (i.e., belt) of Hippolyta, queen of the Amazons. There are varying stories about how Herakles took the belt from Hippolyta. Either Hera stirred up anger among the Amazons, so that they tried to resist Herakles, or Herakles fought the Amazons and then traded his captives for the belt. The belt or girdle represents the entrance into the woman's most guarded, private part, and, in fact, the Amazon women themselves stand as a symbol of social inversion, where women take on the roles of men and pose a threat to male domination.

> "Chrysaor, married to Callirhoe, daughter of glorious Ocean, was father to the triple-headed Geryon, but Geryon was killed by the great strength of Heracles at sea-circled Erytheia beside his own shambling cattle. On that very day Herakles drove those broad-faced cattle toward holy Tiryns, crossing the stream of Ocean."

—Hesiod, *Theogony* 287ff.

In his **tenth labor,** Herakles was sent to retrieve the cattle of Geryon, a three-bodied giant who was son of Chrysaor, "the man with the golden sword." Chrysaor sprang from the stump of the beheaded Medusa along with Pegasus, the winged horse. Geryon's herds were unique and numerous, and guarded by a large dog named Orthrus. They all lived on an island in the far reaches of the Mediterranean, if not in the Atlantic Ocean. Now Herakles had to traverse the vast ocean to reach this island, a feat that he accomplished by borrowing the cup of Helios the sun god. This was the same cup that Helios used to return to the east after sunset every evening. When Herakles reached the island, he struck down Orthrus with one blow of his club, then he slew Geryon with his arrows. Herakles then drove the cattle through Spain, Gaul, Italy and on to Greece.

> "The beautiful island of the gods [Erytheia in the West], where the Hesperides have their homes of solid gold."

—Stesichorus Geryoneis Frag S8 (from Oxyrhynchus Papyrus 2617)

Next, for his **eleventh labor,** Eurystheus bid Herakles to retrieve the golden apples that the Hesperides were guarding in a garden far to the west near Mount Atlas. Gaia had given Hera the apples as a wedding present, and she had planted them in the garden. A beautiful tree sprung up that from then on produced golden apples. Hera was worried that the daughters of Atlas, who lived nearby, might try to steal her apples, so she placed an immortal dragon with one-hundred heads to guard the apples. She also placed the Hesperides, named Aegle (brightness), Erythia (scarlet), and Hesperethusa (evening glow), representing the colors of the sunset, to guard the apples. This was Herakles' second trip to the west where the sun sets and the underworld is located, a clear indication that now Herakles is taking upon himself the heroic task of conquering death, a fact that becomes startling clear in the next labor. At any rate, Herakles traveled across northern Africa on his way to Mount Atlas. At some point during this journey, he went so far to the east that he met up with Prometheus and freed him from the torturous gnawing of Zeus' eagle. In Libya he met the giant Antaeus, who wrestled and killed passers-by. Antaeus was invincible so long as he was attached to his mother Earth. Herakles lifted him on his shoulders and choked him to death. He also met Busiris, a cruel pirate or king who lived in Egypt. He captured Herakles and tried to sacrifice him, but Herakles was able to burst his bonds and kill Busiris and all his companions. Some accounts of the story say that Herakles found Atlas, who was holding up the sky because of Zeus' punishment. This account says that Herakles had to agree to hold up the sky for Atlas so that Atlas could go retrieve the apples himself. When Atlas returned, he refused to take the sky back upon his shoulders, but wanted to take the apples to Eurystheus himself. Cleverly, Herakles pretended to agree to this plan, and only asked that Atlas hold up the sky while he shifts his shoulders into a more comfortable position. When Atlas had the sky once more, Herakles grabbed up the apples and promptly departed. Other accounts say that Herakles found the garden, slew the dragon, and retrieved the apples by himself. After Herakles showed the apples to Eurystheus, Athena returned them to the garden of Hera.

> "Huge Cerberus, monstrously couched in a cave confronting them, made the whole region echo with this three-throated barking. The Sibyl, seeing the snakes bristling upon his neck now, threw him for bait a cake of honey and wheat infused with sedative drugs. The creature, crazy with hunger, opened its three mouths, gobbled the bait; then its huge body relaxed and lay sprawled out on the ground, the whole length of its cave kennel. Aeneas, passing its entrance, the watch-dog neutralized, strode rapidly from the bank of that river [Styx] of no return."
>
> —Vergil, *Aeneid* 6. 417ff.

The **twelfth labor** of Herakles was the last. Herakles had to descend into the underworld and drag up Cerberus, the three-headed guard dog of the underworld, into the world of light. To learn how to enter into the underworld safely, Herakles first became initiated into the Eleusinian Mysteries. In the underworld, most of the shades fled from Herakles out of fear, except for Meleager, the brother of Herakles' future wife Deianeira. While in the underworld

Herakles came across the imprisoned Theseus and Pirithous, two heroes who had come to the underworld to engage in the mischief of kidnaping Persephone, the queen of the underworld. The goddess permitted Herakles to free Theseus, who was stuck in the chair of forgetfulness, but not Pirithous. Then Herakles challenged the dog Cerberus, who keeps the souls in the underworld with his growling and barking, and with his bare hands dragged him up to Eurystheus. When Eurystheus saw the dog, he jumped again into his clay pot to hide. The dog was then returned to its master Hades.

With his new found freedom, the adventures of Herakles only continued. He mounted many expeditions against various enemies, including the Trojans (Herakles lived one generation before the famous Trojan War), Augeas, Pylos (in the Peloponnesus), and Sparta. He came into contact with many characters such as Priam and Nestor who were in the twilight of their life when later the Trojan War began.

Herakles had promised Meleager in the underworld that when he returned to the world above, he would marry his sister Deianeira of Calydon. When Herakles returned, he did head for Calydon, where he found Deianeira being wooed by the river-god Achelous. This river god, by nature of his watery composition, could turn himself into any creature that he wished. When Deianeira expressed the desire to marry Herakles instead of Achelous, the two suitors found themselves locked in mortal combat. In the end Herakles defeated Achelous while the latter was in the form of a bull. Herakles ripped off one of his horns, at which point Achelous conceded defeat and gave to Herakles the hand of Deianeira. The two of them had a son, named Hyllus.

Later, Herakles won another girl in an archery contest; her name was Iole. Because her father had refused Herakles even though he had won the contest, Herakles had to take her by force. According to some versions he killed her father. Most versions agree that in a fit of madness he killed her brother, who may have been a supporter of his, and so had to atone for his sins again as in the previous case with Megara. The oracle at Delphi, however, was so appalled by his repeat crime that it refused to give an answer. Herakles became enraged, took the tripod of the Pythian priestess, and threatened to set up his own oracle. Apollo arrived, and the two came to blows. Fortunately, Zeus' thunderbolt was able to separate them and to dissuade Herakles of any further rage. The oracle then told Herakles that to purify himself he must become a slave of Omphale, queen of Lydia, for three years. She liked to dress Herakles up in feminine clothes, and to take on his lion skin and club for herself. The two of them made a ridiculous transvestite pair, and Herakles even learned weaving from her.

Deianeira, meanwhile, had become jealous that Herakles was being accompanied by Iole; she was afraid that he might begin to love her more than herself. It so happened that one day, while crossing a particularly dangerous river, a strange incident took place that eventually led to Herakles' ultimate downfall. When Herakles came with Deianeira to the river, he was not sure how he would get her across safely. A centaur named Nessus arrived, and promised that she could ride on his back safely to the other side. On the other side, however, Nessus decided to take advantage of Deianeira, since Herakles was still across the river. Herakles, upon seeing what was happening, shot one of his poisonous arrows into Nessus to kill him. Before Nessus died he told Deianeira to take some of his blood because it had special qualities to it: "If ever Herakles begins to lose affection for you," he told her, "this blood can be used to restore his love." It was a trick, though, since the blood had been tainted by the highly venomous arrows (with the Hydra's poison on them), and would surely destroy even the great Herakles. When Deianeira finally decided to act, she rubbed some of this supposed love-potion on a shirt and sent it to Herakles to wear. When he put it on, it burned his skin like napalm, and nothing he did could counteract the fiery acid.[1] When the agony reached such an intense level that he could bear it no more, he built a funeral pyre for himself on Mount Oeta, and climbed on top. He begged servants and passers-by to light his pyre, but no one ever would until the young Philoctetes of Thessaly wandered by and lit it. As a reward, Herakles gave him his unfailing bow and arrows. In some mysterious way, the fire only purged Herakles of the mortal parts, so that with a clap of thunder and the descent of a cloud, Herakles was lifted up to heaven to live with the gods there. Some versions have it that the mortal side of Herakles dwelt with the other shades in the underworld. The now divine Herakles was reconciled once and for all with Hera and even married Hebe, the goddess of youthfulness.

---

[1] The clothing of the ancient Greeks, because of the way it was made, was highly flammable. Both the Greeks and the Romans sometimes punished criminals by dousing their clothing with naphtha and setting it ablaze. Such a garment was later known as "tunica molesta." On this see Adrienne Mayor, "Fiery Finery," *Archaeology* 50 n2 (March–April 1997) 54f.

CHAPTER FIFTEEN
Cretan Myths

"From that point the Argonauts were to cross to Crete, the greatest island in the sea. But when they sought shelter in the haven of Dikte, they were prevented from anchoring to the shore by Talos, a bronze giant, who broke off lumps of rock from the cliff to hurl at them. A descendant of the brazen race that sprang from ash-trees, he had survived into the days of the demigods, and Zeus had given him to Europa to keep watch over Crete by running round the island on his bronze feet three times a day. His body and his limbs were bronze and invulnerable, except at one point: under a sinew by his ankle there was a blood-red vein protected only by a thin skin which to him meant life or death. He terrified the Argonauts, and exhausted though they were they hastily backed water."

—Apollonius Rhodius, *Argonautica* 4. 1638 ff.

To understand the mythological stories of Crete, we must first begin with Europa, the daughter of Agenor and Telephassa in Phoenicia (modern day Lebanon). She had several brothers, including one named Phoenix, meaning "The Phoenician," and Cadmus, who eventually founded the cities of Thebes and could count among his descendants Dionysus and Oedipus.

According to a version of story told by Ovid in his *Metamorphoses*, Zeus became enamored with Europa and desired to take her for his own. Driven by lust and apparently unconcerned that he is demeaning his majesty, he deliberately transforms himself into a bull "as white and smooth as snow that no foot has trod nor wind has stirred." Appearing on the seashore where Europa is playing with his friends, he proceeds to win Europa little by little through his beauty and gentleness. Gradually the young girl becomes intrigued by this almost supernatural creature. She feeds him flowers; he kisses her hands, dances, and rolls in the sand for joy. She pats his breast and winds garlands around his horns. Boldly and unaware of the hidden danger she leaps upon his back as if playing a game.

The seductive Zeus in his taurine disguise edges slowly toward the sea. Carefully, playfully, he steps into the water, and then is off at full speed into the deep. Europa, trembling, looks astonished back at the receding shore and her disappearing friends: She understands that she is being abducted by this strange beast. As she holds on to a horn with one hand, she grips his back with the other. Inside she feels the shiver of fear and dread of the unknown, but, oddly enough, also the shiver of delight in anticipation of the coming sexual event.

L. Valerius Acisculus, 45 B.C. Silver denarius. Diademed head of Apollo with star above. On the reverse, Europa riding a bull.

At length the two arrive at Crete where Zeus throws off his animal guise and makes love to the object of his desire. Some ancient writers say he consummated his love for her in the very cave where he was reared as a child, as if to demonstrate that love-making is merely the return to the source from where you once exited. Others say that he loved her under a huge plane tree which thereafter became evergreen in response to the great act of fertility.

Although for a modern reader this story appears on the surface to describe an unwelcome sexual advance and rape on the part of the divinity, the ancients read something different into it. Here was the inception of a great race of people, endowed by this very act with divine seed and a fortitude comparable to that of the bull. In ancient art, for example, Europa seems less a victim and more a great mother earth goddess who rides confidently and triumphantly on the back of the bull. In other words, the great mother of the Cretan/Minoan race came striding out of the sea bringing with her a powerful, virile symbol of fertility and manifestation of the national character.

In the end, Europa had three sons by Zeus: Minos, Sarpedon, and Rhadamanthys, all of whom loomed large over the Cretan civilization as legendary figures. The god also gave her three significant gifts: a spear that always hit its mark, a dog that allowed no prey to escape, and a giant made entirely of bronze; this was Talos, the guardian of the island, whom the Argonauts would meet as they journeyed home from their expedition. Now these three brothers were quarreling over who should rule Crete when Minos declared that he could prove that the kingdom belonged to him. The gods, he said, would send him anything that he asked for. He prayed to Poseidon for a worthy sacrificial victim to arise from the sea, and the god immediately obliged by sending to him a magnificent bull from the water. Minos' claim to the throne was vindicated, but the bull was so handsome that Minos neglected to sacrifice it. His wife Pasiphae, the daughter of Helios, the sun god, fell in love with the bull, either as a punishment from Poseidon or as a punishment from Aphrodite against Helios, who revealed to Hephaestus her affair with Ares.

There was on the island, in the court of Minos, a craftsman named Daedalus who was famous for his many inventions and creations. Daedalus originally lived and worked in Athens, but once he had fallen into a jealous rage and killed his own nephew for inventing the saw after looking at the backbone of a fish. The Athenians had convicted him of murder and sent him into exile to Crete, where he took up residence in the palace of king Minos.

Pasiphae went to Daedalus for help to satisfy her lust for the bull. At her request the artisan built a hollow image of a cow with space to accommodate the queen in the proper position for mating with the bull. The artificial cow bore such a close resemblance to a real cow that when Daedalus rolled it into the fields with Pasiphae hidden inside, the choice bull of Poseidon was duped and mounted it. Now Pasiphae had other children with Minos, including Ariadne and Phaedra, but now she had a monstrous child, a bull's son, which had the body of a man and the head of a bull. The creature was given the name "Minotaur" ("Minos' bull"). Minos was furious with Daedalus for helping Pasiphae to carry out this bestial love affair. He told him that he would never be able to leave the island and demanded that he create a prison for the monster. Daedalus did as he was told and built at Knossos a labyrinth, a maze so complex with so many winding turns and rooms that no one put inside could find his way out. The king then shut the Minotaur into this labyrinth. Now it so happened that around this same time Minos and his "Minoans" had succeeded in mastering the seas and the lands nearby, including Greece. After conquering Athens, he demanded a yearly tribute of seven boys and seven girls that must be sent to Crete as live food for the Minotaur. In this way the king was able to terrorize the rest of the Greeks and satisfy the cravings of this horrible half-man, half-bull monster living on his island. The Minotaur continued to feed on young Athenians until one day the hero Theseus came and slew him with the help of Minos' daughter Ariadne.

As outlandish and fanciful as the myth of the Minotaur and labyrinth obviously is on the face of it, some historical realities may lie behind it. At the site of ancient Knossos, the main Minoan city of Crete where Minos is said to have ruled and where the Daedalus' maze was supposedly built, archaeologists have uncovered an enormous, labyrinthine "palace" that may have indeed inspired the story of the Minotaur's prison. Furthermore, the meandering structure itself parallels, not other palaces in the Mediterranean, as once thought, but religious economic complexes found in the region of ancient Sumeria. These Mesopotamian temples served both as places of sacrifice and as distribution centers for the wealth of the population. Rooms for feasting and sacrificing stand side-by-side with large concentrations of storage magazines. It is certainly possible that the image of the Minotaur reflects the appearance of priests who, wearing the head of a bull as a symbol of the source of their power, conduct human sacrifice within the labyrinth. In addition, the sexual surrender of a female victim as a substitute for her sacrifice is a common pattern in early religions. Such a pattern may be behind the tale of Pasiphae, who couples with the bull from the sea. Sent by Poseidon, the bull is in a sense Poseidon himself, lord of the sea, with whom the Minoans as a seafaring people claimed a special relation. Young girls may have surrendered their maidenhood to a priest dressed as the bull in a cultic ritual to appease the god.

The story of the king and queen of Crete does not end with the birth of the Minotaur. Minos, it is said, continued to be on good terms with his father Zeus, with whom he spent nine years learning laws which he then imposed on Greece, much in the same way as Moses receives Yahweh's laws on behalf of the Israelites. Unlike Moses, however, Minos carried on many love affairs, much to the dismay of his wife. In response, Pasiphae, who as a daughter of Helios the sun god had family connections with the witches Circe and Medea (see the stories of Odysseus and Jason respectively), plied him with drugs so that he would infect any woman he made love to with a virulent poison. Minos received a cure for his condition from Procris, the daughter of king Erechtheus of Athens and guest in his court at Knossos temporarily as she patched up her marriage with Cephalus of Athens. He rewarded her with the magic hound and an unerring spear that Zeus had once given to Europa. But these presents turned out to be detrimental. When later she was reconciled to her husband and living in Athens again, she became suspicious that his frequent hunting trips were a cover for infidelity. The story goes that while he was out hunting certain friends of Procris overheard him calling out to a certain "Aura" to come soothe him as he rested under a tree. From these reports Procris surmised that Cephalus was having an affair with some girl named "Aura," not also taking into account the fact that the word "aura" simply means "breeze." So she determined to go out to the mountains to spy on him and catch him by surprise. As she followed him she rustled some bushes. Cephalus turned and, assuming a wild boar was about to rush him, hurled his spear into the thicket, mortally wounding his wife. As she lay dying in his arms, she begged him not to marry this Aura, at which point the grieving husband understood the whole chain of events.

We have already mentioned the fact that Ariadne helped Theseus when he came from Athens to slay the Minotaur. Ariadne had in turn obtained help from Daedalus himself, who told her how to use a thread tied to the entrance of the labyrinth to create a trail by which to return. This is the very method Theseus used to emerge safely from the maze. When Minos learned what Daedalus had done, he shut the artisan up in the labyrinth along with his son Icarus. But Daedalus then made wings out of feathers and attached them to their shoulders so they could fly from the island. He advised his son not to fly too close to the sun lest the wax melt, nor to fly too close to the water, lest the feathers become wet and heavy from the mist, but to keep to the middle path, which is always best. His son ignored his warnings, though, and flew too close to the sun. When his wax melted, he plunged into the sea, which thereafter forever bore his name.

Minos grew angry beyond measure at the escape of Daedalus and pursued him westward. Daedalus had first reached Cumae in Italy and later found safe haven in Sicily at the court of king Cocalus, but Minos had great difficulty finding him. None of the kings in Italy or Sicily would tell Minos where the fugitive was hiding. The king presented the rulers he suspected of harboring the refugee with a spiral shell, saying that to whomever could pass a thread through it, he would give a great reward. When Cocalus returned the shell threaded, Minos knew where Daedalus was. Daedalus, you see, had told the king to tie the thread to an ant, and let the ant walk through the shell. Daedalus, however, used the daughters of king Cocalus to trick Minos into taking a bath in a tub specially designed to heat quickly. The tub became so hot that Minos was instantly scalded and died.

THREE JUDGES OF THE UNDERWORLD

Three of the sons of Zeus by mortal women gained a new role when they entered the underworld. Minos and Rhadamanthys, sons of Zeus and Europa, distinguished themselves so in life as just rulers that they continued to act as judges in the next life:

"Europa gave birth to almighty Zeus' sons. They were all glorious leaders of wealthy men—Minos the ruler and just Rhadamanthys and noble Sarpedon, the blameless and strong."

Both Sarpedon and Rhadamanthys vied with Minos for the throne of Crete and lost. Both fled Crete and took up kingdoms in other places, Sarpedon in Asia Minor and Rhadamanthys in Greece. We are lacking detailed information for what happened to Sarpedon while in Asia Minor, though we are tempted to think that he is the same Sarpedon, son of Zeus, who fought in the Trojan War on the Trojan side and whose death is recorded in a spectacular vase painting dating to 510 B.C. The chronology of Rhadamanthys is also confusing. At some point he seems to have devised the Cretan code of laws that became a model for Greek law, then fled Minos to Boeotia in Greece. In this version, some authors fashion him into a son of Hephaestus and great-grandson of Cres, the eponymous hero of Crete. A third child of Zeus, Aeacus, was born of the nymph Aegina, whom Zeus loved and who gives her name to the island off the coast of Athens. The island of Aegina was quite bereft of inhabitants, making Aeacus feel cheated that, though he was a son of Zeus, he had no kingdom. At his request, then, Zeus turned the ants of the island into human beings, who took on the name "Myrmidons," or "ant people." Aeacus gained a reputation for great piety and justice, which he exercised even against his own sons when he discovered that they had committed murder. One of those sons, Peleus, was to become the father of Achilles, who eventually led the Myrmidons into battle at Troy.

The most important thing to remember is that these three wise lawmakers were rewarded with judgeships in Hades. Their specific tasks are delineated through time in various ways. We see in art that Aeacus holds keys and a scepter and makes decisions on cases involving Europeans. Rhadamanthys holds residence in the Elysian Fields and judges the Asians. Minos, however, appears to have held the supreme position of the three, "because he ruled wholly in accordance with law and paid the greatest heed to justice" (Diodorus Siculus, *Library* 5.79.2). Thus in Homer Odysseus describes what he saw when he came to the entrance to the underworld:

"I saw Minos the son of Zeus holding a golden sceptre and delivering judgments among the dead. There he sat, and around him the others sat or stood in the ample-gated house of Hades, seeking from this master of justice the firm sentences of the law."

What exactly these judges are judging is another matter. Plato considers their courtroom to be a first stop on the journey into Hell, where the judges can decide whether one has lived piously and righteously enough to enter into the Land of the Blessed or if he deserves punishment. Vergil (*Aeneid* 6.541ff.) stresses that these judges ferret out sins that were never found out during one's life:

". . . here Rhadamanthus rules, and most severe his rule is, trying and chastising wrongdoers, forcing confessions from any who, on earth, went gleefully undetected—but uselessly, since they have only postponed till death their atonement, sat once Tisiphone, the avenger, scourge in had, pounces upon the guilty."

The Furies often stand beside these stern judges, ready to exact any vengeance and punishment they deem fit to mete out. Other ghostly creatures stand around, point the finger accusingly or glaring with disdain.

This is an old idea, familiar to most readers, the notion that nothing one does in life escapes ultimate punishment, even if it escapes notice now. We all stand before the judgment throne to watch every hidden wrong, every secret evil thought, replayed out in the open for all to see. No pity remains for those who plead. No tears move these judges. Crimes are punished with fair penalties from the wisest lawgivers who ever lived.

CHAPTER SIXTEEN
Theseus and Perseus

THESEUS

"Crete rising out of the waves; Pasiphae, concealed in secret, cruelly fated to lust after a bull; the Minotaur, the hybrid offspring of that monstrous union, a memento of their unnatural love."

—Vergil, *Aeneid* 6.24ff., on what Aeneas saw carved on bronze doors when he arrived in Italy

The myth of Theseus, king of Athens, explains the taming and subjection of the land around Athens and accounts, in mythological terms, for the fall of Crete and the Minoan Civilization there and the rise of the Greek civilization.

Theseus was the son of Aegeus, the fifth king of Athens. The story goes that Aegeus, despite two marriages, was unable to have any children, thus leaving him without an heir. To ascertain the source of the problem, Aegeus went to Delphi to consult Apollo's oracle, where he received the "loxian" advice that he "should not unloose the opening that lets the wine gush out of the wineskin" before he reaches "the highest point in the city of Athens."

Aegeus was puzzled by this advice, so he stopped by Troezen in the Peloponnese to ask his friend Pittheus, the king there, what he thought about the matter. The clever Pittheus immediately understood what the oracle meant, namely, that the next woman that Aegeus had intercourse with would bear him a child, but he did not tell Aegeus. Instead, he got Aegeus thoroughly drunk, then sent him in to his daughter to make love. That night, Aegeus impregnated Aethra, who later the same night was instructed by a dream to swim to a nearby island to offer a sacrifice. On the way, however, she was abducted by Poseidon who also made love to her, mingling in some of his seed, so that the child in Aethra's body had two fathers, one mortal and one divine.

When Aegeus learned that Aethra was pregnant, he led her to a large rock, under which he placed his sword and a pair of sandals, instructing her to rear and train the child well until he was strong enough to lift the rock and remove the items. At that time, strong enough to face any rivals for the throne that might await him, the youth should come to Athens to join Aegeus in his palace.

C. Servilius, Silver denarius, c. 136 B.C. Helmeted head of Roma with wreath behind. On the reverse, the Dioscuri brothers.

By the time Theseus reached the age of sixteen he had proven himself heroic and strong enough to learn the secret of his birth. Aethra informed him of the strange circumstances of his birth and instructed him to make his way to Athens. She showed him the stone where Aegeus had hidden the sword and sandals that would aid his journey. Although it would have been easier for Theseus to make the relatively short and safe trip by sea, he knew that he could never demonstrate his heroic qualities if he took the easy way out. Therefore, he decided to travel by land through a hazardous region populated with numerous bandits and monsters, all of whom inflict punishments on travelers. Theseus was determined to inflict the same punishment on them in turn.

First, near the town of Epidauros he met Periphetes, son of Hephaestus, who was bludgeoning his victims to death with an iron club and then robbing them. Periphetes had the club in the first place to use as a crutch to support himself, since his legs were weak (like those of his father). Theseus met the ruffian on the road and, pretending to admire the weapon's workmanship, asked to hold it in his hands. He then beat the helpless Periphetes to death with it. From that point on Theseus carried the club as his own weapon.

Next, he met Poseidon's son Sinis, a brigand living at the Isthmus of Corinth. This unsavory character would ask passers-by to stop and help him bend down a pine tree, but when the pine tree was down to the ground, he would let the tree go, sending the poor traveler sailing through the air as if catapulted (in some versions Sinis ties his victims between two bent pine trees which tear them apart). Theseus smartly let go of the pine tree before Sinis could so that Sinis met the fate to which he so often subjected others.

Then, just north of the isthmus near the village of Crommyon, Theseus met Phaea, the giant man-eating sow, named after the old woman who cared for it. This sow was so ferocious and so formidable that it ravaged the countryside at will and was killing many human beings. Theseus set an ambush for it and used his club to kill it. It is possible to detect in this exploit Theseus' rite of passage, since for young boys, as we have noted, hunting boars prepared the way for manhood. But Greek author Plutarch (*Theseus* 9.1) knows another variation on the story:

> "Now the Crommyonian Sow, which they called Phaea, was no insignificant creature, but fierce and hard to master. This sow he went out of his way to encounter and slay, that he might not be thought to perform all his exploits under compulsion, and at the same time

because he thought that while the brave man ought to attack villainous men only in self-defense, he should seek occasion to risk his life in battle with the nobler beasts. However, some say that Phaea was a female robber, a woman of murderous and unbridled spirit, who dwelt in Crommyon; she was called 'sow' because of her life and manners, and was afterwards slain by Theseus."

Near Megara Theseus ran into Sciron, an outlaw whose name means "limestone" and who lived at the edge of some tall cliffs. He was a kind of local hero who blocked the pass along the cliffs and made all comers bend down to wash his feet. He would then kick them into the sea where a gigantic turtle would eat them. Theseus bent down, feigning submission, but immediately grabbed Sciron's feet and threw him off the cliff to the turtle, thus ending his reign of terror.

At Eleusis Theseus met up with Cercyon, a son of Poseidon or Hephaestus who forces everyone making his way from Megara to Eleusis stop to fight him. Because he was semi-divine and particularly strong, he would invariably wrestle his victims to death and then seize their possessions. Theseus, who had always been an expert fighter himself, held him high in the air and then dashed him to the ground, thereby killing him.

Last, near Athens Theseus came upon Procrustes who ran a roadside hotel. The name of this rascal means "stretcher." He possessed a hammer and a saw, and had an odd fetish that people should fit into his bed precisely. Those who were too short, he hammered out until they were long enough (or stretched them out), while those who were too long he sawed until he had shortened them to just the correct length. Theseus turned the tables on Procrustes by forcing him to lie down on one of his own beds, then cutting him off until he was the right length. The term "procrustean" in English has come to refer to an arbitrary standard to which exact conformity is demanded.

The news of Theseus' many triumphs preceded him to Athens. Everyone in town was wondering who this man coming their way is. When Theseus arrived, Aegeus had no idea that Theseus was his son. Because of the rules of hospitality, however, he received Theseus into the palace and proceeded to take care of him. Since the time that Aegeus had begotten Theseus, he had come under the influence of the sorceress Medea, who had promised Aegeus that she would give him the heir he long sought. In fact, she had already become pregnant with Aegeus' child. Medea understood immediately who Theseus was and that he would win Aegeus' heart over her own child, and so that night at the banquet she tried to convince Aegeus to poison Theseus. Right at the moment that Theseus was about to drink the poisonous drink that Aegeus had offered to him, however, Aegeus saw the sword that was his long ago and realized that this is his son. He swiped away the poisonous cup and welcomed Theseus with open arms, rejoicing. Medea sneaked away into the night.

There is also the story that Medea had tried to get rid of Theseus by convincing him to go to the region of Marathon (just north of Athens) to catch a large bull there that was ravaging the countryside. The bull, in fact, seems to have been the Cretan bull that Herakles brought back during one of his labors. He breathed fire from his nostrils and was extremely large. But Theseus got the best of him, chained him up, and brought him back for sacrifice. It is said that when Theseus pulled out his sword to perform the ritual of sacrifice for Apollo that Aegeus recognized the sword and his son at that time.

While at Athens Theseus learned that the city was under a heavy burden: Every year (some say every nine years), seven young men and seven maidens had to be sent to Crete to be fed to the Minotaur as a kind of tax or tribute. King Minos of Crete had imposed this penalty on Athens because he believed that the Athenians were guilty for the death of Androgeos, his son (in fact, Androgeos was killed by the Marathonian Bull). Theseus decided that he would go as one of the youths in order to try to defeat the Minotaur, thus saving Athens from this disgrace. His father did not want him to go, but reluctantly allowed it, only requesting that the son do him one favor: Normally, as the youths sailed away to Crete, they did so under a black sail. Aegeus asked that if Theseus was successful, he should hoist a white sail as he returned, so that even at a distance he would know the outcome. Theseus agreed.

The Minotaur's originated from a sordid chain of events involving the royal family on the island of Crete. The details are variously told, but the basic story line runs as follows: Minos, son of Europa, was attempting to prove that he should rule over Crete by divine right. He sacrificed to Poseidon and asked that the god send him up a splendid bull. A bull did appear out of the depths of the sea, but it was so magnificent in every way that Minos did not want to sacrifice it. Instead, he sent the bull out into a meadow to graze and to act as a stud for his herd. The gods punished this selfishness by causing Minos' wife, Queen Pasiphae, to conceive an enormous lust for the creature. In her passion she employed the Athenian craftsman Daedalus to devise a way that she could fulfill her desires for the bull. Daedalus helped her by building a hollow decoy cow that he rigged up and rolled out into the meadow with Pasiphae inside. From this union Pasiphae gave birth to the hybrid child Asterion (meaning "starry one," perhaps connecting him to the constellation Tauros), a half-human, half-bull creature that devoured human flesh. An oracle told Minos to have Daedalus to build a twisting, winding cage spreading over several acres in which he could contain the creature. The cage took on the name "Labyrinth," a word which we still use today. It was said that once you entered, you could never escape or perceive the exit because of the convoluted windings of the passageways.

At Crete in the city of Knossos (Cnossus) the daughter of the king, Ariadne, quickly fell in love with Theseus and wanted to try to help him survive his ordeal with the Minotaur (women often provide crucial help for heroes in Greek myths). She enlisted the aid of Daedalus, the Athenian artisan and captive living on Crete, to show her a way for Theseus to slay the Minotaur and exit the Labyrinth where he lived. Daedalus gave Theseus a thread which he tied to the entrance of the Labyrinth, and he gave him a sword to conceal under his cloak. When Theseus met the Minotaur in the Labyrinth, he attacked with the sword, then used the thread to exit along with the surviving youths. Ariadne had readied a ship, meanwhile, and together, along with Ariadne's young sister Phaedra, they all escaped Minos and the island of Crete.

On the way home, Theseus stopped off at the island of Naxos (sometimes called Dia) for supplies and rest. While sleeping there with Ariadne, he was told by Dionysus to abandon Ariadne so that the god could have her for himself. Theseus obeyed, and as Ariadne slept he grabbed up his sandals and left for the boat. When Ariadne woke she saw him departing over the horizon, leaving her confused and bewildered. Catullus describes the pathetic scene this way:

"Ariadne, with uncontrolled passion in her heart, looking out from the shore of Naxos with its sounding waves, saw Theseus receding into the distance with his fleet at full speed. Not yet could she believe her eyes, for she had only just been wakened from deceitful sleep and saw that she was alone, unhappy, upon the shore. But the young man, forgetful, parted the waves with his oars in flight, leaving his promises unfulfilled to the gusts of wind."

Dionysus finally revealed himself to Ariadne, though, and the two of them lived happily from then on.

Meanwhile, Theseus forgot to hoist the white sail, so as he sailed toward Athens, he sent a false signal to his father as he watched from the cliffs everyday for his son's return. Upon seeing the black sail, and thinking that he had lost his son, Aegeus jumped off the cliff into the sea and drowned. It is from him that the sea receives its name, Aegean.

With Aegeus out of the way, Theseus now is ruler over Athens; eventually he will marry Ariadne's sister, Phaedra, though she may have been too young when he first returned. In the beginning of his reign, Theseus ruled well and made laws that benefitted the Athenian people. But Theseus was not satisfied with conducting the day-to-day business of government. His heroic blood yearned for adventure. It was during this period that Theseus joined the fateful expedition of Herakles against the Amazon women on the shores of the Black Sea, or, as some mythographers say, made his own separate trip. In either case, Theseus is said to have abducted the queen of the Amazons, Hippolyta, or perhaps a princess named Antiope, and taken her back to Athens to be his bride. By this Amazon Theseus had a son by the name Hippolytus, whom later Phaedra tried unsuccessfully to seduce. This encounter with the Amazons brought trouble upon the Athenians. The Amazons invaded the region of Attica and besieged the city of Athens. Only after desperate fighting in the very streets of the city did the Athenians finally prevail and slaughter all the Amazon women. For the Athenians this incident was a clear example of the dangers of social inversion.

Theseus was ever one for finding trouble and in fact found a partner for this, a fellow named Pirithous. Pirithous was the son of Ixion and ruler over the Lapiths who lived in Thessaly (north central Greece). Pirithous had heard of the exploits of Theseus, so he decided to put him to the test. He began raiding Theseus' flocks that he kept in the area of Marathon, until finally Theseus was able to catch him in the act. Pirithous so admired Theseus for his good looks and physique, that he offered to be Theseus' slave. But Theseus too was impressed with Pirithous, so he instead extended his hand in a gesture of eternal friendship. In fact, the two became fast friends and carried out many heroic deeds together.

At this time Pirithous was set to marry a girl named Hippodamia, and of course Theseus was invited to the wedding. Pirithous also invited the Centaurs, who were cousins of his by way of his father's immoral assault on Hera. The Centaurs were monstrous and so lacking in self-control that when they had imbibed enough wine during the celebration, they become wild and attacked the bride. This is the famous battle of the Centaurs and the Lapiths, the symbolic struggle of humans trying to be civilized against the forces of violence and wildness represented by the Centaurs. The famous frieze on the Temple of Zeus at Olympia depicts Apollo, the god of reason, rising up in the midst of this battle at the wedding, as if to say that reason will eventually prevail over the irrational.

After the death of Hippodamia, Theseus and Pirithous swore to help each other find "fantasy" wives. As it turned out, Theseus decided that he wanted Helen (future wife of Menelaos), who at this time was still just a young girl. The two were able to abduct her at Sparta, but she was later rescued from their clutches by her two brothers, Castor and Pollux (the Dioscuri). Pirithous, unfortunately, decided that his fantasy woman was Persephone, queen of the underworld. When the two arrived, Persephone (or Hades) invited them to sit down in two chairs, but these two chairs caused them to forget everything, including how to get up! It wasn't until Herakles arrived that Theseus was pulled from the chair and rescued. Pirithous, however, was required to remain there forever in the chair, because it was he who planned the expedition.

Herakles returned Theseus to an Athens that was in total chaos. Theseus had really made a mess of things. When Helen had been rescued, the Dioscuri brothers had also taken his mother Aethra captive to be her slave. The Athenians were still trying to recover from the death and destruction brought about when the Amazons attacked the city. While he was in the underworld his wife Phaedra had committed suicide over an incident between herself and Theseus' son Hippolytus. The king reacted rashly by sending his son into exile and causing his death. Theseus was beginning to look like a bad tyrant. In the end he was forced to flee, and he chose the island of Scyros in the Aegean for his refuge, hoping that he would find hospitality from the king there. Instead, the king led him to a cliff on the island as if to show him the survey of the land, but pushed him off to his death. Such was the humiliating end to Theseus. Years later, though, when the Athenians were fighting the Persians at the battle of Marathon, they claim that they saw a man of enormous size fighting on their side heroically. Figuring that the man must be Theseus, the Athenians made a point to retrieve the remains (the bones) from Scyros and return them to a magnificent burial in Athens. In a sense, then, Theseus became immortalized in the end.

PERSEUS

"Also depicted on Herakles' shield was Perseus, the son of rich-haired Danae: his feet did not touch the shield and yet were not far from it—a marvel to tell, since he was not supported anywhere; for lame Hephaestus had so fashioned him in the gold with his hands on purpose. On his feet he had winged sandals, and his black-sheathed sword was slung across his shoulders by a cross-belt of bronze. He was flying as swift as one can think. The head of a dreadful monster, the Gorgon Medusa, covered the broad of his back, and a marvelous bag of silver contained it. From the bag bright tassels of gold hung down. Upon the head of the hero lay the dread cap of Hades which reeked the awful gloom of night. Perseus himself, the son of Danae, was straining his body to the limits, like one who hurries and shudders with horror. And after him rushed the Gorgons, unapproachable and unspeakable, longing to seize him. Under the trample of their feet, the hard shield rang sharp and clear with a loud clanging. Two serpents hung down at their girdles with heads curved forward; their tongues were flickering, and their teeth gnashing with fury, and their eyes glaring fiercely. And upon the awful heads of the Gorgons great Phobos (Fear) was quaking."

—Hesiod, *Shield of Heracles* 216ff

In the northeastern region of the Peloponnese is a grouping of three cities that in ancient times always had close connections: Argos, Tiryns, and Mycenae. It so happened that at some point Argos was ruled by a certain Acrisius, while Tiryns was ruled by his brother Proetus. The two had quarreled from the earliest days, even in their mother's womb, much as in the Bible Jacob and Esau were said to have done. At any rate, the two distrusted each other so that they constantly vied for supremacy and worried about the other's strength. Proetus employed the Cyclopes to build walls around Tiryns using huge stones, and even today the "Cyclopean" walls can be observed there.

Acrisius was concerned because he himself had only a daughter, Danae, but no male heir. After a quick check with the oracle about the matter, he learned that Danae would indeed have a son, but that this grandson would also bring about his demise. As many of these characters in myth do, he tried to find a way to thwart his fate as proclaimed by the oracle. He built a bronze chamber which he mostly submerged underground, with holes just big enough to slip in food and water. That way, he assumed, no man could ever reach her. But Zeus saw the girl, found her beautiful, and decided that he wanted her for himself. He descended upon her in a shower of golden rain through the crack in the chamber and impregnated her.

As time went by, the pathetic Danae bore her child while continuing to live a miserable existence in the chamber. Eventually, the news got out as people heard the baby crying. Acrisius was understandably upset and confused, not wanting to believe that she had given birth to a child of Zeus, as rumors indicated. So he removed her from her chamber, built a wooden box for her that looked something like a coffin, and nailed her and her child in it. He ordered his henchmen to toss the box into the boisterous sea. Essentially, he was burying his own daughter alive so that he could avoid the oracle's prediction.

The gods determined that Danae should live. Soon, a fisherman named Dictys ("Netman") pulled her out of the sea and took her to the little island of Seriphos where he allowed Danae and her baby, Perseus, to live with him. Perseus grew fast and strong, exhibiting a strength and athleticism that far surpassed that of anyone on the island. The king of the island, Polydectes, who happened to be Dictys' brother, had designs on Danae, but Perseus thwarted his every effort. Polydectes, therefore, plotted Perseus' ruin: While pretending to get married to some girl on the island, the king demanded that everyone on the island give him a present of an outstanding horse. Perseus was too poor to own a horse, so he told the king he would give him whatever the king requested he go get in place of the horse. Polydectes seized the opportunity by telling him to go get the head of the Gorgon Medusa, a seemingly impossible task, since the Medusa, like the other Gorgons, could turn people to stone with one look. Even if Perseus could cut off the head of Medusa, the other Gorgons, immortal and winged as they were, would quickly pursue him. The Gorgons protected Medusa even though she was not originally their sister. In fact, she was the only mortal Gorgon, having been transformed into one by Athena in a fit of rage. Medea had once been a beautiful priestess of Athena, but she incurred the goddess' wrath because she had "allowed" herself to be raped by Poseidon in her temple. Women often took the blame and suffered for the sexual indiscretions of the gods.

Before Perseus could find and behead the Medusa, he first had to find three old women, hags really, called the Graiai (or Graeae, meaning "the gray ones"). These women were so old and hideous that they shared among them one eye and tooth. Their one task was to bar the road that lead to the Gorgons, their sisters. Perseus went to them and stole their eye. Versions of the story differ here. Either they possessed the knowledge necessary for dealing with the Gorgons, or, probably an older version, they just watched the road. At any rate, it could be that Perseus learned from them the location of the Gorgons, or he learned that he needed certain equipment, with which some nymphs supplied him: the cap of Hades, which would make him invisible ("Hades" means "unseen"), the winged sandals of Hermes, a purse called a *kibisis* for carrying the Gorgon's head, and a scimitar, a kind of curved sword. Despite what the movie "Clash of the Titans" says, Perseus did not ride around on Pegasus, the winged horse.

Perseus used his winged sandals to fly over the ocean to where the Gorgons had their abodes. On the advice of Athena, he used the reflection in his shield to back up to the Medusa and behead her. He stuffed her head in the purse, without looking, then used his winged sandals and the cap of invisibility to escape the other Gorgon sisters.

On the way, Perseus seems to have been flying over North Africa, Libya to be exact, and the blood dripping from his purse turned into snakes as they hit the desert. Somewhere, either in Ethiopia or in Judea, at a port city called Joppa, Perseus spied a strange scene: There beneath him was a swarthy maiden tied to a stake near the ocean, while her parents hid fearfully behind a rock. He flew down, checked the woman out (Andromeda), decided he wanted to marry her, and went over to talk to the parents. As it turned out, Andromeda was waiting for a sea monster to come out of the sea to devour her, a payment demanded by the sea nymphs because Andromeda's mother had boasted that her daughter is more beautiful than they are. Perseus asked if he rescued her from the monster would they let him marry her. The parents gladly agreed, and Perseus waited for the monster. A tremendous battle ensued between Perseus and this monster named Ceto (the word simply means "sea monster"), with Perseus darting in and out, stabbing it with his sword, until finally it curled up into the sea like a coral reef, dead. But all was not well. The parents of Andromeda forgot to tell Perseus that she was promised to someone else. When the rival showed up to their wedding with his band of hooligans, all hell broke loose. Perseus, however, had a secret weapon. At just the right moment, he whipped out the Medusa's head, showed it to them, and turned them all into stone.

Afterwards, Perseus flew back to Seriphos to show Polydectes the head of Medusa. He found Polydectes harassing his mother, so he marched into the king's palace, pulled out the head of Medusa again and startled the king with it. The scene is described in the ancient text as follows:

> "When he reached Seriphos, Perseus found that his mother along with Diktys had sought refuge at the altars from the violence of Polydectes, so he entered the royal palace where Polydektes was entertaining his friends, and with his own face turned aside he displayed

the Gorgo's head. When they looked at it, each one turned to stone, holding the pose he happened to have been striking at that moment. Perseus made Diktys king of Seriphos, and gave the sandals, kibisis, and helmet back to Hermes, and the Medusa's head to Athena. Hermes returned the aforementioned articles to the Nymphs, and Athena placed the Gorgon's head in the center of her shield. (It is affirmed by some that Medusa was beheaded because of Athena, for they say the Gorgon had been willing to be compared with Athena in beauty.)"

—Apollodorus, *The Library* 2.45–46

Perseus then turned his flight to Argos to find his grandfather, Acrisius. When Acrisius learned that Perseus was coming, he fled north to Thessaly, assuming that some harm would come to him from Perseus. At some point, the king of Thessaly was holding some athletic games, which Perseus attended to participate in. While throwing the discus, Perseus slipped, the discus flew into the crowd and hit an old man there. Not surprisingly, given the old oracle, that old man was Acrisius. The oracle was fulfilled after all, since now Perseus had killed his own grandfather, though by accident. When Perseus returned to Argos he was so ashamed of the accident that he traded his city for that of Tiryns, and then founded nearby Mycenae. He and Andromeda lived and ruled there for many years until their death, when Athena turned them into a constellation.

"The art of the flute that long ago Pallas Athena invented, weaving in music's rich refrain the ghoulish dirge of the fierce-hearted Gorgons. This in their anguished struggle from those dread maiden's lips was heard streaming, and from those writhing serpent heads untouchable, when Perseus over the third of those fell sisters launched his cry of triumph, and brought fatal doom to Seriphos by the sea—doom for that isle and for her people. Yes, for he had made blind the grim offspring of Phorkys, and bitter the wedding-gift he brought to Polydektes, thus to end his mother's long slavery and enforced wedlock—that son of Danae, who reaped the head of fair-cheeked Medusa . . . But when the goddess maid delivered from these labors the man she loved, then she contrived the manifold melodies of the flute, to make in music's notes an image of the shrill lamenting cries, strung from Euryale's ravening jaws. A goddess found, but finding, gave the strain to mortal men to hold, naming it the tune of many heads."

—Pindar, *Pythian Odes* 12

CHAPTER SEVENTEEN
The Trojan War

"My mother Thetis, the goddess of the silver feet, tells me I face two sorts of destiny in regard to the day of my death. Either, if I stay here and fight beside the city of the Trojans, my return home is gone, but my glory will be everlasting; but if I return home to the beloved land of my fathers, the excellence of my glory is gone, but there will be a long life left for me, and my end in death will not come to me quickly."

—Homer, *Iliad*

Troy, also called Ilium, was a city situated on the western shore of what is now Turkey (ancient Asia Minor) near the Hellespont, which is the entrance to the Black Sea. It reached its height of power sometime around 1300 B.C., about the time that the Mycenaean Greeks centered at Mycenae and Argos were flourishing on mainland Greece. The two States clashed, though the reason is not exactly clear. Myth tells us that Paris, the son of king Priam of Troy, stole Helen away from her husband, king Menelaos of Sparta. Since Menelaos was brother of Agamemnon, king of Mycenae, and Helen was sister of Agamemnon's wife Clytemnestra, Paris' rape of Helen triggered a chain of events that resulted in the annihilation of Troy by the Greeks. We can surmise more likely reasons for the epic clash between these two peoples, however: Possibly the Trojans were harassing the Greeks as they tried to enter the Black Sea along trade routes. Whatever the cause of this clash, we do know that the story of the Trojan War is not all fiction, rather a complex weaving together of historical fact, as proven by archaeology, and mythic imagination.

The story of the Trojan War must be introduced by pulling together a number of threads. The story begins with what is called "the house of Atreus," that is, the regal line that includes the ruler Atreus and his children (see also chapter 19 on Agamemnon). The story runs as follows: Tantalus, a ruler in Lydia (Asia Minor), was favored by the gods and invited to one of their banquets. Wanting to test the clairvoyance of the gods, he chopped up his own son, Pelops, and brought it as a casserole to the feast. None of the gods were taken in by the trick, except for Demeter, who was brooding over the fact that Persephone was in the underworld. She ended up eating the shoulder of Pelops before the trick was exposed and Tantalus was punished. Hermes and Hephaestus then took the butchered Pelops, boiled his

Julia Paula, Bronze coin, c. 220 A.D., from the region around Troy. The reverse shows Apollo Smintheus ("mouse slayer"), standing on a pedestal and holding a bow and a patera (ritual bowl) in front of a flaming tripod.

body parts together with a few magic herbs, and, voila! the child was reconstituted. His missing shoulder (now in Demeter's belly) was replaced by an ivory one.

Pelops grew up and traveled to Elis near where Olympia is in southern Greece. There ruled a certain king Oenomaus who had a lovely daughter named Hippodamia, for whom he himself had developed an incestuous love. Now Hippodamia was being wooed by many young men in the kingdom, but her father had devised a means to put them off so that she would never marry. He was demanding that before anyone could have her hand in marriage, they must first beat him in a chariot race across the peninsula to Corinth. The problem was that Oenomaus' horses were as swift as the wind, so that even when he gave the suitors a head start, he was able to catch up with them. When he did catch them, invariably he would spear them in the back, drag them from the chariot, and cut off their heads, whereupon he nailed the decapitated heads to his palace door. Fewer and fewer people thereafter were willing to try their hand at chariot racing. But when Pelops showed up, he decided to try, undeterred as he was by the show of heads. The night before the race, Pelops bribed Myrtilus, chariot driver of the king, to lose the race by rigging the chariot. He promised Myrtilus that if he did this, he could spend the first night with Hippodamia. Myrtilus complied, replacing the bronze linchpin of the wheel with a wax one. The next day when the chariot wheel heated up, the wax melted and the wheel flew off. Oenomaus himself was unprepared for this and so became tangled up in the reins and killed. Myrtilus then rode on with Pelops and Hippodamia to Corinth to win the race. But as the group stopped and Pelops went off to find some water, Myrtilus decided it was time to cash in on his reward: Pelops returned to find Myrtilus on top of Hippodamia trying to have his way with her. Pelops could not bear the sight, so he grabbed Myrtilus and threw him off the cliff. As Myrtilus fell, however, he cursed Pelops that his family would suffer the worst evils, a curse that came to pass, as we shall see. The ancients believed strongly that a curse uttered by a dying person has special efficacy.

Now Pelops was king and the entire peninsula became known as the island of Pelops, or "Peloponnesus." With his new wife he had four sons, Pittheus, Chrysippus, Thyestes, and Atreus. Meanwhile, on the other side of the peninsula, Eurystheus, the king of Mycenae who had sent Herakles on so many labors, died without an heir. An oracle said that a son of Pelops, either Atreus or Thyestes, should have the throne. The two both wanted to rule there, so they had to find some resolution. It was agreed that whoever of the two could produce the golden fleece of a sacred lamb (a seemingly impossible thing) could have the throne. Now Atreus had such a fleece which he had hidden in a locked trunk and not told anyone about but his wife, whose name was Aerope. Little did he know, however, that Thyestes was having an affair with his wife, and she had already given the fleece to him, so, in fact, Thyestes was able to produce the fleece, much to the bewilderment of Atreus. Atreus would not give up so easily: He predicted that the sun would rise in the West on the next day as a sign from the gods that he himself should rule Mycenae. The next day the sun did rise in the West, forcing everyone to admit that was a powerful sign in favor of Atreus.

Atreus began to rule over Mycenae, but the solution to the puzzle of the golden fleece dawned on him. He finally realized that Thyestes had been watering Aerope's garden, so to speak. He devised a plan of revenge. He invited the now exiled Thyestes back to Mycenae on the pretense of reconciliation. Meanwhile, he took Thyestes' two children (their names are not important to us), chopped them up, and made a stew out of them. So when Thyestes came for dinner, he was fed, of course, his own sons. While poking around in the stew, he came across some recognizable part of one of his children, chocked and gagged, and ran off cursing Atreus and swearing that he would one day get revenge.

His revenge was complicated. He went to the Delphic oracle to ask the oracle how to get revenge on Atreus, but the oracle told Thyestes he must find his long lost daughter, Pelopia, and make love to her. So Thyestes obediently set out to find his daughter. One night during his journey, while camping out under the stars, he came across a young girl whom he could barely see in the flicker of the campfire and the darkness; in his desperation for entertainment, he attacked her, drug her into the bushes, and made love to her. In doing so, he left his sword behind by accident, which she retained in her possession. Little did Thyestes know, though, the young girl was indeed Pelopia, and she became pregnant with their son, Aegisthus.

But the story takes another turn. Shortly after her rape by the lusty Thyestes, Pelopia returned to the court of Atreus, who took her in and made love to her as well, with the result that he thought the eventual child was his own. In the meantime, Atreus sent his two sons, Agamemnon and Menelaos, whom he had begotten with Aerope, his first wife, to Delphi to consult the oracle concerning Thyestes. Thyestes had also returned to the oracle at the same moment in frustration that he could not find his daughter. The young men captured him and drug him back to Mycenae in chains. Atreus sent in his other son, Aegisthus (who was in reality Thyestes' son), to kill Thyestes as a sign of loyalty and manhood. Aegisthus took a sword into the room where Thyestes was so that he could kill him, but Thyestes recognized the sword as the one he had lost in the bushes long ago. He put together the incident, the oracle, and the present sword to realize that Aegisthus was his own child. The two ran to Pelopia to verify the whole story. When she realized that she had had intercourse with her own father, she committed suicide, but first confirmed everything. Aegisthus then went in and murdered Atreus instead, creating a bitter enmity between Agamemnon and Menelaos on one side and Aegisthus on the other.

There's more. In Sparta, where Tyndareus ruled, a problem was brewing. Tyndareus' beautiful daughter Helen was being courted by far too many noble and heroic young men, and he was worried that fighting would break out among them. Agamemnon and Menelaos both wanted her, but so did many, many others, including Odysseus and other future generals of the Trojan War, such as Diomedes, Ajax, Philoctetes, and Patroclus. Odysseus was especially clever and surmised that the situation with Helen was hopeless. He had taken a hankering toward a niece of Tyndareus, anyway, whose name was Penelope. He therefore went to Tyndareus with a plan: "If you give me Penelope," he said, "I will show you a way to prevent fighting among all these great heroes." Tyndareus was happy to comply, and so Odysseus told him to make all the heroes swear an oath, the famous Oath of Tyndareus, whereby they pledged to respect Helen's choice of a mate and not try to take her from him or to let anyone else do so. The heroes willingly pledged this oath, whereupon Helen chose Menelaos as her husband. Agamemnon settled on Helen's sister Clytemnestra as a kind of second prize.

We can chart the family line in this way (including the three children of Agamemnon):

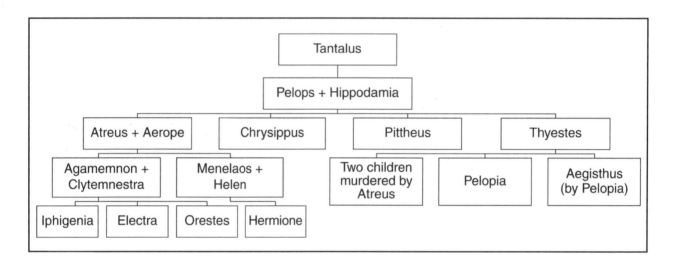

We now come to the story of the wedding of Peleus and Thetis. Zeus had long been interested in the pretty sea nymph named Thetis, one of the most impressive of all the sea nymphs, but an oracle had told him that the son of Thetis would be greater than the father. Zeus was concerned, then, that she might have a powerful child that would challenge his throne. He therefore arranged that she would marry Peleus, a mortal king of Phthia in Thessaly (north central Greece). She was not at all pleased with this situation. Concurrently, Zeus was under discussions with Themis, the old Titaness, about the problem of human population. During this time, it so happened, the world had become overly populated, and Zeus was wanting to do something about it. The two gods devised a terrible plan and enlisted the help of Eris, the goddess of strife, and sister of Ares. She created an apple of gold on which she wrote the simple words, "To the Fairest."

When the wedding of Peleus and Thetis was in full swing with all the gods and goddesses present except for Eris, who never got invited to such functions, the goddess of strife unexpectedly showed up, and rolled the golden apple into the midst of the gathering. Three goddesses in particular saw it and lunged for the apple, assuming that "To the Fairest" referred to them: Aphrodite, Hera, and Athena (who should have known better). A fight broke out, with the three goddesses rolling around on the floor, scratching each other's eyes and pulling hair. Finally they came to Zeus and asked him to decide which of the three should get the apple. Zeus knew that if he made a choice he must necessarily alienate two goddesses, which he was not stupid enough to do. So he told Hermes to take the three goddesses along with the apple to the region around Troy to a certain shepherd there named Paris to let him make the decision. Paris was actually the son of the king of Troy, Priam, but had been sent off as a child to live with shepherds when his mother, Hecuba, dreamed that she had given birth to a firebrand that destroyed the city. It was assumed that Paris was that firebrand and that he would somehow take an action that would result in the city's demise. Paris had proven himself an excellent shepherd and had even gained the name "Alexander" for his skill in warding off marauders ("Alexander" means "warder off of men").

At any rate, Hermes presented the three goddesses to the surprised Paris, and each of the three tried to bribe Paris in some way according to her own attribute. Hera offered him world domination, Athena wisdom or military distinction, Aphrodite the most beautiful woman as his wife. Foolishly, Paris granted the apple to Aphrodite and then asked that Helen be made his. But Helen belonged to Menelaos, and there's the rub. Paris traveled to Sparta and entered into the palace of Menelaos and Helen. In accordance with the rules of hospitality, Menelaos took Paris in and let him stay as a guest of the house. But when Menelaos went off to Crete on some official state business, Paris grabbed Helen (whether she went willingly or not was much debated in antiquity) along with the treasure of the house and left for his ship. In this way the power of Aphrodite made Helen leave her husband, their child Hermione, and her reputation behind.

At this point the Oath of Tyndareus kicked in. All the heroes who had pledged to protect the inviolability of the marriage of Helen and Menelaos had to gather up armies to prepare to win her back from the Trojans. Back at Troy, despite his sister Cassandra's warnings, Paris had been received back into the royal household along with the treasure and Helen. In Greece, Agamemnon took charge of the huge expedition that was getting under way there. Together the heroes went around from place to place gathering up all those who had sworn the oath. Among the many they enlisted are included the following:

1. Ajax, son of Oileus, king of the Locrians, who had 40 ships full of soldiers. He eventually would rape Cassandra on the altar of Athena at the end of the Trojan war and bring destruction down upon himself.

2. Odysseus, who was now married to Penelope with a one year old son named Telemachus. He did not really want to join them, so he feigned madness. When the Greeks came to his island of Ithaca, they found him ploughing the seashore with salt behind a yoked team of an ox and a mule. Suspecting a trick, the heroes placed Telemachus in front of his plough, thinking that if he were really insane, he would plough his son under; otherwise, he would stop and have to reveal himself. Odysseus had to give in and admit that he was not insane.

3. Ajax, son of Telamon, king of Salamis. He killed himself at the end of the Trojan War because the Greeks would not give him Achilles' armor.

4. Philoctetes, to whom Herakles had given his bow and arrows. He spent most of the war suffering on the island of Lemnos from a gruesome snake bite that stank rancidly and caused him to curse incessantly. He finally joined the Greeks at the end of the war after he was cured. He became partner with Neoptolemus, son of Achilles, who also joined the war late.

5. Nestor, old and garrulous king of Pylos (his palace is a relatively recent archaeological discovery) who brought with him ninety ships.

6. Calchas, a seer who told the Greeks that they had to bring the young Achilles with them to the war if they ever hoped to win. Achilles had not sworn the oath or courted Helen (probably he was still very young), so he technically did not have to go. His mother Thetis had tried to protect him from the heroes by placing him on the island of Scyros dressed as a girl, but Odysseus found out his trick. Achilles had been made nearly immortal by his mother when she dipped him in the river Styx; he was only mortal where she held him, namely, on his heel.

7. Diomedes, king of Argos. He had eighty ships and was skilled at the spear. During the Trojan War he distinguished himself by sneaking into Troy and stealing the image of Athena called the Palladium. He also wounded Aphrodite on the battlefield, for which she made his wife be unfaithful.

The Greeks first set sail (Helen had the face that "launched a thousand ships") from Aulis, but the winds blew them to southern Asia Minor where they accidentally attacked Telephus, a son of Herakles. In a bizarre story, Telephus was later cured of a wound by rust from Achilles' spear. At any rate, the Greeks recouped in Aulis again, but trouble appeared. While Agamemnon was hunting for food for the many soldiers, he struck and killed a deer that Artemis held sacred (probably a young deer, given what we know of Artemis). She demanded that Agamemnon repay her by sacrificing his own daughter to her, else she would cause adverse winds to blow, keeping the Greeks from ever being able to sail to Troy. Agamemnon, driven by greed and lust for battle, or perhaps afraid to disappoint the army, summoned his own daughter Iphigenia to Aulis under the pretext that she would marry Achilles. He then killed her at the very altar where she thought she was about to be married. The Roman poet Lucretius describes the pathos of the scene in this way, adding a slam against religion at the end:

> "At Aulis the altar of Artemis was foully defiled by the blood of Iphigenia, shed by chosen leaders of the Greeks, chieftains of the host. So soon as the wedding ribbon had bound her maiden tresses, falling in equal lengths down either cheek, so soon as she saw her father standing sorrowful before the altar, and by his side attendants hiding the knife, and the people shedding tears at the sight of her, dumb with dread she sank to the ground upon her knees. Alas, poor girl! no help could it be to her at such a time that she first called Agamemnon father; for uplifted by the hands of men, all trembling she was brought to the altar, not that amid solemn and sacred ritual she might be escorted by loud wedding song, but a clean maiden to fall by unclean hands at the very age of wedlock, a vic-

tim sorrowful slain by a father's hand: all in order that a fair and fortunate release might be given to the fleet. Only religion has the power to persuade to such evil deeds."

With that the Greeks were able to sail to Troy to start their ten-year long siege of the great city. We cannot repeat all the details of the Trojan War here, because there are far too many. Suffice it to say that there were many turns of fortune during the war. At times the Greeks seemed poised to bring down the city walls, and certainly they had easily mopped up Troy's surrounding allies by making raids on small towns, looting and raping as they went. At times, according to Homer who writes about the ninth year of the war in his epic, the *Iliad*, the Trojans were ready to throw Helen off the walls down to the Greeks (most of the Trojans had grown to hate Helen, who seemed content to stay in Troy). Sometimes the Trojans pushed the Greeks back all the way to their ships, even burning some of them and nearly bringing the war to an end. This occurred when Achilles withdrew with his troops from battle, sulking because he had been insulted by Agamemnon. Often, one-on-one battles transpired, usually with no decisive outcome, except when Achilles killed Priam's son Hector, the chief general on the Trojan side, in retaliation for the death of his best friend Patroclus. Patroclus had foolishly donned Achilles armor and pretended to be the great hero in an effort to rally the Greek troops, but he was slain in the fighting and a terrific battle arose over the body and Achilles armor. Before Achilles could come back into the fray, his mother Thetis had to go to Hephaestus to have some new armor made.

There were raids, spy missions, intrigue, insurrections, and so on, but in the end no one could win. It was not until Odysseus with the help of Athena concocted the stratagem of the Trojan Horse that the Greeks were finally able to bring down the city.

Odysseus encouraged the Greeks to build a huge horse, hollow inside with a trap door that would allow twelve soldiers to hide within. The Greeks sailed away, leaving behind the horse and an actor, named Sinon, who claimed that the Greeks had given up the fight and left the horse as a present to Athena. Sinon also claimed that the Greeks had tried to sacrifice him to the horse, but that he had escaped and now hates his own people. He told the Trojans that if they could drag the horse into the city, that they would please Athena and be invincible. Despite warnings from Cassandra and other clear signs, the Trojans dumbly drug the horse full of Greek soldiers into their city, then threw a huge party celebrating the end of the war. That night, when the drunken revelry had ended, the Greek soldiers climbed out of the horse, opened the gates, and signaled for the Greeks to sail back (they were hiding at the nearby island of Tenedos). Such was the downfall of Troy after a bloody, horrific night of street fighting and brutality. A few Trojans escaped, including the famous Aeneas, who sailed off to found the Roman race in Italy. Most Trojan men were killed, while the women and children were taken off into slavery in Greece.

HOMERIC WELTANSHAUUNG

The question as to the historical accuracy of Homer's depiction of late Bronze Age Greeks leads us into many complicated problems. If Homer composed the *Iliad* around 800 B.C., as we think, then he is some five hundred years removed from the Trojan War. In other words, he is telling a tale in a time when Greeks had no written historical records and believed in the existence of fabulous divinities about an event that took place half a millennium before his lifetime. In fact, Homer mentions several technological advances that archaeology has shown could not have belonged to the Trojan War era. Thus, some of Homer's description is easily recognizable as anachronistic. But we should remember too that Homer was a professional bard, and so he would have inherited his craft and his stories, at least in part, from bards that went before. It is likely that Homer's poems represent a long legacy of tales about the Trojan War, some of them stretching back to the years immediately following the war itself. Therefore, Homer's *Iliad* may reflect a historical reality held in the memory of the bardic tradition. This mixture of truth and fiction has proven difficult to sort out.

Even so, we can clearly identify in Homer what we might call a *Weltanschauung*, that is, a "world-view." Homer's characters exhibit a definite set of core values that govern their actions and make the story as a whole work in a consistent manner. From the very outset of the *Iliad*, the prologue, so to speak, of the poem itself, this world-view is discernible:

> "Wrath, sing it, goddess, the destructive wrath of Achilles, son of Peleus, which caused much pain for the Greeks, and hurled many brave souls of heroes down to Hades, and made their bodies booty for dogs and feast for the birds—and the will of Zeus kept being accomplished—ever since the son of Atreus, king of men, and divine Achilles separated, quarreling."

The very first word of the poem, "wrath," (translating the Greek word "menis"), carries with it certain definite connotations beyond the simple idea of "anger." *Menis* is a particular kind of anger, arising, not from jealousy or frustration, not from thwarted plans or any innate cause, but from violated honor. Honor and glory, or what the Greeks call *kleos*, that is, receiving the respect that one has earned by one's accomplishments and one's family connections, drives the action of this entire story. An offense against Achilles' *kleos* signals the first motivation to action in the story: wrath.

This underlying notion of *kleos* that drives the characters is further hinted in the opening lines with the phrase, "son of Peleus." In Greek, "son of Peleus" is one word, what we call a "patronymic." Patronymics occur often in the *Iliad*; they name the characters in the story by reference to their father or some famous ancestor. Homer, by naming Achilles' father along with his name, immediately signals certain things about the hero, such as his noble status (his father was a king), his semi-divine birth (any Greek would know the story of Peleus and Thetis), and his inherited heroic qualities (Peleus participated in the Calydonian boar hunt, the quest for the Golden Fleece, and the battle with the Amazons led by Herakles). It was important to have a heroic past to go bolster the credibility of one's own courage and heroicness.

Homer's opening passage also refers to three separate planes of existence that are constantly at interplay in the *Iliad*. Achilles' anger has led to brutal and costly battles on the plains before the walls of Troy. Greek and Trojan warriors struggle on this human, worldly plane with heroic valor that, if they are successful, can increase the respect they receive here on earth. What they are struggling *against*, however, is the descent to the lower plane: The brave souls of many heroes are headed for Hades, while their more substantial bodies lie helpless and unanimated on the earth as food for the animals. Their souls in the underworld continue to carry on an existence, continue to think and feel emotions such as fear and anger, but without bodies they are shadowy and insignificant. In this dark, unpleasant realm they can only vaguely mirror their former selves. Meanwhile, above the heroes who are struggling on the earthly plane exist the gods. In the heavenly realm they also conduct their lives in a manner parallel to the humans below them, but on a higher level. They laugh and banquet, they quarrel among themselves and lie to one another, they devise ways to work affairs to their advantage, just as the humans do below them. But they are bigger, happier, and better in every way and, in fact, they control the events unfolding beneath them. It is on this higher plane that humans themselves wish to live and to which they strive with all their might to gain entrance with their heroic deeds on the battlefield and with their nobility of character among their peers.

Finally, throughout the *Iliad* the world-view of the Bronze Age Greeks shines through in the conversations of the actors themselves. In every case, the heroes indicate that they believe *kleos* overrides all other goals and all other moral prerogatives. The hero can conceive of no other lifestyle but one that aims at glory and gains the prize. We might say, "Whoever dies with the most toys wins." Peleus, for example, addresses his son Achilles before he enters the battle with the following advice: "Always be the best, and superior to others." When Sarpedon, a child of Zeus who fought on the Trojan side fell in bettle, a huge struggle broke out on the battlefield between Trojans and Greeks over his armor. Throughout the Greek army the battle cry arises, "Let us kill or be killed, win glory or let it go to others." And at another time, when Greek soldiers were faltering in battle, Odysseus runs through their ranks and encourages them, "Only cowards retreat; a man who wants honor in battle must stand fast and kill or be killed." Such were the two options for a Bronze Age Greek: Glory or death, there is nothing in-between.

CHAPTER EIGHTEEN
Odysseus

"Odysseus spoke, and aimed a bitter arrow at Antinous. Now he was on the point of raising to his lips a fair goblet, a two-eared cup of gold, and was even now handling it, that he might drink of the wine, and death was not in his thoughts . . . But Odysseus took aim, and struck him with an arrow in the throat . . . and the cup fell from his hand as he was pierced."

—Homer, *Odyssey* 22.8–18

"Tell me, Muse, about the man of many turns, who many
Ways wandered when he had sacked Troy's holy citadel;
He saw the cities of many men, and he knew their thought;
On the ocean he suffered many pains within his heart,
Striving for his life and his companions' return.
But he did not save his companions, though he wanted to:
They lost their own lives because of their recklessness.
The fools, they devoured the cattle of Hyperion,
The Sun, and he took away the day of their return."

So begins Homer's *Odyssey*, the long and complicated story about the return of Odysseus from Troy. Odysseus has spent ten long years with the Greek army besieging the city of Troy, and now, because of his own foolishness and the mistakes of his men, he is destined to wander another ten years far from his beloved island of Ithaca. There he has his palace, his faithful wife Penelope, and his dear son Telemachus (his name means "fighter from afar"), who is only reaching manhood about the time Odysseus makes his return.

The story begins with a description of the situation back in Ithaca. Times are bad. When the story begins, Odysseus has been gone about nineteen years (later in the *Odyssey* he recounts his adventures in the earlier years), and his family doesn't know where he is. No one has heard from him. In fact, a hundred or so suitors, convinced that Odysseus is dead, have overrun the palace and are vying for Penelope's affections. They see the young man Telemachus as an obstacle and a threat, since he may prevent one of them from marrying Penelope in the hope that his father may one day return. But these suitors, who for all

C. Mamilius Limetanus, Silver denarius, 82 B.C. Head of Mercury, wearing winged petasus, caduceus over shoulder. On the reverse, Ulysses walking right, holding staff and extending hand towards his dog, Argus.

intents and purposes live in the house, are not good guests: They are rapidly consuming all the food and are corrupting many of the younger household slave girls. And notice too, from the quote above, how they enjoy Odysseus' fine wine in golden-eared goblets, truly making themselves at home.

Furthermore, they intimidate Telemachus, making him afraid to stay in his own home, and they harass Penelope whenever she comes down from her bedroom. Penelope, though, stays faithful to her husband and clings to the hope that one day he may return. Still, without the man in the house, she has no protection, not for her property or for her own body.

Telemachus decides that it is time that he search for his father. He sets sail for mainland Greece and arrives at Sparta, where now Helen and Menelaos rule, fresh on their return from Troy. The suitors back in Ithaca meanwhile plot to ambush Telemachus when he returns, kill him, and then say that he drowned. At any rate, Telemachus finds Menelaos henpecked by a dominant Helen—as the world's most perfect beauty she is able to seduce her angered husband again at the end of the war—but no one knows where Odysseus is. Even so, they offer plenty of predictions that he will return home soon.

In the meantime, Odysseus finds himself stuck on the island of Ogygia under the control of Atlas' daughter Calypso, a goddess who uses him as her sexual plaything. He has been there for seven years, remaining eternally youthful yet unhappy. The story of what leads him to this predicament is one of the most interesting adventures in all literature, and forms the central story of the *Odyssey*. It is on this story that we should concentrate our attention. In the end, it should be stated, Odysseus will make it home, now in disguise, and plot together with his son the overthrow of the suitors. Together as champions of justice they slay all the suitors and, after some tense moments, Odysseus is reunited and reconciled to Penelope. The relatives of the suitors show up eventually, seeking revenge, but fortunately (else the retaliation will never end) Athena intervenes and tells them to forgive and forget, thus ending the saga.

Let us return, though, to the travels of Odysseus. When the city of Troy fell, the Greeks gathered up their belongings and the spoils of war and headed home. Those traveling with Odysseus occupied a dozen ships or so. Instead of aiming straight for home, as any reasonable person would have done, Odysseus decided that he and his men needed a few more spoils of war, so he sailed north toward Thrace (he should have followed the coast homeward, or perhaps sailed southwest into open sea). There they conduct a pirate raid on the land of the Cicones, a people famous for their strong Ismarian wine, used by many in the worship of Dionysus. They storm the place, kill the men who resist them, then plunder the villages and enslave the women. Odysseus tries to get his men back to the ship, but they refuse, and instead butcher sheep on the shore to make gluttons of themselves. Meanwhile, the fugitive Cicones go for help inland, to other Cicones, who happen to ride horses and to be better skilled at warfare. All day the Greeks fought these Cicones in a fierce pitched battle. The Greeks were driven back to the shore, desperately trying to defend their ships from fire, until that evening they barely escape. Six benches on every ship stand empty from the battle, and the Greeks mourn the missing men greatly. Greed, gluttony, and the heroic mentality cost them dearly. The Greeks did spare one of the Cicones, though, a man named Maron who bribed them by giving them a healthy supply of Ismarian wine, which later will come in handy when the Greeks meet the Cyclops Polyphemus.

A north wind blows against Odysseus and his men that drives them for ten days straight, past Cytherea at the southern edge of Greece then all the way to Africa. There they find the Lotus-Eaters, a people who mainly eat the honey-sweet fruit of the flowering lotus tree (the date plum). This is the same plant that Ovid mentions in his *Metamorphoses* as he recounts how the nymph Lotis is transformed into it in her effort to escape the clutches of Priapos. From then on, this tree was sacred to the phallic god. Odysseus stops in the land of the Lotus-Eaters for water, and, as is his way, sends envoys inland to meet the locals. The locals show that they are friendly people and wish to do Odysseus and his companions no harm. They offer the lotus flower to the envoys, in fact, but it has a strange effect on them: It takes away their desire to ever return home. They don't even think about reporting back to Odysseus, rather, they sit with the Lotus-Eaters eating lotus flowers all day. Homer calls this a loss of their "nostalgia," that is, their longing for a homecoming. Odysseus has to find his men and drive them back to the ships wailing. He forces them on board, puts them to the oar, and sternly orders the others to rush from that place or else lose all hope of returning home.

Tired and hungry, Odysseus next comes to what we will call, for lack of a better name, Goat Island. There the Greeks find a virgin place where no hunters ever come, and where flocks of wild goats and other animals roam untouched. They have all their needs met here abundantly. But in the distance Odysseus sees peering from the mist another island, with signs of human-like life and activity. He decides that he will lead a small expedition over so that he can exchange gifts with those people and spread the glory of his name.

With one ship, therefore, Odysseus arrives at the island of the Cyclopes. Odysseus and a few companions find a cave (it belongs to Polyphemus, who is away pasturing his sheep), where they see a cheese-making operation, lambs and kids orderly in pens, vessels full of whey, and pails for milking. The men want to take everything and run, but Odysseus wants to stay to find out what the owner of this place has to offer him. They build a fire, help themselves to all they can eat and drink, and wait. Unfortunately, the gigantic Cyclops Polyphemus, orb-eyed man-eating child of Poseidon, returns with a crash, takes a huge stone and places it in front of the cave, and begins milking his ewes while working with his cheeses. When his chores are done, he glares at Odysseus and his men and asks, "Who are you, and why have you come here to plunder my livelihood?" Their knees knock and their hearts fall to their stomachs. Odysseus tells him generally that they are Greeks from Troy (but doesn't give his name) and reminds Polyphemus of Zeus, who oversees hospitality. He is still hoping to acquire gifts. There are no ships, he says slyly, because they all wrecked in one of Poseidon's storms. Polyphemus' response is that the Cyclopes don't fear Zeus or obey his rules of hospitality (this is a change from Hesiod's claim that the Cyclopes serve Zeus by making his thunderbolts). Then, he clutches some of the Greeks and beats their brains out on the floor like they "were squirming puppies." He dismembers them and eats them until he has had enough. This scenario happens again the next night, and each time Polyphemus uses the immense stone to keep Odysseus trapped in the cave.

Finally, Odysseus has seen enough. The "man of many turns" devises a plan. First, he offers Polyphemus some of the strong Ismarian wine to "wash down the men with." Polyphemus is used to drinking milk only, so he does not know to control his intake of wine. He drinks to his heart's content, until he is totally intoxicated. Then he turns to Odysseus and says, "What's your name, anyway?" Odysseus cleverly responds, "My name is Nobody." Polyphemus thanks him for the wine and promises to eat him last as a reward.

> "You, too, Centaur Eurytion, were undone by liquor and you, too, Polyphemus, by the wine of Ismarus."
>
> —Propertius, *Elegies* 2

So Polyphemus falls asleep (or rather, he passes out drunk). Then, on the orders of Odysseus, several of the men ram a sharpened and heated stake into the single eye of the Cyclops. He howls, clawing at his face in agony. Other Cyclopes hear him screaming, but when they come to ask him who has hurt him, Polyphemus replies, "Nobody." The others then turn away, shaking their heads and exclaiming that their brother must have gone insane.

Odysseus laughs at the trick. He next ties his men under the rams and waits for morning. Then, as Polyphemus removes the heavy stone (this is why Odysseus didn't kill him outright) to let out the sheep, he feels the animals' backs to make sure no Greek is escaping. Little does he know or suspect that the men are tied to the bottom, while Odysseus himself is clinging to one with his great strength, until all are free. In a touching moment of the *Odyssey*, Polyphemus actually addresses one of his sheep, his favorite, with deep fondness, imagining that he must be lingering in the cave because he pities his master's blindness.

> "You that I love best, why are you last of all the flock to come out through the cavern's mouth? Never up until now have you come behind the rest: before them all you have marched with stately strides ahead to crop the delicate meadow-flowers, before them all you have reached the rippling streams, before them all you have shown your will to return homewards in the evening; yet now you come last. You are grieving, surely, over your master's eye, which malicious Nobody just now put out, along with his evil friends, after overmastering my wits with wine; but I swear he has still not escaped destruction. If only your

thoughts were like my own, if only you had the gift of words to tell me where he is hiding from my fury! Then I would hurl him to the ground and dash his brains here and there across the cave; then my heart would find some relief from the tribulations he has brought me, unmanly Nobody!"

That should be the end of that episode. But as Odysseus is sailing off, he calls back to Polyphemus, who is now standing by the shore, simply to taunt him: "Cyclops! Did you think you were going to make a feast of my companions? Am I puny in the big caveman's hands? How do you like the beating that we gave you, you damned cannibal? Guest-eater, Zeus and the gods have paid you!" Odysseus' men beg him to stop. Polyphemus hurls rocks in their direction, endangering the ships, but still Odysseus recklessly continues: "Cyclops, if ever mortal man inquires how you were put to shame and blinded, tell him Odysseus, raider of cities, took your eye. I am Laertes' son, whose home is on Ithaca!" That was a huge mistake: Once Polyphemus has detailed information such as this he can call on his father, who happens to be Poseidon, to avenge him. This curse will plague Odysseus on the rest of his journey.

Next, the Greeks come to the island of Aeolia, where Aeolus, lord of the winds, rules. He keeps the winds locked up in his hollow mountain, only letting those escape which the gods order for whatever purpose. He welcomes Odysseus, eventually giving him the right wind for going to Ithaca, and giving to Odysseus a sack full of all the other winds which he should not open until he is safe on shore in Ithaca. Odysseus leaves gleefully, and he and his men soon arrive within sight of their dear island. Thinking he was as good as home, Odysseus falls asleep on deck, but his men distrust him and suspect that he really has loads of treasure in the bags. They foolishly open the bags, letting the winds swirl out and blow the ship off course. Now they are really lost.

Seven days later Odysseus and his men arrive on the coast of the Lestrygonians, a giant cannibal tribe that spear-fishes from the high cliffs overlooking the harbor. Most ancient authors place this, as well as the island of the Cyclopes, on Sicily, though some say that Helios the Sun God passes the land of the Lestrygonians on his way back to the East every night as he travels the northern circuit of the Ocean stream. These men are ruled by Antiphates, who eats any guest that visits his palace. When Odysseus and his men arrive, they become the "fish," until Odysseus sails off having salvaged only one ship, his own. All others are lost.

Afterwards, they come to the island of Aiaia, where Circe, a witch, lives in the center of the island. This master of metamorphosis and necromancy was the child, by some accounts, of Helios, and by others of Hecate, the black-magic goddess of the moon. She was sister to Medea, the sorceress whom Jason took on as a common-law wife. She turns many of Odysseus' men into swine and would have done so to Odysseus himself had Hermes not come to Odysseus and given him a special immunity drug. When he does not turn into a pig, Circe is startled, and Odysseus pulls out her sword and forces her to have sex with him. But the gods warn Odysseus, "Don't let her turn you into a coward or unman you." Ah, but the sex does just that, for a year in fact, until finally Odysseus' men demand that he get hold of his senses and depart for the ship.

Before long, after a brief encounter with Hades, where Odysseus learns that life is precious and not to be squandered, Odysseus is sailing the seas again. He passes the Sirens, strange, birdlike women who live along the rocky shores and sing beautiful songs that make men want to drive their boats onto the rocks to hear them, until they meet their doom. They had originally been the handmaids of Persephone before she was abducted by Hades. After the abduction, Demeter had given them wings to seek out her daughter, but when they failed, they settled on the rocky shores of a flowery island. Odysseus plugs up the ears of his men as they pass by, but has himself tied to the mast so he can hear their song. He nearly goes mad trying to escape his bonds as he hears their songs, but he cannot. The best we can tell, the Sirens seem to sing songs that praise and glorify the listener; that is one song we're all dying to hear.

Odysseus and his men must also sail past the Scylla and Charybdis, two monsters that live in the straits between Italy and Sicily. They represent the idea of being "between a rock and a hard place." The Scylla is a female monster who lives in the cliffs on the Italy side of the straits. She once had been a beautiful woman, but Circe changed her into this monstrous creature out of jealousy over a certain lover named Glaucus. Scylla has six huge dogs protruding from her belly, which devour any sailors who pass by. Actually, they can only eat six sailors from any given ship. On the other side lies the Charybdis, a kind of giant crab that lives under the water and creates a whirlpool with all his sucking and blowing. This whirlpool is worse than the Scylla because it takes down the *entire* ship. So Odysseus, without telling his men of the dangers, sails his ship past Scylla, losing six sailors in the process, but saving the ship as a whole.

The tired crew lands the ship at an island where Hyperion the sun god keeps his cattle. Odysseus warns his men to respect the god by staying away from the cattle, no matter how hungry they are. With that warning he goes off to sleep. The next thing he knows the insubordinate men are having a big barbeque. Their foolhardiness will be their downfall. Hyperion goes to Zeus and says that he will "go down to Hades and shine among the dead" if Zeus doesn't do something to avenge this outrage. So, when the Greeks set sail again, Zeus sends a thunderstorm, driving their ship back to Charybdis and wrecking it. Odysseus himself barely survives by holding onto an overhanging fig tree, then riding on the back of a turtle (or a plank from the ship). None of his men, however, survive. After days on the sea, he finally arrives at the island of Ogygia, where he spends the next seven years under the whims of the goddess Calypso, in obscurity. Finally, the gods pity him, and order her to let him go.

> "Thus was Calypso affected by the Ithacan's departure, when long ago she wept to the lonely waves: for many days she sat disconsolately with unkempt tresses uttering many a complaint to the unjust sea, and although she was never to see him again, yet she still felt pain when she recalled their long happiness together."
>
> —Propertius, *Elegies* 1.15

So now we come around to the end of the tale, when Odysseus arrives back in Ithaca. The last few chapters of his story show him trying to reconnect with his old friends. He carefully tests each one as he remains disguised to see how loyal they still are to him. Only when he has completely scouted out the situation and determined who his true allies are does he feel prepared to take action against the one hundred suitors who are ransacking his house. He bonds with his old and faithful dog, his former nurse, his wife, son, and aged father. This is the psychological *nostos* that follows upon his physical *nostos* (homecoming).

ODYSSEUS IN THE UNDERWORLD

As we have noted already, Odysseus has a brief stint in the underworld (*Odyssey* bk. 11). He goes there to talk to the old seer Teiresias to learn about his future. The somewhat bizarre exchange between the two touches on many important points, but most of all it directs our attention to the importance of the homecoming. Odysseus is telling the story:

"Then came also the ghost of Theban Teiresias, with his golden scepter in his hand. He knew me and said, 'Odysseus, noble son of Laertes, why, poor man, have you left the light of day and come down to visit the dead in this sad place? Stand back from the trench and withdraw your sword that I may drink of the blood and answer your questions truly.'

So I drew back, and sheathed my sword, whereon when he had drank of the blood he began with his prophecy.

'You want to know,' said he, 'about your return home [**nostos**], but heaven will make this hard for you. I do not think that you will escape the eye of Poseidon, who still nurses his bitter grudge against you for having blinded his son. Still, after much suffering you may get home if you can restrain yourself and your companions when your ship reaches the Thrinacian island, where you will find the sheep and cattle belonging to the sun, who sees and gives ear to everything. If you leave these flocks unharmed and think of nothing but of getting home [**nostos**], you may yet after much hardship reach Ithaca; but if you harm them, then I forewarn you of the destruction both of your ship and of your men. Even though you may yourself escape, you will return in bad plight after losing all your men, in another man's ship, and you will find trouble in your house, which will be overrun by high-handed people, who are devouring your substance under the pretext of paying court and making presents to your wife.

When you get home you will take your revenge on these suitors; and after you have killed them by force or fraud in your own house, you must take a well-made oar and carry it on and on, until you come to a country where the people have never heard of the sea and do not even mix salt with their food, nor do they know anything about ships and oars that are as the wings of a ship. I will give you this certain token which cannot escape your notice. A wayfarer will meet you and will say it must be a winnowing shovel that you have got upon your shoulder; on this you must fix the oar in the ground and sacrifice a ram, a bull, and a boar to Poseidon. Then go home and offer hecatombs to the gods in heaven one after the other. As for yourself, death shall come to you from the sea, and your life shall ebb away very gently when you are full of years and peace of mind, and your people shall be prosperous. All that I have said will come true.'

This exchange, as we have stated, contains a wealth of details. But for all its intricacies, one principle stands true here as it has throughout the entire tale of Odysseus: Our hero always wants to "know," and for him to know he must make a journey. His journey always takes him to strange places, places he cannot imagine, where he is not recognized and does not recognize, where his greatest skills (such as sailing) and his long-held assumptions (for example, that an oar is an oar) are constantly questioned and redefined. Only as a traveler, as a constant explorer who encounters new ways of looking at old things, can Odysseus gain the critical skills he needs to be truly wise.

CHAPTER NINETEEN
The Return of Agamemnon

Cassandra, in prophetic trance speaking of the curse on the house of Atreus, Agamemnon's father: "Now bear me witness, as, like a dog hot on the trail, I catch the scent of a track of brutal crimes done long ago [the crimes of Atreus and his brother Thyestes]. For from their house's roof never departs a choir chanting in unison, but singing no harmonious tune; for their song is menacing. And so, gorged and drunk on human blood, so as to be the more emboldened, a revel-rout of kindred Furies haunts the house, hard to be driven away. Lodged within its halls they chant their song of hate and primal sin; and, each in turn, they spurn with loathing a brother's bed, for they bitterly spit curses on the one who defiled it [Thyestes began the deadly blood feud when he seduced his brother Atreus' wife]. . . . Bear witness upon your oath that I know the deeds of sin, ancient in story, of this house."

—Aeschylus, *Agamemnon* 1184ff.

Agamemnon was the proud ruler of the city of Mycenae, the most powerful of all Greek city-states during the late 14th Century B.C. The citadel of the city was surrounded by the huge Cyclopean walls, made of stones so large the ancients believed those giant brutes must have set them in their places. The famous "lion's gate" guarded the entrance. Mycenae was engaged in commerce and politics throughout the Mediterranean world; by this time it had already eclipsed the Minoans on Crete. Agamemnon's brother, Menelaos, ruled over another rich and militaristic city, Sparta, and was married to Helen, a child of Zeus. Agamemnon was married to Helen's sister, Clytemnestra. The two brothers stood at the height of their power when the opportunity came for them to lead a pan-Hellenic expedition against Troy. This was the first time that all of the Greek city-states had banded together for one purpose.

But in the very heart of Agamemnon's glory there was heartache and pain. A dark cloud hanged over his "house," that is, his family line. His father Atreus and his uncle Thyestes, children of Pelops and grandchildren of Tantalus, had carried on a bitter feud that eventually was passed on to their children. Thyestes, as the passage above indicates, carried on an affair with Atreus' wife. The latter took revenge by killing two (some say three) of Thyestes' children, chopping them up, and making a stew out of their body parts. He then invited Thyestes to his house on the pretense of making amends over a feast of stew. Thyestes

A silver tetradrachm from Sicily dating to about 414 B.C. The obverse shows two eagles devouring a hare, an allusion to the omen that said Agamemnon and Menelaos (the two eagles) would destroy Troy (the hare). The reverse shows Scylla and Charybdis.

stained his soul with the abominable though unintentional act of eating his own children. Atreus had forever heaped guilt upon his head for carrying out the unholy act. Even the Helios the sun god recoiled from his usual course when he observed it. The two brothers parted, heaping curses upon one another. Then, to make matters worse, Thyestes had an incestuous affair with his own daughter, producing the child Aegisthus, who made it his goal in life to take vengeance on Atreus' family. He killed Atreus first, and then, when Agamemnon was off fighting at Troy, he started up an affair with Clytemnestra, Agamemnon's wife. Clytemnestra was ready and willing to engage in the affair because of another murderous event: Agamemnon had sacrificed their daughter Iphigenia to Artemis in order to gain favorable winds for the voyage to Troy. Clytemnestra never forgave him for this act.

The story gets worse. When Troy fell, the Greek chieftains drew lots to see who would receive what Trojan captive as a slave. Cassandra, daughter of Priam and priestess of Apollo, went to Agamemnon, the general-in-charge on the Greek side. This was a terrible blow to Cassandra, who had already suffered rape at the hands of Ajax and had watched her boyfriend butchered before her eyes. Now she had to suffer the humiliation of serving the very man who brought about the destruction of her dear city. But she also had forebodings that something awful would happen to both Agamemnon and herself upon their return to Mycenae. Her divinely induced suspicions were correct. The story of Agamemnon's return was one of the momentous events in the history of Greece, forever changing the way Greeks thought and lived. The Greek playwright Aeschylus, who lived and flourished in the first half of the 5th century B.C., tells the story of Agamemnon in a series of three plays that we refer to collectively as the *Oresteia*. The individual plays were entitled *Agamemnon*, *Libation Bearers, and Eumenides*. What follows here is a summary of those three plays:

The Agamemnon

After the Greeks took Troy and sacked the city, they lit signal fires that through a sequence of stations sent a message all the way to Mycenae, announcing the end of the war. Back in Mycenae there is much discussion about the war: so many young men were killed in a war that was unjust, all ten years of bloodshed for the sake of one single woman. The citizens (who serve as the chorus in Aeschylus' play) remember the sacrifice of Iphigenia, which they interpret as a sign of Agamemnon's evil desire for war. He could have refused to go: Who would fault him? They also talk about Clytemnestra's bitter brooding as a result of the sacrifice of her child, her hatred of her husband, and her desire for vengeance. Meanwhile, she has taken to herself a boyfriend, Aegisthus, the surviving son of Thyestes, brother of Atreus (you may recall that Atreus, Agamemnon's father, had long ago killed Thyestes' other two sons and tried to feed them to his brother at a banquet, giving rise to a bitter enmity that is now passed on to the sons). Furthermore, the people of Mycenae are critical of the war, because news has come that the Greeks, in destroying the city, also dishonored the gods and destroyed their shrines.

Therefore, a kind of dark cloud of anticipation hangs over the city, an expectation that some great suffering is about to occur. Their words in the play are meant to create a sense of dread in us. Invoking Zeus to unravel the complexities of the story and to reveal his mysterious plan, they address him as follows:

> "Zeus, who guided men to think,
> who has laid it down that wisdom comes alone through suffering.
> Still there drips in sleep against the heart
> grief of memory; against our pleasure we are temperate.
> From the gods who sit in grandeur
> grace comes somehow violent."

Then, recalling the horrific sacrifice that Agamemnon made of his own daughter Iphigenia at Aulis, they ominously observe,

> "Justice so moves that those only learn
> who suffer: and the future
> you shall know when it has come; before then, forget it.
> It is grief too soon given.
> All will come clear in the next dawn's sunlight."

Amid this air of anticipation, the herald of Agamemnon announces his arrival from Troy:

> "He comes, lord Agamemnon, bearing light in gloom
> to you, and to all that are assembled here.
> Salute him with good favor, as he well deserves,
> the man who has wrecked Troy with the spade of Zeus
> vindictive, whereby all their plain has been laid waste.
> Gone are their altars, the sacred places of the gods
> are gone, and scattered all the seed within the ground.
> With such a yoke as this gripped to the neck of Troy

he comes, the king, Atreus' elder son, a man
fortunate to be honored far above all men
alive . . ."

The herald, at least, believes strongly that Agamemnon has accomplished the
destruction of Troy righteously with the aid of Zeus.

With this grand announcement up rides Agamemnon to the palace gate,
newly returned from the war, and carrying with him in the chariot his greatest prize: Cassandra. Before he even steps off the chariot, he begins to brag
about his unmatched glory, his divinely sanctioned victory at Troy, his military skills, and, echoing the herald before him, he proclaims confidently how
he exacted the proper punishment on Troy. He fully expects the citizens and
his wife to welcome him home as a brilliant leader!

In the meantime Clytemnestra arrives to greet her husband, followed by her
servants who are carrying a purple tapestry which they spread out next to
the chariot. This purple tapestry, or "tinted splendors" as Agamemnon calls
it, she took from the temple of the gods: Only gods should walk on this
tapestry, and for any mortal to do so is to make a claim for divine status for
himself, that is, to equate himself with the gods.

At first Agamemnon refuses to walk on the purple, knowing that it will be a
sacrilege. But gradually Clytemnestra flatters him, and convinces him that
only someone who is really a god could have led the Greek army and sacked
the city of Troy. So without further hesitation, Agamemnon unlaces his
shoes and enters the palace.

Clytemnestra looks at Cassandra: "Come on in deary, the knife is sharpened
and we're going to make a sacrifice to the gods." Cassandra, who can see
the future, and can see what's about to happen in the house, begins to call
Apollo for help, and then, in a sudden fit of dementia, exclaims, "Ah, let the
bull beware! It is a robe she wraps him in, and strikes! Into the bath he
slumps heavily, drowned in blood. Such her skilled handicraft." Cassandra
also sees her own death coming, but no one outside the palace believes her.

Shortly after Cassandra herself is forced to enter the palace, the townspeo-
ple hear Agamemnon shout from within. "What's the matter, Agamemnon?"
"I've been struck a mortal blow!" he replies. Clytemnestra has him wrapped
up in a robe, pushed down into the bath tub, and she's hacking away with
an axe. The shouting, the shock of the bystanders, the hacking all continues
until Agamemnon is dead. Cassandra is then hacked to death too.
At this moment, Aegisthus comes in, supposedly her accomplice in all this
(some ancient authors have Aegisthus ambushing Agamemnon on his
return), and exults over the dead body of Agamemnon. Together they think
of 1) revenge for the death of Aegisthus' brothers, 2) revenge for the sacri-

fice of Iphigenia to Artemis, 3) revenge for the affair with Cassandra, and 4) revenge for the way Agamemnon destroyed the shrines and walked on the carpet. So the first play ends.

The Libation Bearers (sometimes called by its Greek title, Choephoroi)

Several years later, after Clytemnestra and Aegisthus have been living in the palace and ruling over Mycenae with impunity, Clytemnestra has a dream. She dreams she gives birth to a snake, who immediately turns around and bites her on the nipple. She is afraid this is a terrible omen of things to come. She and Aegisthus have done all they can to ensure that no harm comes to themselves. They have sent the son of Agamemnon, Orestes, off into exile, lest he turn on them as he gets older and take revenge. They have taken Agamemnon's other remaining child, Electra, and essentially locked her up, so that no young man of Mycenae might fall for her and thus become her ally in revenge.

But now Clytemnestra sends out Electra to pour libations on the tomb of Agamemnon in hopes of appeasing his spirit. Electra, however, sits at the tomb, weeping, wondering where Orestes is, or who will ever come to overthrow her mother and avenge her father. Suddenly, Orestes appears, together with his friend Pylades, returned home from exile, driven by the Furies, who avenge murders, and by the commands of Apollo, who ultimately has a nobler plan in mind. After a rather ridiculous recognition scene (the two siblings haven't seen each other for years and years, but recognize each other by comparing footprints and such nonsense), Electra and Orestes together plot the murder of Clytemnestra and Aegisthus, invoking the spirit of Agamemnon for strength and the proper amount of righteous indignation. Orestes then enters the palace disguised as a traveler announcing, ironically, the death of Orestes. Clytemnestra is thrilled with the news, and so sends a servant to summon Aegisthus. When Aegisthus comes, Orestes meets with him privately and kills him. But during the act Clytemnestra hears the screams of her new husband, who shouts the enigmatic, "Help! The dead are killing the living!" She realizes what's going on, and calls for her "man-slaying" axe, but it's too late. Orestes enters with his sword drawn.

As Orestes backs Clytemnestra into a corner, she pleads for mercy, reminding him that she cared for him as a child, and that his father deserved to die. In a last desperate move, she rips off her upper garment and exposes her breasts to Orestes, asking him if he will now bloody the very breasts on which he suckled as a baby. Orestes hesitates, but Pylades reminds him of his duty (the *lex talionis* leaves no room for mercy) and the commands of Apollo. So he rams the sword through her chest, ending, or really continuing, the chain of murders.

But even though he had to do it, even though he had to commit what ordinarily would be unthinkable, Orestes feels guilt. Once again the Furies come, this time sent by Clytemnestra ("bloodhounds of my mother's hate"), because no one else is left to avenge her death; they begin to chase Orestes and drive him mad: "They come like gorgons, they wear robes of black, and they are wreathed in a tangle of snakes . . . repulsive for the blood drops of their dripping eyes. I can no longer stay." He flees Mycenae (Argos) as the chorus of libation bearers reviews the tragic events thus far:

> "Here on this house of the kings the third
> storm has broken, with wind
> from the inward race, and gone its course.
> The children were eaten: there was the first
> affliction, the curse of Thyestes.
> Next came the royal death, when a man
> and lord of Achaean armies went down
> killed in the bath. Third
> is for the savior. He came. Shall I call
> it that, or death? Where
> is the end? Where shall the fury of fate
> be stilled to sleep, be done with?"

So the second play ends.

The Eumenides

Orestes flees to the temple of Apollo at Delphi, but the Furies pursue him there, and Clytemnestra goads them on in the form of a ghost, demanding justice. Inside the temple, where Orestes has found some measure of refuge, Apollo tells Orestes to flee to Athens, if he can make it, to Athena's temple on the Acropolis, because only she in her wisdom can free him from the Furies' tortures and the tortures of guilt.

To make a long story short, Athena sets up the first trial by jury, comprised of twelve Athenians, on the Areopagus (Mars' Hill), with herself as judge. On the prosecution side, the Furies must argue their case, then Orestes must stand up and speak in his own defense.

The Furies argue on their side that they are the oldest law in the universe and cannot be overturned no matter what. It is their right; justice, to their mind, is simple vengeance. At any rate, they say, if they aren't honored, they will destroy Athens.

Orestes argues that, first, Apollo commanded him to kill Clytemnestra, so he really had no choice. Furthermore, he argues, that the true parent is not the mother, who merely carries the child, but the father, whose seed the mother receives. To prove this he uses the analogy of planting, where the earth is just the receptacle and nurturer, while the sower provides the actual seed. Knowledge of DNA came later! His point is this: No one can accuse him of killing his *parent*, which is the charge at hand, since his mother is not a true parent. The argument is lame, but it's all Orestes had to work with.

The vote of the jury is a tie (Orestes needed a majority to win), but Athena casts the deciding vote in favor of Orestes. The Furies are angry still, but she appeases them by giving them a new role and name, Eumenides (Kindly-minded Ones), and a grotto in the city of Athens where they will be honored. They agree that this arrangement is satisfactory, and so the third play ends.

ORESTES AND IPHIGENIA

You may wonder what happened to Orestes, his friend Pylades, and Iphigenia after the blood feud was ended by Athena. The sacrifice of Iphigenia had brought about the anger of Clytemnestra and the horror and disgust of the citizens, but in reality Iphigenia survived the events at Aulis. Artemis, some ancient mythographers relate, rescued her from the altar at the last second and, unbeknownst to the onlookers, substituted a deer in her place. Some depictions of the sacrifice of Iphigenia on vase paintings show Agamemnon's daughter morphing, so to speak, into a deer. According to this version, Artemis whisked Iphigenia away to a distant, barbaric land called Tauris, which is identified with the modern-day peninsula Crimea on the northern side of the Black Sea in modern Ukraine. There she was made to serve in the temple of a somewhat uncivil manifestation of Artemis worshiped there. This Artemis demanded that all foreigners who came to the shore of Tauris be sacrificed to her in the temple. Thus Iphigenia is commissioned with carrying out the same gruesome task that she herself fell victim to at Aulis.

Some mythographers say that Orestes, still driven mad by Furies who were unsatisfied with Athena's decision, came by chance to the very shores of Tauris where Iphigenia served as priestess. Both Orestes and Pylades swing their swords wildly into the empty air and shriek and moan madly because they themselves sense the presence of their oppressors, the Furies. After some tense moments when it seems that Iphigenia will sacrifice her own brother Orestes unawares, the two siblings recognize each other. Since Iphigenia is held at Tauris against her will by the local king Thoas, the two plot an escape. They also plan to rescue the image of Artemis from the temple and to take it with them. They had almost made their escape good when king Thoas realizes what is happening and calls his soldiers to cut them off. In the end, Athena again has to intervene. She tells Thoas that everything that is taking place, the arrival of Orestes, the escape of Iphigenia, and the stealing of the sacred statue, all were ordained by Apollo. Then she orders Orestes to return to Athens and near there, in a place called Halae, to erect a temple to Artemis as a shrine for the newly recovered image. There, she says, Greeks will come to celebrate the fact that once the gods demanded human sacrifice and blood to pay for sins, but now they allow for a substitute, just as a deer had been substituted for Iphigenia at Aulis. Athena ordered Iphigenia herself to Brauron, also near Athens, where she is to hold the keys to the temple of Artemis there and to teach young girls how to put to death their old selves, so to speak, as they make the transition from girlhood to womanhood.

CHAPTER TWENTY
Oedipus

"Whom have the gods and divinities that share their altar and the thronging assembly of men ever admired so much as they honored Oedipus at that time when he removed that baneful, man-raping plague called 'the Sphinx' from our land."

—Aeschylus, *Seven Against Thebes* 773ff.

The story of Oedipus begins with Labdacus, a king of Thebes and grandson of Cadmus, the founder of Thebes and slayer of the dragon of Ares who once presided over that land. You may recall from the story of Dionysus that this is the family that includes Pentheus, Agave, Semele, and Dionysus himself. Although Labdacus only ruled a short time, and was fairly insignificant at that, the line of kings that he produced is from then on called "The House of Labdacus." His one great distinction is that he lost a battle with Athens over a border dispute and died shortly thereafter. He left behind, however, an infant son, Laius, who was too young to take the throne at his father's death. Regency, temporary rule, was given to a fellow named Lycus, who, as you might expect, enjoyed his power and devised ways to rid himself of the eventual true heir to the throne. Because of the threat, supporters of the descendants of Cadmus whisked the infant Laius away to live with Pelops in Elis near Olympia. Their main desire was to preserve the Cadmeian line. Some authors say that the child was sent into exile by Lycus himself.

Regardless, Antiope, the niece of Labdacus, had relations with Zeus and became pregnant. Lycus thought she brought shame on the family and on the city, so he sent her off to live in another city. Later, however, he became worried that somehow she might produce new heirs to the throne, or something like that, so he dragged her back to Thebes. On the way, she bore two sons and left them in the bushes in the mountains. They were "exposed," that is, left out to die in the elements, but eventually a shepherd rescued them and reared them to be tough. He named them Amphion and Zethus. As you may have already recognized, there are many elements in this story that match the Romulus and Remus one—the niece becomes pregnant, bears Zeus' twin sons who are rescued by a shepherd, and so on.

A silver denarius minted by T. Carisius, 46 B.C. Head of Sibyl and seated Sphinx.

These kinds of stories follow a predictable pattern.

Meanwhile, back at Thebes, Lycus is ruling with terror and violence, and his wife Dirce spends her free time torturing poor Antiope whom she keeps locked up in a cell. Years later, when the boys reach manhood, they hear the whole story from the shepherd, and naturally become enraged. So one day when Dirce is on the mountain worshiping Dionysus, they track her down, tie her to the horns of a bull, and let her be dragged to death. Then Amphion and Zethus make their way to Thebes, where they overcome Lycus, seize the throne and free their mother. As rulers they gain fame for building the city walls of Thebes, known for its seven large gates. The two rule together peaceably, Amphion using his skills as an artist to help the city, Zethus being a man of action. Unfortunately, the two boys die young, leaving the throne vacant again.

Now, at long last, the throne is open for Laius, the rightful heir. As you recall, he is living with Pelops in Elis. Pelops, whose father Tantalus had once attempted to feed him to the gods, was himself the father of Atreus (father of the Greek general of the Trojan War, Agamemnon) and Thyestes, but also two other boys, Pittheus and Chrysippus. After all those years of living in the palace, Laius has fallen in love with Pelops' young son Chrysippus, so that one day, on the pretext of giving him chariot lessons, he kidnaps the boy and rides off with him. Pelops utters a curse on the house and line of Laius, which proves accurate and fatal.

Laius goes to Thebes, seizes the empty throne, and marries a woman named Jocasta, daughter of a Theban aristocrat and sister of an impressive young man named Creon. Together the two set themselves up as absolute rulers over Thebes. Sadly, though, the two cannot have children, and since heirs are crucial to rulers, Laius goes to consult the oracle at Delphi to find out why. The loxian (ambiguous) answer comes back: "You will have a child that will kill you and marry your wife." Laius' reaction to the oracle is typical: He imagines that he can thwart the oracle by taking some course of action, whereas that very course of action sets the oracle's predicted chain of events into motion. When he returns to Thebes, he and Jocasta decide to abstain from sex, but one day he became drunk and impregnated Jocasta anyway. They kept the child for six months, since obviously they cherished it and wanted one so badly, but the oracle's words kept gnawing at them, so they decided to get rid of it through the ancient practice of exposure. They gave it to one of their household servants and told him to expose the baby on the mountain (Mt. Cithaeron, to be exact). They drive a stake through the poor baby's ankles so he can't crawl away or come after them when he's dead.

The servant who took the baby (as yet unnamed) to Mt. Cithaeron, did as he was commanded, leaving the crying child in the bushes to die. But the servant took pity on the baby, so when he chanced upon a Corinthian shepherd pasturing his flocks on the mountain, he told him about the abandoned child and begged him to rescue the baby. The shepherd, it turns out, worked for the king of Corinth, so he turned the child over to his master. King Polybus and Queen Merope reared the child as their own and named him "Oedipus," which means "swollen foot," a name that refers to the stake driven through his feet as an infant.

One day, after many years had passed, Oedipus was attending a banquet in his father's palace. One of the guests, who had become drunk with wine, began to taunt the arrogant young Oedipus that he was not actually the son of King Polybus and did not deserve to think so highly of himself. Oedipus was distraught and confronted his parents, but they insisted that he was really their birth son. Oedipus doubted, however, and decided to pack his bags and head for the oracle at Delphi to check on the veracity of their claims. So, despite his parents' vehement objections, Oedipus left Corinth never to return.

When Oedipus arrived at Delphi he posed his question to the priests and the Pythian Sibyl there. He wanted to know, specifically, if Polybus and Merope were his true parents. The enigmatic reply came back that he would one day kill his father and marry his mother. To Oedipus, this did not seem to relate to the question that he had asked, or, perhaps, it assumed that Polybus was his real father and was predicting that he would kill him. Therefore, Oedipus determined to stay as far away from Corinth as he possibly could, and thus, like Laius before him, try to thwart the prediction of the oracle. As he left Delphi, though, he came to a crossroads where he met a man on a chariot accompanied by a large train of servants. Since Oedipus did not want to yield the right-of-way to this obviously important individual, nor did the stranger want to yield to Oedipus, an altercation broke out among them. Oedipus cut in front of the stranger's chariot, and the stranger took his scepter (he was a king) and struck Oedipus on the head, a kind of early road rage. Oedipus struck back, and before it was over, he had killed the king and all of his servants save one, who managed to escape.

Oedipus continued his journey away from Delphi and Corinth until he came to the outskirts of the city of Thebes. There he found the city oppressed under a heavy curse. Hera had become angry that Laius had loved Chrysippus, Laius' son, and so had sent the monstrous Sphinx (see below) to plague the city (according to one prominent tradition among many explanations about her origins). She sat outside the city and harassed anyone who came in or out of the city, and vowed that she would not go away until someone answered her riddle. If any passerby or inhabitant of the city attempted and failed, she would tear him apart. Creon, who was temporarily ruling over the city, offered the kingship to anyone who could solve the riddle.

In this context, Oedipus, decked out with his traveling hat and carrying a walking stick, met her as he approached the city of Thebes. She stopped him and demanded that he answer her riddle: "What creature," she said, "goes on four legs in the morning, two at noon, and three in the evening, and is strongest when walking on the least?" Oedipus contemplated the question, knowing that his life was in danger, and then gave the correct response: "Man, who crawls on four in the morning of his life, walks on two in the prime of his life, and then uses a cane in the eve of his life." At least one ancient author says that Oedipus had learned the answer in a dream sent from the gods. The Sphinx shrieked in horror that someone had answered her riddle "that had baffled earlier brains" (Ovid, *Met.* 7.759) and immediately threw herself from the rock on which she was perched. She died. Some versions of the myth say that she was so startled that she let her guard down and Oedipus attacked her with his sword. In either case, she died according to the terms of an oracle from Delphi, which had set the conditions of the curse over Thebes.

Fresh from his success with the riddle, Oedipus entered into the city an instant hero. The people rejoiced and rewarded him with the hand of the recently widowed queen in marriage, making Oedipus king of Thebes. The queen, as you may have guessed, was Jocasta, and the two of them had four children, the most famous being Antigone. After ten years of marriage, however, a new plague came upon the city, this time as a result of the mysterious and unresolved murder of King Laius years before.

It is at this point that the well-known story told by the Greek playwright Sophocles in *Oedipus the King* picks up. In short, Oedipus discovers that he has killed his own father, as the oracle of Delphi had predicted, and married his mother. Jocasta hanged herself in despair, while Oedipus blinded himself out of shame for seeing what he never should have seen. Jocasta's brother Creon takes over the throne and sends Oedipus into exile, where he is accompanied by his faithful, loving daughter Antigone. Eventually, Oedipus' two sons, Eteocles and Polyneices, battle for the throne of Thebes, resulting in the death of both of them simultaneously. Oedipus himself dies in Colonus near Athens during the reign of Theseus and is taken up to live with the gods as a hero. Oedipus died in misery and shame, but his tomb was venerated as a source of power and redemption.

The story of the death of Oedipus at Colonus is full of religious feeling and mystery, but the stories of what happened to his children after his death are marked by misery. The two sons were supposed to share power in Thebes in alternate years, but their stubborness resulted in the famous "seven against Thebes" myth. As mentioned, the end of this story has the two sons fighting in one-on-one combat and killing one another. Meanwhile, Antigone, who was set to marry a young man named Haemon, son of Creon, killed herself in protest of Creon's refusal to bury one of her brothers, Polyneices, since he had attacked Thebes to win the throne. In essence, the family line ended disastrously (though Eteocles and Polyneices did have children), and it seemed to any onlooker that the gods had planned it that way from the very beginning.

The story of Oedipus played well with the Greeks. It became a vehicle for them to talk about some of the most important problems of human existence: personal guilt and predestination; our limitations as human beings and the import of the maxim, "know yourself"; the possibility for redemption and forgiveness in the face of horrific transgression; and the tenuous nature of success and happiness. All these are complex issues and not easily resolved by the telling of one story, but it is interesting to see that the story of Oedipus envisions a universe in which, if gods and men work in tandem, each in their respective roles and meeting specific responsibilities, all things work together for the good.

A Note on the Sphinx

An ominous and colorful description of the Sphinx appears in the Roman poet Statius' work entitled *Thebaid* (2.500ff.):

> "At a distance from Thebes two hills bear close upon each other with a grudging gulf between; the shadow of a mountain above and leafy ridges of curving woodland shut them in . . . Through the middle of the rocks threads a rough and narrow track, below which lies a plain and a broad expanse of sloping fields. Over against it a threatening cliff rises high, the home of the winged monster of Oedipus [the Sphinx]; here long ago she stood, fiercely uplifting her pallid cheeks, her eyes tainted with corruption and her plumes all clotted with hideous gore; grasping human remains and clutching to her breast half-eaten bones she scanned the plains with awful gaze, should any stranger dare to join in the strife of riddling words, or any traveler confront her and parley with her terrible tongue; then, without more ado, sharpening at once the unsheathed talons of her ashen hands and her teeth bared for wounding, she rose with dreadful beating of wings around the faces of the strangers; nor did any guess her riddle, until a hero that proved her match caught her, with failing wings—ah! horror!—from the bloody cliff she dashed her insatiate belly in despair upon the rocks beneath. The wood gives reminder of the dread story: the cattle abhor the neighboring pastures, and the flock, though greedy, will not touch the fateful herbage; no Dryad choirs take delight in the shade, the sacred rites of the satyrs seem unfit for this place, and even the lowliest of birds fly far from the abomination of the grove."

The Sphinx was a monstrous creature having the wings of a bird of prey, the body of a lion, the talons of a vulture, the tail of a serpent, and the face and upper body of a woman. She may have been the child of one of the giants that Gaia sent against Zeus in the Gigantomachy, perhaps also of Geryon's dog. One ancient historicizing explanation even presents her as a daughter of Laius who was attempting to keep rivals away from his throne. As for her place of birth, the Greeks themselves believed that she originated from Ethiopia or Egypt, which suggests that she is a modification of the Egyptian creature of the same name. Even so, there are important differences between the two. The Egyptian Sphinx has no wings and typically guards the entrances to temples or watches over religious sites. The Greek Sphinx takes on any pose the artists desires and can adorn tombs or the facades of public buildings. On the throne of Zeus in his temple at Olympia the artist depicted several of them ravishing small children. The playwright Aeschylus describes a warrior's shield on which is bolted down an image of "the Sphinx, who eats men raw." Whatever her lineage and origins, for the Greeks she was almost exclusively associated with this story of Oedipus.

Hera, as we have noted, sent her to Thebes to punish the city for Laius' sins. She plagued the city by demanding that the inhabitants answer her riddle(s), else she would devour one citizen per day. She is also said to have perched herself on a nearby mountain to devour passers-by if they could not answer her riddle. Besides the riddle that she asked Oedipus, we know that she also asked a riddle about two sisters: "There are two sisters: one gives birth to the other and she in turn gives birth to the first." The answer (it makes more sense in Greek) is "Day and Night."

CHAPTER TWENTY-ONE

Jason and the Argonauts; Medea

"When Medea's witch-poison had consumed Jason's new bride, and the sea on either side had seen the royal palace all in flames, her wicked sword was drenched in her sons' blood; and, accomplishing in this way a mother's vile revenge, she fled from Jason's sword. Her Dracon team, the Titan-Dracones, carried her away to Athens."

—Ovid, Metamorphoses 7.391ff.

JASON AND THE ARGONAUTS

The story of Jason and the Argonauts contains many elements common to folk tales: magic, mystical creatures and dragons, an evil stepmother, a sacrificial ram, a man with one sandal, a dangerous voyage to complete an impossible task, the help of a girl who staves off the evil king by throwing impediments in his path. The story is so complex that we can only imagine that it must have accrued many details over the centuries and been used for many purposes. In the form that the tale has come to us we can detect a keen interest on the part of its composers in geography, sailing, and expansionism.

We must begin in Orchomenus, a town in central Greece near Thebes, where King Athamas had two children by the name of Phrixus and Helle. For whatever reason, Athamas divorced his first wife and married Ino, who turned out to be an evil stepmother. She was so jealous of Athamas' children by his first marriage that she devised this trick: She had the women of Orchomenus roast the crop seeds before they were to be planted so that they would not grow. When the farmers noticed that the crops were not springing up, the oracle at Delphi was consulted, but Ino had bribed the priests to say that Athamas must sacrifice his son Phrixus to Zeus in order to recover the fertility of the seeds. Athamas was ready to cut his son's throat at the altar when an amazing ram appeared with a fleece spun of gold. Possibly Athamas' first wife had appealed to the gods to rescue her son from doom. At any rate, the ram, which could talk as well, instructed Phrixus to mount his back, along with his sister Helle, and off they flew to the east toward Asia. The two children clutched tightly to the ram's back, but at some point Helle could not hold on any longer and fell into the sea

161

An Electrum Hekte from Cyzicus, near where Jason and the Argonauts encountered the Harpies. The reverse shows a Harpy holding a tunny fish.

where she died. The place where she fell, the spot where Europe and Asia meet, took on the name "Hellespont." Later it was called "Dardanelles."

Phrixus made it all the way to Colchis on the eastern end of the Black Sea, a region ruled by king Aeetes. Phrixus put the ram to death—such gratitude!—sacrificing him to Zeus. After making good with the king, Phrixus married his daughter Chalciope. Soon an oracle came to king Aeetes that a Greek stranger would destroy his kingdom, and so, assuming that Phrixus was the stranger, he killed him. Phrixus' four sons were able to escape to a nearby island, however, from where they eventually served as guides to the Argonauts in the last stages of their journey.

Well, that's how the golden fleece made its way to Colchis. But who was Jason? Jason was the son of Aeson, rightful king of Iolcus (modern-day Volos, whose promontory today is dominated by a Medieval castle, and which sits at the foot of Mt. Pelion in Thessaly). Pelias, Aeson's half brother, usurped the throne and imprisoned the king. Jason, who was still a child, was sent by his mother into hiding under the tutelage of Chiron, a benevolent centaur who trained other heroes as well (Achilles, Asclepius). Thessaly, as you recall from the story of Theseus and Pirithous, was the land of the Centaurs. As the years went by, Pelias received an oracle that he should "beware of a man with one sandal." Sure enough, during a certain festival when the people were making sacrifice to Poseidon, Jason, now grown, showed up to reclaim his rightful throne. On the way, by chance, he had helped an old woman (some say she was Hera in disguise) to cross a flooded stream, where he lost his sandal. Jason's minor show of heroism helped to fulfill the old oracle.

Now Pelias was not exactly surprised to see Jason show up one day, but he was distressed that, because it was a sacred festival time, he could not kill him outright. Anyway, Jason had many supporters, and the rules of hospitality demanded more tact. Pelias acknowledged Jason's right to the throne, but said that he should prove his worthiness by first fetching the golden fleece, which was in itself a symbol of royal power, of gold, and the wealth of Greece stolen by the East. Jason jumped at the chance for adventure.

Up until this time the Greeks had not done much boating or sailing, so a particularly gifted craftsman, Argus, had to be employed to build a ship that could handle such a long journey. Some of the wood used for the ship came from Dodona where Zeus had his ancinet oak tree through which he gave oracles. For this reason, the ship Argo, as it was called, had the ability to speak. Meanwhile, Jason invited heroes from all over Greece, with their special talents, to join him on his expedition. He assembled an amazing crew: Orpheus the musician, Pollux the boxer, Zetes and Calais, winged sons of the North Wind, Herakles and his boyfriend Hylas, Peleus, father of Achilles, and so on.

When the ship was completed and fitted with sails, the Argonauts (i.e., "sailors on the Argo") set forth on their journey from Iolcus to Colchis in the Black Sea. Their journey took them on countless adventures, not all of which can be recounted here, but certainly the highlights, as told in the novel *Argonautica* of the Hellenistic writer Apollonius of Rhodes, are worth noting.

The heroes first sailed past Mt. Athos in northern Greece and made their way to Lemnos, an island in the Aegean. There they found that the island was inhabited only by women. They came to this husbandless condition by insulting Aphrodite in some way, who punished them by causing an intolerable smell to come from their bodies. Their husbands refused to have sex with them, and, in fact, went over to Thrace and stole some women who subsequently bore them children. The Lemnian women were understandably jealous, so in a single night rose up and killed all the males on the island, down to the last boy. By the time the Argonauts arrive, though, the women are sex-crazed. But, then, so are the Argonauts, who apparently didn't notice the bad smell and so had their first adventure in the Lemnian bedrooms. Herakles himself preferred to stay onboard the ship with his boyfriend Hylas. After waiting for some time, he sent a grouchy letter to the men, congratulating them on their fabulous lovemaking, which was so full of irony that they all came back in shame to the ship.

The next major stop, after passing through the Hellespont into the Propontis, the anteroom, so to speak, to the Black Sea, was a headland called Bear Mountain where King Cyzicus ruled over the Doliones. An oracle had told him to be kind to strangers, so day and night he entertained the Greek heroes. Later, when the Greeks were back onboard their ship and setting sail, a wind caught them and blew them back at night. The Doliones thought some enemy was attacking them, and so a tremendous battle broke out. By morning their mistake became clear. Jason himself had killed Cyzicus with his spear in the throat. Many apologies were exchanged and the Argonauts sailed away a bit nervously.

Soon, the manly Herakles broke off his oar from his ferocious paddling. The heroes stopped at Mysia so they could cut down a tree for another one, and, in the meanwhile, Hylas went off to look for some water. While he was passing one particular pond, a water nymph saw him and dragged him under. Herakles heard his scream, but couldn't find him. In his distress he told the Argonauts they must sail on without him, because he couldn't give up his search.

Now the Argonauts reached the land of Bebryces, where a huge ugly brutish braggard named Amycus challenged all passers-by to box. Polydeuces, one of the Dioscuri brothers, floated like a butterfly and stung like a bee until one of his blows rammed a bone into the challenger's skull, at which the bully dropped dead.

In the northern edge of the Propontis the Argonauts found Phineus, punished by the gods for revealing too many secrets through his prophet powers. The gods blinded him and let him grow very old. Furthermore, they sent Harpies to torture him by defecating on all of his food. Zetes and Calais set a trap for the Harpies and defeated them, driving most of them away. Phineus repaid them by telling them about their future course in great detail, especially how to sail through the Symplegades, the "clashing rocks" that guarded the entrance to the Black Sea. These rocks would smash any ship that tried to pass through.

When the Argonauts reached the Black Sea, they sent a dove through the Symplegades first. When the rocks crashed together, as if some sort of trap had been sprung, the dove barely got through by losing a few tail feathers. Immediately, as the rocks recoiled, the heroes rowed through furiously. Of course, the recoiling of the rocks caused a whirlpool, but with a push from Athena, the heroes made it through, losing only the back tip of their ship, just as the dove had done. From then on the Symplegades remained stuck in place.

The Argonauts had many other adventures in the Black Sea: They saw Prometheus being gnawed at by Zeus' eagle, and they observed the special fluid called "ichor" that drips from his veins from which springs up a special flower with magical properties, later to be used by Medea. They saw the land of the Chalybes who dig for iron with never a holiday, whose resulting soot and smoke turn the sky black with pollution. They saw the Mossynoeci who had an opposite morality, doing what we do behind closed doors at home out in the open, and vice versa.

Finally Jason and the Argonauts reached Colchis. Aeetes received them badly, telling Jason he could take the fleece only if he first yoked two fire-breathing, bronze-hoofed bulls, then plowed up the ground, sowed dragons teeth left over from the monster that Cadmus had killed in founding Thebes, and then destroyed the armed warriors who would spring up from the teeth. Jason became depressed and gave up. In fact, Jason appears as an anti-hero throughout this whole story, constantly making poor decisions and exhibiting too little fortitude when it was needed. Fortunately, though, Medea, a daughter of Aeetes and perhaps Hecate, the goddess of sorcery, had fallen in love with him by the influence of the gods and so came to help him. She gave him an ointment that would protect him from the bulls' fire, and then told him that by throwing rocks between the warriors he could defeat them.

Thus Jason succeeded in foiling Aeetes. The king suspected Medea, but, before he could act, Medea led Jason to the fleece which stood in the grove sacred to Ares, put the dragon that guarded it to sleep, and helped Jason grab the prize. Medea, taking her brother along, joined Jason on board the Argo to sail away with him back to Greece. The brother proved useful, but not as he himself might have hoped. As Aeetes pursued the Argonauts, Medea cut off parts of her brother and threw them into the water. Aeetes felt obligated to retrieve those body parts so as to give them proper burial, thus slowing his progress until the Argonauts got away.

Back in Iolcus, the rumor spread that the Argo had sunk with all hands aboard. Pelias congratulated himself on being the first human to escape the fate predicted by an oracle and decided to finish off his half brother Aeson; he graciously permitted the old man to kill himself by drinking bull's blood (a deadly poison!) at a sacrifice. Aeson's wife, Jason's mother, ran screaming into the palace, cursed the king, and killed herself with a sword. She left a young son, but Pelias killed him too.

Jason's voyage had lasted four months. When he unexpectedly returned and presented the fleece to Pelias, the haughty king accepted it but showed no sign of relinquishing the throne. Medea saw a way of getting rid of him which required the aid of his daughters. Pelias, whose power only old age could challenge, could be made young again through her magic, Medea explained. To show what she meant, she cut up a decrepit old ram, threw the pieces into a pot, threw in some special herbs and bat gizzards and so forth, boiled them for several hours, then removed the top. Out popped a frisky young lamb and scampered off to the meadows.

The daughters were persuaded that Medea could help their father. That night they sneaked into their father's chamber, chopped him into pieces, and brought the pieces to Medea. She cooked them for several hours, then removed the lid to reveal a thick, murky, evil-smelling soup, not at all the young king she had promised them. She apologized profusely, admitting that she must have omitted an important ingredient or two.

The Iolcans were shocked and appalled by her barbaric inhumanity. For them she fit the stereotype of the eastern woman: exotic, magical, uncivilized, and dangerous. Thus, after they gave the dead king state honors, they drove out Medea and Jason from the city forever.

The couple then traveled to Corinth and settled there in a kind of common-law marriage (Greeks could not legally marry foreigners). Jason dedicated his ship at a shrine of Poseidon nearby. They lived relatively happily for years and Medea bore two sons. But Jason was running out of money, was tired of the foreign woman and the life of retirement, and arranged with King Creon to marry his daughter Glauce, or Creusa. He needed only to get rid of Medea to fulfill his ambitions, and since he didn't hold her in much esteem anyway, the task seemed a minor obstacle. Jason's attempts to rid himself of Medea is the subject of Euripides' famous play *Medea*.

MEDEA

Euripides' well-known story of Jason's abandonment of Medea and the subsequent tragedy is one of the most striking and controversial tales to come out of antiquity. Here we have the insensitive Jason playing the part of the typical male chauvinist pig by dismissing his long-held companion and mother of his children without a thought or care for her well-being or for anything but himself. As a male in a male-dominated society, he has certain powers and advantages that he is all too willing to abuse for his own benefit. "It would have been better far for men," he proclaims to Medea, "to have got their children in some other way, and women not to have existed. Then life would have been good." Jason can only see women as a nuisance and a means to a self-serving end. Medea, however, is not at all the compliant, weak and sniveling female the average Greek would have been used to. She was a sorceress and foreigner, and unwilling to be trampled upon by Jason's aspirations. One consideration drives the plot of the entire story, therefore: With what can Medea, suffering intensely the common plight of women, find some leverage to exercise her own power and take charge of the situation. In other words, how can she do battle with Jason who has all the obvious advantages?

Medea does indeed find the strength that she possesses. "A woman," she says, "dreads the sight of cold steel, and shrinks from contending with the sword face to face with a man, but wronged in love no other soul can hold so many thoughts of blood." She turns to her own "magical powers" as a woman to fight back. True, Medea was the niece of Circe, the magical goddess whom Odysseus would face, and she worshiped the goddess of black magic, Hecate, but to concentrate our attention on *that* kind of magic would be to miss the point of the story. Medea turns to the same magical powers with which Pandora was once endowed and that all women possess: She has the ability to charm and seduce, to make men weak with her womanly wiles; she faces her foe with deceit and machinations rather than with head-on confrontation; and, most of all, men need her to have children, their protection against old age and their only hope of immortality. By procreation, men pass on their seed and in a sense can live forever. Medea, therefore, taps into her own sources of womanly power to do battle with Jason, to harm him in the most brutal and profane way imaginable, to cut him off from immortality by ending his present bloodline and blocking any chance he has of starting over again. Her victory will be personally devastating but nonetheless unyielding. She has one goal, to crush those who crossed her and to be "dangerous to her enemies." Medea escapes punishment at the hands of Jason and the citizens of Corinth by escaping on her grandfather Helios' chariot drawn by flying dragons. She makes her way to Athens where she joins Aegeus and plays a role in the Theseus saga. Jason, on the other hand, dies in shame and despair underneath the Argo hanging in the temple of Poseidon at Sounion. Some authors, however, say that Jason returned to Iolcus where, with the help of the Dioscuri brothers, he seized control of the town and ruled for many years.

CHAPTER TWENTY-TWO
Roman Myths

"People nowadays may ridicule religious ceremonies, saying, 'What does it matter if the sacred chickens don't eat or are slow in leaving their coop [the Romans used chickens to divine the will of the gods]?' These are trivial things. But our ancestors made Rome great by not despising these trivial things, whereas we profane all rituals, as if there was no longer any need for the *pax deorum* ("peace of the gods")."

—Livy 6.41

Although we often lump the Greeks and the Romans together to speak about a "Greco-Roman" this or that, in fact the Romans were significantly different from the Greeks in many ways. The Romans had culturally unique influences from their geography, racial origins, historical experiences, and language that created in them religious and social patterns of thought as well as economic and political institutions distinct from those of the Greeks. The Romans themselves, for example, recognized that they possessed superior skills of organization and administration that allowed them to run an empire on a grand scale with a Senate and a well-tuned bureaucracy at the helm. Everyone knew his or her place in the social order. They had running water (aqueducts), sewers, public baths, regular recreational events, welfare programs, etc., things we take for granted because we derived them from the Romans.

Romans also believed that they were more practically minded than the Greeks. The Roman thinker Cicero observes that the Greeks muse endlessly about grand theoretical problems, such as the nature of man, epistemological difficulties, and mathematical theorems. The Romans, he says, concern themselves with how to build a better catapult, or how best to instill valor and virtue in the populace, how to govern more efficiently, how exactly to balance clemency and law, and how to obtain and distribute grain for the masses.

For the Romans, myth was bound up in their history, for which reason we think of them as legends more than myths. Most of their myths were designed to elicit support for certain social ideals and ways of behaving; to help define what is important for the populace; and to help the people make decisions about behavior (such as self-sacrifice for the common good). In the end, it did not matter so much if the story that they told was true; to the

Sextus Pompeius Faustulus, 137 B.C. A silver denarius, c. 137 B.C. Helmeted head of Roma (personified Rome). The reverse show the she-wolf suckling Romulus and Remus beneath a tree with the shepherd Faustulus behind.

Romans, it was true enough if it served its function. Our story of George Washington and the cherry tree is similar. But for the Romans, all myth, legend, and religion could be viewed this way. The Roman poet Ovid once said, "It is convenient to suppose that gods exist and, since it is convenient, let us so suppose." Whatever worked, whatever provided some social, ethical, or political benefit, that's what the Romans wanted to believe.

The earliest Roman gods, before the influence of Greeks from southern Italy, were remote and colorless *numina*, or "divine wills." The Latin word *numen* (pl. *numina*) comes from the verb meaning "to nod," that is, to indicate with the movement of the head one's assent or disapproval. Thus the earliest Roman gods were simply "the nodders," nebulous, mysterious powers that pervade everything, countless in number. Every object, every duty, every action had some *numen* attached to it. There were even divinities concerned with beard cutting or the wailing of babies. And, of course, there were more important divinities who watched over boundaries between properties (the god Terminus), gods to keep weeds out of gardens, or to watch over gateways (the god Janus). Still, these were not divinities with personalities or stories attached to them. What was more important to the Romans was the interconnection between their divinities, particularly the family relationships, and the means to obtain the *pax deorum*, a peaceful and harmoniously relationship with the gods (see the Livy quote at the beginning of this chapter).

The Romans had a very legalistic approach to dealing with these divinities. For example, the divinity Robigo ("blight of the crops") was sacrificed to regularly on April 25th of each year. In a well-choreographed ceremony, a priest would offer Robigo a bribe of wine, incense, the gut of a sheep, and the entrails of a filthy red dog. This precise sacrifice was part of a deal struck with the gods, a legal transfer of ownership of this stuff to the *numen*. In return, the *numen* was supposed to fulfill its function of keeping blight off the crops. Thus the Romans were very ritualistic and concerned with precise language of prayers, invocations, oaths (like the language of a legal contract), and they saw their priests as lawyers of a sort. In fact, if a single mistake was made during the ceremony, the Roman priest would have to start the whole ritual over again from the beginning.

As the Romans came into contact with the Greeks, they applied the stories of that people to their own *numina* that most closely touched on the related function. Jupiter, who had been a vague *numen* of the weather, was equated to Zeus and took on his stories. At times the matches were not very precise: Minerva, a goddess of weaving, was equated with Athena, who wove, true, but much more. Apollo had no counterpart among the Roman *numina*, so he was taken over name and all.

The Romans too had their own gods for which the Greeks had no equivalent: the Lares and Penates, for example, very important to the Romans, were household gods who watched over the people and things in the house. Janus, the biform god, is also unique. Then, too, the Romans made more of Vesta (= Hestia, goddess of the hearth) than the Greeks ever did, because they believed that the State was one large family. Therefore, they had a State religion, complete with Vestal Virgins and public sacrifices, devoted to Vesta to ask her to keep the populace united as one big happy family. The Vestal Virgins kept a flame lit in the temple of Vesta that was supposed to be a reminder of the hearth of a home, symbolizing the fact that the State is simply an enlarged and extended family.

THE FOUNDING OF ROME

The Romans believed that the their race began from remnants of refugees who escaped from Troy on the night the Greeks ransacked the city. These refugees built ships over the course of the year after Troy fell and set sail westward, uncertain where they should relocate. They were led by the Trojan hero Aeneas, who was bringing with him his little son Ascanius (later called Iulus) and the "household gods," the Lares and Penates. Aeneas himself was the child of Anchises, a son of Zeus, and the goddess Aphrodite. A prophecy given before his birth predicted that he and his descendants would rule over the Trojans for all eternity. After years of adventures on the high seas, this weary and decimated group reached the western shores of Italy at a place called Latium. There, after many battles and much intrigue, they allied themselves with the Latins and even made friendships with the Greeks who were living in southern Italy. Aeneas founded the city Lavinium, while his son founded the city Alba Longa. In making contact with some Greeks in the area, Aeneas, according to Vergil, visited the site of future Rome, where king Evander governed a small settlement called Pallanteum (the Romans later called one of the seven hills of Rome the "Palatine"). This is the same Evander who some years before Aeneas' arrival honored Hercules with an altar and cult after the hero had destroyed the monster Cacus.

After the death of Aeneas, the power of this Trojan-Latin race shifted to Alba Longa, where Aeneas' descendants ruled. First Iulus ruled, then Aeneas' grandson Silvius. Generations passed, about five hundred years, in fact, but still Aeneas' descendants held power in Alba Longa. That firm grip began to slip, however, during the reign of a certain Numitor. Although king Numitor was the rightful heir to the throne, he had tried to share some of his good fortune and wealth with his brother Amulius. Not satisfied with a portion of the inheritance, Amulius plotted against Numitor and eventually seized the throne itself. He imprisoned his brother and made the former king's daughter Rhea Sylvia become a Vestal Virgin. Since Vestal Virgins were supposed to abstain from all sexual contact, he figured, she would not be able to produce a rival for him.

Despite her status as a Vestal Virgin, Rhea Sylvia became pregnant and gave birth to twin boys. She defended this sacrilege and pollution of her sanctified body by insisting that the god Mars had come upon her and fathered the children, but Amulius turned a deaf ear to her declarations. He imprisoned Rhea Sylvia and had his servants cast the two boys into the nearby Tiber river. Now the Tiber at that time was overflowing its banks because of recent heavy rains. The servants who were supposed to throw the boys into the river were not even able to reach it, so they placed them into a basket and pushed it into the overflow. The basket floated for awhile, but soon the waters receded and left the basket on dry land. Miraculously, a she-wolf who was suckling her own pups at the time discovered the crying infants and shared her milk with them. The she-wolf moved the boys to a spot that was later called the "Lupercal" (in Latin "lupus" means "wolf") at the foot of the Palatine hill, where a large fig tree grew and a spring bubbled up out of a cave.

Before long a shepherd named Faustulus stumbled upon the strange scene of a wolf suckling two human boys. He drove off the animal and took the boys to his wife to rear. Already, though, we see that the boys in the myth are beginning to fulfill the typical heroic pattern. They had a miraculous birth (the god impregnated a virgin), they faced danger in infancy (they were thrown into the Tiber), and experienced a sign of divine favor (a she-wolf suckled them in the wild). In the house of the shepherd they have their time of withdrawal and preparation. As they grow, they exhibit the marks of their noble and divine parentage. In their teenage years they are able to defeat and drive off the bandits who harass the shepherds and farmers in the area around the Tiber. When they reach manhood, their adoptive father tells them about their rescue from the wolf and how their discovery coincided with the exposure of the twins born to Rhea Sylvia. Convinced of their regal heritage, Romulus and Remus, as they are called, determine to restore their father to the throne while freeing their mother. Leading a group of herdsmen to the house of their uncle Amulius, the twins make a surprise attack and kill him. The people of Alba Longa welcomed this turn of events— Amulius had been anything but benevolent to them—and gladly acclaimed Numitor as their rightful king.

Romulus and Remus were satisfied that they had avenged the wrong done against their family, but they were much too heroic and adventuresome to stay at Alba Longa under their father's rule. They decided to return to the spot where they had been discovered as infants to found their own city. Each of the young men with their band of followers went to the hills on the banks of the Tiber and began to build city walls, Romulus on the Palatine hill and Remus on the Aventine. A dispute arose among the two groups, however, about what the new city would be called and who would be the king. Each looked for a sign from the gods. The followers of Remus began to rejoice when they saw six vultures flying over the Aventine hill, surely a sign that the gods favored his undertaking. Shortly thereafter, though, Romulus' followers spotted twelve vultures flying over the Palatine hill. Was it better to see six vultures first, or twelve vultures second? Remus was not happy. He leapt over Romulus' partially built walls and declared, "This is what your enemies are going to do to you!" The angered Romulus drew his sword, and while driving it into his brother exclaimed, "And this is what will happen to them!" After that, the dispute was settled. Romulus would be the first king and the city would take the name Rome.

Romulus ruled over the fledgling city of Rome for thirty-three years. During his reign the so-called "rape of the Sabine women" occurred. In this incident the rag-tag collection of shepherds, fugitives, and suspect characters that made up the Roman citizenry attempted to obtain wives from the nearby Sabine people. During a horse-racing festival for Neptune Equester arranged just for the occasion, the Romans seized the unwed daughters of their guests the Sabines and drove their relatives out of the city. In time the Sabines gathered strength and attacked the city, but during hand-to-hand fighting in the streets of Rome an amazing thing happened: The Sabine girls who were now married to the men fighting their fathers and brothers rushed in to the midst of the combatants and pleaded with their relatives to lay down their arms. The Romans had treated them so well, they admitted, that now they wanted to remain with them. It is interesting to note that a parallel story is told in the Bible concerning the tribe of Benjamin and the daughters of Shiloh in Judges 20 and 21. In that story, the men of the tribe of Benjamin capture the maidens of Shiloh as they are dancing at a festival and the other Israelites defend their marriage against the fathers of Shiloh.

It should be clear by now that Romulus' major accomplishment was the founding of Rome. One day, when Romulus was out reviewing his troops on the Campus Martius, Rome's training ground, a storm suddenly arose and enveloped the army and onlookers. An unexpected eclipse of the sun added to the darkness. When the darkness dissipated and the light returned, everyone was astonished to see that Romulus had disappeared. Later, a certain Julius Proculus claimed that he had seen a vision in which Romulus told him that he had ascended to heaven in a cloud and become the god Quirinus, an old Sabine god of war (no one seemed to question how a human could transform into an already existing deity). Through his spokesman, Romulus ordered the Roman people to construct a sanctuary for him on the Quirinal hill, where the Sabine community had been located, and to worship him there.

After Romulus followed six more kings, some of whom established Rome's religious institutions, others who bolstered Rome's military prestige. In the end, however, Rome's kings became so oppressive that in 509 B.C. the Romans turned to a new form of government, the Republic, which itself lasted until the time of Augustus Caesar.

One of the most important mythological/religious landmarks in Rome was the temple of Capitoline Jupiter on the Capitoline Hill, containing what is known as the Capitoline Triad: Jupiter Optimus Maximus ("the greatest and best"), Juno Regina ("the queen"), and Minerva, the goddess of wisdom. Previously, the Romans had an archaic form of this triad made up of Jupiter, Mars (as an agricultural divinity), and Quirinus (as a military divinity), thus reflecting a social order of government, farmers, and soldiers. The latter triad, was reportedly built by the Etrusco-Roman Tarquin the Proud, the last king of Rome, and derived from Etruscan models (the Etruscans lived in the area north of the Tiber River), with its one male divinity accompanied on both sides by two female divinities, finds few parallels in ancient Western cultures.

Lecture Outlines

Introduction to Myth

1. Carl Jung on Myth

    a. 1906, the incident of the sun with the oscillating phallus

    b. pneuma, spiritus = breath, wind

    c. ancient papyrus of the Mithraic cult

    d. Medieval portrayals of Mary

    e. theory: the collective unconscious and archetypes

      Example: marriage to death (Iphigenia, Antigone, Alcestis, Eurydice, Artemis)

2. Defining the word "mythology" + some observations about the uses of myth in the societies that spawned them

3. Anthropomorphism = elevation of man as the crowning achievement of creation

4. Myths are about: cosmogony, Titans, Olympian gods, heroes, lesser figures (legends and folklore)

5. The inevitable question: Did the Greeks actually believe their myths? The story of Acts 14:8–15 (Paul and Barnabas in the Asia Minor cities of Lycaonia, especially Lystra)

    a. Scepticism

    b. Xenophanes

    c. Plato

    d. Hellenistic philosophers and allegorism

    e. Euhemerus (St. Augustine thought this was the most believable interpretation for the origins of myths)

    f. Lucretius (Roman)

6. Major regions and sites in Greece

    a. Delphi

    b. Athens & Eleusis

    c. Dodona

    d. Olympia

    e. Corinth

    f. Mycene

    g. Mt. Olympus & Dion

    h. Epidauros

    i. Thebes & Orchomenos

Creation According to the Greeks

1. Some terms:

   a. theogony

   b. cosmogony

   c. titanomachy

   d. gigantomachy

   e. a word about the complexity of "truth" and "falsehood"

2. The three generations of the gods

   a. Gaia & Ouranos

   b. Kronos & Rhea

   c. Zeus & Hera

   d. Attempted overthrow: Gigantomachy

3. Principles & observations

   a. Division into interrelated opposites

   > Chaos ↔ Gaia

   > Night ↔ Day

   > Aphrodite ↔ Furies

   > Aphrodite ↔ Hephaistos

   > Aphrodite ↔ Ares

   b. The universe and the woman's body

   > Sky, Earth, Tartaros

  c. Power established and maintained through intelligence

    Ouranos

    Kronos

    Zeus & Prometheus

    Gigantomachy (beasts vs. human intelligence)

    Prometheus

  d. Knowledge alienates gods and men

    Prometheus and the fire

    Comparison to Adam and Eve

    Io and the seed

    Tower of Babel

  e. The magical power of women

    Pandora = "all gifts"

    mixed blessing

    the meaning of Pandora's box

Ovid's Creation Story

1. Ovid, the poet

   Writings include:

   a. *Ars amatoria*

   b. *Amores*

   c. *Remedia amoris*

   d. *Metamorphoses*

   e. *Fasti*

   f. *Heroides*

   Exiled in 8 A.D.: Tristia, *Epistulae ex Ponto*

2. Some obvious parallels with the Bible

   a. Genesis and the flood story (Gen. 6ff.)

   b. Daniel's vision of the metalic-clay statue (Dan. 2)

   c. Nebuchadnezzar (Dan. 4.28–33).

3. Ovid's *Metamorphoses*, book I

   Purpose of the *Metamorphoses*: to expose philosophy and reason as inferior to the mythic imagination.

   The state of the universe from the beginning and the actions of "some God"

   a. Ovid's chaos is different than Hesiod's

   b. the importance of boundaries

c. is man the *sanctius animal?*

> cf. Gen. 1.27: "So God created man in his own image, in the image of God created he him; male and female created he them."

d. Prometheus and mixtures

The Four Ages of Man

a. Golden Age: ruled by Saturn (Kronos)

b. Silver Age: ruled by Jupiter

c. Bronze Age: surveyors do their work

d. Iron Age: violation of boundaries, giants

The Meeting in Heaven

a. similar to a Senate meeting in Rome on the Palatine Hill

b. the story of Lycaon, the paragon of human presumption

> cf. Plautus, *Asinaria* 495: "Man is a wolf to man, not a man." And, Automedon of Cyzicus (from the *Greek Anthology*): "In the evening, when we drink together we are men, but when daylight comes, we arise wild beasts, preying upon each other." Note, too, Matt. 10.16, that when Jesus sends his disciples out on a missionary task, he warns them, "Look, I send you out as sheep in the midst of wolves."

The Flood Story

a. a remixing?

b. Jupiter tries for a *sanctius animal* also

c. humans now are a composite from many positive and negative sources (There was a proverb among the ancients that said that mortals are all "sprung from oak and stone," and the phrase "talk of oak and stone" came to mean, "to talk about irrelevant, nonsensical subjects.")

cf. Hesiod, *Catalogues of Women*, no. 82: "So out of stones mortal men were made, and they were called people."

cf. Homer, *Iliad* 22.126 (an ancient curse): "May you all turn to earth and water."

Conclusion

Aristotle, *Politics*, 1.1: "Man is either a beast or a god."

Zeus and Hera

1. Zeus as an Indo-European sky god

    DHEU-

    dyaus pitar

    Jupiter

    duw

    Tiw

    Dieu

    Dios

    deity, divine

    Diuvei

    cloud-gatherer

    Dodona (Dione)

2. Zeus who maintains order and justice in the universe

3. Zeus in relation to the Moirai (Parcae)

    Clotho

    Lachesis

    Atropos

4. Zeus and the two jars (*Iliad*)

    Priam and Hector

    Achilles

5. The philosophical Zeus

Cleanthes and the Stoics

Nature

Reason (logos) = providence, fate, will

Law (nomos)

Poseidon, Ares, Hermes, Hephaestus

1. Poseidon

    a. earth-shaker

    b. the violent god

        Scylla and Charybdis

        Medusa

        Polyphemus

        Proteus

        Laocoon

    c. The meaning of the Contest with Athena

2. Hermes

    a. His older function as a sex-symbol

    b. Hermes as mediator (the universe is his playground)

        Hermaion

    c. Hermes and the gift of orderly disorder

        techne

        kakometis

3. Hephaestus (Hephaistos)

Artemis, Protectress of the Young and Athena, Goddess of Crafts

Artemis

1. Artemis in the *eschatiai*

    a. a goddess of transitions and the rites of passage

        cf. Hera and Eilithyia

    b. the worship at Brauron (Arkteia)

        Why bears?

    c. the worship at Halai (10 km north of Brauron, at the temple of Artemis Tauropolos)

2. The significance of the Actaeon story

3. The deer at Aulis (cf. the Isaac story)

    Agamemnon, husband of Clytemnestra, father of Iphigenia

4. Artemis and the moon

Athena

1. Hephaestus

   Erichthonius

   Cecrops

2. Reason's control over elemental force (cf. with Poseidon)

3. The Panathenaia

Cybele, the Great Mother

1. The Mother Goddesses

   a. Cybele (Phrygian) = *Magna Mater* and *Mater De(or)um* (cf. Mary, mother of Jesus), Idaean Mother, Lady Dindymus

   b. Asherah (Adonai), Kybebe (Hittites), et al.

2. Elements of the Story

   a. pomegranate

   b. pine tree

   c. almond tree (agmydal-)

   d. the hair and the little finger

3. The Meaning of her Attributes and Iconography

   a. turreted Crown

   b. lions

   c. tympanum

   d. biga

   e. patera

4. The Worship of Cybele in Greece and Rome

   a. procession and bathing of the cult images

   b. mutilation (Curetes, Corybantes, Galli)

   c. raucous music

   d. Roman black stone (meteorite)

   e. coins, rose petals

5. Interpreting the Cult of Cybele and Attis

   a. the taurobolium

   b. soteriological aspects

Aphrodite

1. Etiological Myth

2. Plato's *Symposium*

3. Aristophanes on the origins of sexual attraction

4. Eros/Cupid

5. The God in the Dew

   a. E = ros?

   b. Latin: cupidus

6. The attributes of Aphrodite

7. Priapus

8. Lotis

9. Silenus' ass

10. Lampsacus

11. Protector of gardens (Pompeii)

Demeter and Persephone

1. The imagery of flowers

    a. flower festivals in Greece

    b. liminal places

    c. Narcissus flower

    d. Catullus: "Don't expect my love anymore. Because of her (that girl) it has fallen like a flower on the edge of a meadow, touched by a passing plough."

2. The significance of Hekate (moon) and Helios (sun) in the story

3. Iambe's carnival behavior

4. The pomegranates and the divine symmetry

5. Eleusinian Mysteries

    a. the city of Eleusis

    b. Lesser Mysteries (spring)

    c. Greater Mysteries (fall)

    d. requirements for initiation

    e. mystes

    f. hiera

    g. washing and sacrificing young pigs

    h. reenactment of the myth

    i. revelations about the afterlife

6. Persephone as Kore

    a. the mother-daughter paradigm

    b. the tradition of kolyva

Apollo

1. Intro: The Attributes and Sphere of Influence of Apollo

    a. Apollo an eastern divinity? Hittite?

    b. Phoebus

    c. Smintheus, Epikourios

    miasma

    Paiawon/paean

    Knossos/Crete

    Python

    Orestes

    Admetus

    Vale of Tempe

    d. Pythian

    The Oracle at Delphi

    Priestess = Pythian Sibyl

    Loxian (the story of Croesus from Lydia)

    "Know thyself" and "Nothing in excess" and " A pledge, and ruin is near."

    ethylene gas

    e. Lykeios, Delphinios

    f. Music

2. The "transcendence" of Apollo (Hyperboreans)

3. Failed love affairs

    Cassandra

    Daphne (Laurel)

    Marpessa

    Hyacinthus

    Cyparissus

    Sinope

4. The interpretation of Apollo and his worship

    kouros

Dionysus

1. Semele at Thebes

2. The attributes and followers of Dionysus

    Sileni

    Satyrs

    Maenads

    thyrsus

3. Meaning and Cult

    Denditres

    Bromius

    Lyaeus

Lenaeus

Other epithets of Dionysus

Later Roman portrayals (Fantasia)

communion and transformation (enthused)

sparagmos

omophagia

4. City Dionysia (Athens)

   March 24–28

   Komos

   Dramatic performances

The Topography of Hell

Observations of Greeks (and Romans) on the Afterlife

1. Individuality of the dead survive as *umbrae*

    domus aeterna

    Polyxena and Achilles

    Anthesteria and Parentalia

    the consultation of the dead

2. Connection of the person with bodily remains

3. Cremation and inhumation

    generative fire

4. The impurity of the dead

5. Hell and the West

6. Tartarus

   Sisyphus

   Tantalus

   The Danaid Sisters (loutrophoria)

   Ixion

   Tityos

7. Does the sun shine in Hell?

8. The rivers Styx and Lethe

Orpheus

1. calming music

2. procress of regeneration

3. Orphism (600 B.C.)

4. Orphica

5. Dionysus—Zagreus

6. Chronus

7. Adrasteia

8. Aether/Chaos/Erebus

9. Phanes/Night

10. Gaia (Gea) and Ouranos

11. Titans, Cronus (Kronos)

12. Zeus and Hera

13. Semele

14. Asceticism

15. purifications

16. expiation

17. transmigration

Herakles

1. The heroic pattern as applied to the life of Herakles (a loose adaptation of Lord Raglan's hero scale as it appears in his classic work, *The Hero: A Study in Tradition, Myth and Dreams*)

2. The interpretation of the heroic persona of Herakles: the mediator between human and divine

3. Herakles and the choice of two paths

4. Herakles' Roman connection

    a. Latium

    b. Evander

    c. Cacus

5. Alexander the Great and Herakles

6. The Hesperides' Golden Apple tree: a connection with the Garden of Eden?

Cretan Myths

1. Minoan Civilization on Crete

   Linear A

   Asia Minor

   Middle Bronze Age

   Palace = Labyrinth

   Mesopotamian (Sumerian) Temples

   Knossos

   Thera

   1628 (Santorini)

   Akrotiri

   Blue Monkeys

Bull Jumping/Vaulting/Leaping

Great Mother Goddess

The Double Axe

Late Bronze Age

Myceneans (Linear B)

1200 B.C.

The Sea Peoples

2. Daedalus and the problem of artisans in mythology

Icarus, Hephaestus

3. Pasiphae and the sacrifice of the maiden

Theseus and Perseus

Theseus

1. Theseus and the heroic pattern

2. Amazons and social inversion

3. Theseus and Helen

   a. Dioscuri brothers

4. Spartan cult of Helen

   a. Sanctuary of Terapne

   b. Ariston

5. Helen: Pirithous/Paris/Deiphobus/Menelaos

Perseus

1. Perseus and the heroic pattern

2. Freud's view of Medusa

3. Neutralizing the horrific female

The Trojan War

1. Heinrich Schliemann (1822–1890)

   Homer

   Crimean War

   1869 to Greece

   Troy—10 layers

   Treasure of Priam

   Mycenae

   Lion Gate

   Beehive Tombs

   Mask of Agamemnon

2. Homer

   Iliad and *Odyssey*

   Dark Ages

   blind bard

   Homeric Question

   Milmann Parry

   Serbo-Croatian poets

   "swift-footed Achilles" and "wine-dark sea"

   formulaic

3. Achilles and Patroclus

   Hubris

   Ate

Odysseus

1. Humans are self-destructive

2. Odysseus' transformation: the abandonment of the Kleos-ethic

3. "Hero on a journey" motif

4. The Cyclops problem

   Zeus Xenios

5. The Lotus-eaters and nostalgia

6. Women in the Odyssey

    a. Circe

    b. Calypso

    c. Sirens

    d. Scylla

    e. Nausicaa

    f. Penelope (vs. Clytemnestra)

The Return of Agamemnon

1. *Lex taionis*

    Dike = justic

    Herald: "Greet him who has dug Troy into the ground with the pick-axe of Justice-bearing Zeus!"

    Ag: "First, it is just that I should pay my respects to the land of Argos and her presiding Gods, my partners in this homecoming as also in the just penalty which I have inflicted on the city of Troy." (p. 502)

    Clytemnestra says that Justice will lead Agamemnon into the home and take care of his needs. And after she murders him she cries out that justice has been done.

    When Aegisthus arrives, he sees Ag. dead and shouts, "0 day that brought justice, now I know the gods exist!"

2. A hint at where this story is going can be found in a statement by the chorus near the beginning of the first play:

"Zeus, who laid it down that man must in sorrow learn and through pain to wisdom find his way. When deep slumber falls, remembered wrongs chafe the bruised heart with fresh pangs, and no welcome wisdom meets within. From the gods who sit in grandeur grace comes somehow violent."

Helen, too, is an integral part of the moral texture of *Agamemnon*

3. Orestes' confrontation with his mother: hesitation and guilt

4. Extenuating and mitigating circumstances

5. Old Testament "cities of refuge"

Oedipus

1. The Story

   Mt. Cithaeron

   Polybus and Merope of Corinth

   Sphinx's riddle: "What creature walks on four legs in the morning, on two at noon, and on three in the evening, and is weakest when it walks on the most?"

   Jocasta

   Antigone, Ismene, Polyneices, Eteocles

   Creon

   Tiresias

   Uses Jocastas' broaches for blinding himself

2. Know thyself theme

   Tiresias: "you are blind in your ears, your brain, and your eyes."

   Oedipus: "O god, I think I have called curses on myself in ignorance!"

   Irony of the Sphinx's riddle

3. Personal Accountability

   the paradox of predestination

   Jesus and the Tower of Siloe (Luke 13)

4. Our "Ephemeros" nature

   Solon

   King Croesus in Sardis in Lydia

   Tellus (fighting against Eleusis)

   Cloebis and Biton (the temple of Hera)

Medea

1. Corinth

2. Palace of Creon

3. Question: How can Medea do the most harm to Jason?

4. Lot of women: kyrios-servant relationship

5. The sword vs. magic

6. King Aegeus

7. The poisoned wedding present

8. Helios (Medea is his granddaughter)

9. Lorraine Bobbitt? Joy Luck Club?

Roman Myths

1. The Seven Kings, 753–509

2. Tarquin the Proud

3. Servius Tullius

4. Sextus—Gabii

5. Tarquinius Collatinus

6. Lucretia

7. Collatinus and Brutus

8. Religious Life

Flamen

Flamen Dialis

augurs

haruspices

9. Some festivals

Lupercalia

Salian priests

Saturnalia